A DICTIONARY OF THE TEENAGE REVOLUTION AND ITS AFTERMATH

A Dictionary of the Teenage Revolution and its Aftermath

Kenneth Hudson

MACMILLAN PRESS
LONDON

Macmillan Reference Books

First published 1983 by
THE MACMILLAN PRESS LTD
London and Basingstoke
Associated Companies throughout the world

ISBN 0 333 28517 4

Typeset by Leaper & Gard Ltd, Bristol

Printed in Hong Kong

Contents

Acknowledgements

The preparation of the *Dictionary* has involved long and sometimes tedious days of turning over the pages of periodicals, in the hope of discovering linguistic nuggets. A large part of this work was carried out by Helen Martin, at the Newspaper Library at Colindale and at Brighton Polytechnic, which holds a number of magazine files not at Colindale. I should like to express my very warm gratitude to her for her solid and imaginative efforts, which provided an indispensable basis for further research.

My heartfelt thanks are also due to Ann Nicholls, who typed and checked, apparently without turning a hair, a manuscript containing certain features not of a drawing-room nature.

Introduction

The philosophical and historical basis of this *Dictionary* will be found in my *Language of the Teenage Revolution* (Macmillan 1983) and there is no need to do more than summarize its conclusions here. What is perhaps more important, however, is to explain the purpose of the present work.

During the 1940s and 1950s, the values and codes of behaviour of Western society began to change rapidly and in a radical way. This was particularly marked among young people and the gulf between them and their parents became wider and deeper than in previous generations. The new Permissive Society, the motto of which might well have been 'Nobody has any right to tell me what to do', produced its own language, made up partly of new expressions and partly of old words used in a different way. To record and interpret this language demands an unconventional type of dictionary, with fuller and more discursive entries and the complete avoidance of such irrelevant labels as 'slang', 'taboo', and 'obscene', which made some sense 50 or 100 years ago, but very little today. They no longer correspond to the way in which a large part of the British people think and behave. In this *Dictionary*, a serious attempt has been made to indicate what kinds of people have been using a particular word or phrase and to trace the curve of the waxing and waning of popularity of new speech habits. The result is a work which many traditionally-minded people would undoubtedly find some difficulty in bringing within their concept of a dictionary, but there seems to be no good reason for denying it the title. It carries out the essential function of a dictionary, to define and explain words, and it sets out these words in alphabetical order. It is intended as a work of reference, but it is also a book which one can dip into according to one's inclinations, a readable book. It makes no claim to be fully comprehensive, in the sense of listing the whole of the teenage vocabulary of the past 30 years. The method has been rather to select and document what seem to be the most significant words and meanings, those which have served to divide one generation from another and to baffle the people who have not themselves used them. But it is worth noting that about one in four of the entries in the present work are not to be found in those modern dictionaries which do call themselves comprehensive.

My own interest in language is social, rather than technical. Over the years I have become increasingly amused by the word 'communication' and increasingly conscious of the power which words have to confuse, mislead and annoy people. Sometimes, it seems to me, this result is achieved intentionally and deliberately, but more often in innocence and ignorance. I have summarized my feelings about this important matter of non-communication in three closely related books I have written for Macmillan – *The Dictionary of Diseased English*, *The Jargon of the Professions*, and *The Language of Modern Politics*. The success of these books has encouraged me to feel that my diagnoses and prescriptions may possibly be having some degree of useful influence, and I am doing what I can to help this process along by preparing *The Dictionary of Even More Diseased English*, which is due to be published later in 1983.

My attitude towards words is not, I think and hope, puritanical. I have not the slightest wish to freeze or fossilize English, or to advocate an Academy control over what I continue to regard as the most marvellously flexible and adventurous language in the world. Many years in the broadcasting business, both on the staff of the BBC and as an unattached person, have helped me to understand the subtle relationships between spoken and written English, and have made me give thanks every day of my life that I live in a country where the prestige of formal language is relatively low. If the British still have any contribution to make to civilization, as I firmly believe they have, it is primarily because their language discourages them from being pompous and pretentious. We are an easy people who, left to ourselves, tend to write much as we talk. It is a blessing beyond price. British English is a language in which one can breathe easily and enjoy the pleasure of being oneself.

But we are also in Britain terribly, terrifyingly class-bound and class-conscious, and our language shows it all too well. British society is characterized by an extremely powerful and omnipresent system of what I have decided to call language labels. It is not unique in this respect, but the British labels are exceptionally complex and subtle, a fact which is not easy to explain to foreigners or for foreigners to understand, even when their mother tongue is English. These labels are one of the most important means by which a cultural group – and we have many – proclaims its identity to the outside world and at the same time strengthens its own morale and cohesiveness. Sometimes they consist of special words, sometimes of ordinary words used in a special sense, sometimes of intonation and phrasing, sometimes of pronunciation, sometimes of peculiarities of syntax. Not all of them are fully capable of being reproduced in print and therefore of being included in a dictionary.

Language labels are always combined with other types of identification, such as dress, hairstyle, motorcars, living conditions, or food and drink. They are only one form of labelling among many. Some labels are of long standing and so well known that the people to whom they are attached have, fairly or unfairly, become stock types, even caricatures. The bowler hat and furled umbrella, the clerical voice, the Jaguar, the policeman's way of giving evidence, are of this type. Others, however, are often not recognized for what they are, partly because the group concerned does not come into frequent or close contact with the rest of society and partly because the clues are so novel and unexpected that outsiders are not sensitive to them. A further obstacle to understanding is the reduction in the range and number of what one might call mixed-group occasions. Railway trains and railway stations, for instance, were for many years great mixers of the classes, remarkably effective places for anyone interested in observing the behaviour of people from a sector of society different from his own. The railway mixed, the motorcar isolates, and television and radio are very selective and imperfect mixers. Viewers and listeners see and hear for the most part only what producers and editors decide they shall. Any mixing that takes place within the framework of broadcasting is tightly controlled and carefully sifted.

In previous books I have analysed with some care the language of the high prestige groups, the lawyers, doctors, estate agents, art critics and the rest. These are the groups for whom the possession of a special vocabulary and of a different way of assembling and presenting words constitute an important part of the equipment for earning a living. Some at least of their language labels, one could say, are exchangeable for cash and are deliberately acquired and cultivated with this in mind. In the present book I am more concerned, not with what one might call the officers in British society, but with the other ranks, those who live their lives by instinct rather than by theory, and who are more interested in present satisfactions than with future prosperity and security. These people are at the same time much concerned with a style of speech which helps to bind them closely to other members of their group and to distinguish friends from enemies. The attempts of outsiders to copy their language are often ludicrous, involving the use of what are imagined to be in-words long after the people inside the group have abandoned them and passed on to newer, fresher and more magical expressions. I am very interested in the origin and pedigree of these tribal words and phrases, in their stamina, in the extent to which society as a whole understands what they mean, and in the barriers which exist to their becoming more widely adopted. I make no apology at all for concentrating so heavily in the present *Dictionary* on the drug, pop music, hippy and near-hippy cultures, and on the many aspects of sexual behaviour and violence. These are the special characteristics of the post-war world, the most powerful marks of difference between three generations, the fields of greatest ignorance and misunderstanding.

Within a primitive society, everyone is expected to think and behave in the same way, to observe the same religious rites, practise the same customs, wear the approved clothing and ornaments, sing the same songs, dance the same dances and use words in the same rigid fashion. There is and can be only one culture and any tendency to deviate from it is unthinkable.

Developed societies, of the type with which we are familiar in the West, are characterized by a different pattern of organization and a different set of assumptions. There is a dominant or core culture, which the educational system is more or less expected to perpetuate, which the government and state institutions encourage and to which ambitious and successful people take care to conform, at least outwardly. Within this broad national culture, an infinite number of minor variations are possible. Citizens are not permitted to travel naked to their place of work but, within certain limits, they may wear or not wear what clothes they please, indulge in a wide range of religious practices, choose their own style of hairdressing, their own reading matter, and their own music. In exceptionally liberal and tolerant societies, they are free to advocate political programmes entirely opposed to those of the government in power and indeed to demand that society shall be organized in a completely different way.

In such societies, work has become increasingly specialized and social conditions vary a great deal, both within a local community and over the country as a whole. Groups of people with similar tastes, occupations, incomes, aspirations and attitudes will tend to form identifiable groups and classes. Where these display certain characteristics which are markedly different from those of the controlling groups of the society in question, one is entitled to speak of a sub-culture, a culture within a culture.

Most social groups do in fact form part of the established order of society, although some are more closely and more obviously tied to it than others. Lawyers, doctors, art critics, bishops and Conservative Members of Parliament are social groups, with recognizable characteristics, especially of speech and dress, but they do not represent sub-cultures. Their values, in general, are those of the upper levels of British society as a whole. They are, it is true, people for whom the possession of a special vocabulary and a different way of assembling and presenting words constitute an important part of their equipment for earning a living. Their style of speaking and writing is, one might fairly say, exchangeable for cash and it is deliberately cultivated with this in mind. It marks them off as the professionals and experts they are, and it helps to bind one member of the group to another.

But – and this is of great importance – the bishops, lawyers and other categories of people instanced above are alike in more ways than they are different. A well-informed and observant person can sometimes distinguish them by their specialized manner and appearance and by their characteristic turns of phrase, but their tastes and habits, and the general quality of their life, will probably not differ a great deal from one profession to another. They do not, properly speaking, belong to a sub-culture, any more than policemen or long-distance lorry drivers do. Their roots are in a class. They live their lives and earn their living within an established tradition, which they are content to accept, just as the great majority of American doctors, lawyers, stockbrokers, widows living in Florida, and airline pilots are content to take American capitalism and anti-socialism as they find it. They have their own professional associations and their own methods of defending their interests, but in their social life they are accustomed to mix freely with people whose occupations are quite different from their own, but who have similar incomes, live in similar houses and marry similar wives. Their style indicates to the world that they consider themselves successful and in the UK, but to a much lesser extent in the USA or Australia, their speech is an important part of that style.

To belong to a true sub-culture, however, is not merely to assert one's difference, but to make fundamental criticisms of the central tradition of the dominant culture. One is protesting against things as they are and, in order that the protests shall be clearly seen and understood, every external detail of one's life, every point of contact with the public, has to be regarded as a signal. Objects – clothes, food, possessions of any kind – become style, and style, as one shrewd observer has recently pointed out, is 'a gesture of defiance or contempt, a smile or a sneer. It signifies a refusal.'[1]

Within this context, all objects, all words have a double function. 'On the one hand,' says the same writer, 'they warn the 'straight' world in advance of a sinister presence – the presence of a difference – and draw upon themselves vague suspicions, uneasy laughter, 'white and dumb rages'. On the other hand, for those who erect them into icons, who use them as words or as curses, these objects become signs of forbidden identity, sources of value.'[2]

Any sub-culture, Hebdige believes, is essentially aggressive. It expresses 'a fundamental tension between those in power and those condemned to subordinate positions and second-class lives'.[3] This, he thinks, has always been the case – the Christians, in Roman times, behaved as members of a true sub-culture – and, with rare exceptions, those who have given their allegiance to the sub-culture are committed to ending the status quo and to the renewal and reshaping of society. They regard social consensus as a dangerous myth and consider it to be their duty to carry out a continuous campaign of offending the silent majority and of challenging the principle of unity and cohesion.

To some extent, this reflects the battle between the generations, which has always existed, but during the past 30 years or so the disagreement, mutual contempt, or whatever else one may choose to call it, has taken an extreme form, with many, but by no means all, of the new teenagers insisting that the past of their society and the values of their parents have no meaning for them and no relevance to their lives. They have emphasized this by doing everything possible to shock and outrage their elders and to convince the world and themselves that a new breed of humanity is in the making. Punk is the extreme form of this attitude. No other non-religious sub-culture has taken such pains to detach itself from normality and from the taken-for-granted basis of living or to bring such strong and outspoken public disapproval upon itself. But, precisely by their extremism, the punks have made it clear that they cannot be considered typical. Because their appearance is so outrageous, it is obvious that they constitute only a tiny fraction of the young people of the same age-group. They are symbols, rather than models.

[1]   Dick Hebdige, *Subculture: the Meaning of Style*, 1979, p. 3.
[2]   ———— pp. 2–3.
[3]   ———— p. 132.

We have been bedevilled by absurd generalizations about our adolescents. In 1965 Dennis Chapman, for instance, was writing with wild exaggeration about 'the present generation of young people, a generation largely independent of, and isolated from their elders'.[4] In the same year, George Melly suggested, more reasonably, that the 'young affluents' who set the tone and gave journalists something to write about were 'not strictly anyone between the age of thirteen and twenty, but a moneyed group between those ages who are able to afford what they want and decide their own pattern of life, which is very different from their parents. They come from the upper working and lower middle class.'[5] This could have represented between a third and a half of all adolescents, certainly something much less than 'a generation'.

In 1963 Britain was still in the first flush of excitement over a phenomenon that was being called the Teenage Revolution, and journalists, television producers and sociologists were busy discovering that there were interesting differences between the adolescents of the 1930s and the adolescents of the 1950s and 1960s. By the end of the decade, however, more sceptical observers had begun to wonder if this revolutionary generation was quite as remarkable and all of a piece as it had been made out to be. In an article, well titled 'Non-Swinging Youth',[6] Bernard Darwin pointed out that there was plenty of evidence that 'everything that is young does not swing'. His researches in the northern industrial districts of the UK had revealed large numbers, possibly a majority, of working-class boys and girls who were neither big spenders nor stylish dressers, and who seemed to have much the same sort of problems that their parents had had at the same age, although some of them, it is true, made a rather sad attempt to acquire a swinging veneer during the pathetically brief period before the care and responsibilities of adulthood finally descended upon them. What then, Bernard Darwin sensibly asked, are the real parameters of this thing called 'youth culture'? How many sub-species is it permitted to have before it ceases to have any validity as a 'culture'?

It might, however, be more accurate and more helpful to consider the situation in terms, not of species and sub-species, but of active and

---

4   *The Listener*, 17 Jan 1963. The great value of *The Listener* is that it reproduces what has been said, not written, and that publication follows quickly on the heels of thought.
5   *The Listener*, 9 May 1963.
6   *New Society*, 3 July 1969.

passive followers of a trend. There have been, beyond doubt, many teenagers who have been bored by pop music, discos and all that goes with these cultural manifestations, but who have found it convenient to suppress their real feelings and go along with the herd, because the thought of loneliness and ostracism frightens them. Being a teenager is to belong willy-nilly to one of the toughest trade unions we have. There have been many, too, who understand perfectly well the cult language of their contemporaries, but who rarely, if ever, use it themselves. One could, perhaps, make a comparison with respectable, refined middle-aged ladies who are privately and surprisingly familiar with the full range of obscenities, but who would never dream of using such expressions themselves. In this respect, their membership of society is entirely passive.

The point to be emphasized is that very few of the teenagers whom Bernard Darwin met in the North of England formed part of the sub-culture described by Hebdige, although from superficial evidence one might quite possibly have arrived at a different conclusion. Perhaps every sub-culture, like every trade union and every religion, necessarily has two categories of member, the militants and those who merely pay their dues, the attenders and supporters on the one hand, and the true believers on the other. But, if both observe the same rituals, how is the outsider to distinguish between them?

Most generalizations have some truth in them. In the 1950s and 1960s, it made a certain amount of sense to refer to 'the autonomous generation' and 'the young affluents'. Compared with their parents and grandparents, the majority of those who were growing up at this time were able to lead more independent lives and to do things which would previously have been impossible for most people in this age group. Equally, no doubt, the teenagers of the 1970s considered their immediate predecessors in the 1960s to have been quaintly old-fashioned in many ways and without a number of the advantages which they considered themselves to have. It is probable that those who are 16 and 18 today, in the early 1980s, often marvel at the low prices of 10 years ago and at the ease with which jobs and money were available. We may soon find them being described as 'the deprived generation', or something similarly pitiful and newsworthy.

What matters, however, is not the generalizations of journalists and academics, which are devised to meet particular needs, but what individual people, of all ages, feel about society and their place in it. What do they want to do, what kind of people do they see as their friends and enemies, which groupings and allegiances make them feel happier, more confident and more secure? What concessions, compromises and adaptations are they prepared to make in order to be respected by members of this or that group? Everyone is aware, however vaguely, of the social or cultural group to which he belongs and everyone is likely to resent any attempt from outside to place him in a category where he knows he has no business to be.

People have a regrettable habit of defying classification by the social scientists. They foul up the computer, the teenagers who hate discos, the quiet, studious, exam-passing blacks, the intellectuals who do not read *The Guardian*, the art students who favour representational art and who can actually draw, the doctors and dentists who have no wish to own a boat. To draw attention to such people is not to say that all attempts to classify and categorize humanity should cease forthwith, but rather to point out that society is exceedingly and wilfully complex and that every member of it is linked to another by a multitude of crisscrossing lines. The human situation is marvellously, deliciously untidy, which creates a heaven for the artist and a hell for the social scientist.

Obligingly, most people in any modern society do approximate remarkably closely to the stereotypes laid down for them. But it is the extent to which we do not fit the stereotype, do not conform to the generalization, which makes us interesting and significant. The sociologists and the psychologists cannot have it both ways. It is not reasonable to construct norms and categories, which must always involve some distortion of the facts as they really are, and then get angry with those people who, for one reason or another, fail to match up to them. The person with extra-large feet does, regrettably, exist, however much the shoemaker and the shopkeeper may try to pretend otherwise.

But mass-production does not like the man with big feet or non-standard ideas. The humanist, with his roots in the past, emphasizes human differences and urges toleration towards eccentric views, tastes and habits. The present-worshipping mass media, on the other hand, depend for their acceptance and prosperity on the concept of the average man, of standardized attitudes. For the mass media, the market cannot be too big or too homogeneous. The culture to which they give their immensely powerful support is based on the creed that everything can and must be made effortless, foolproof, and immediately understandable, which implies culture at a very low level. The concept of the teenager is the perfect reflection of this philosophy. It has led to the creation of an artificial stereotype, based on the individual who left school at the earliest possible moment, who went into an unskilled and dead-end job – if indeed he went into any job at all – the person who lives only for his free time and for whom all satisfactions must be facile and immediate. 'It is,' observed the sociologist, B. Sugarman, 'no accident that the heroes of youth culture – pop singers, clothes designers and others – have mostly achieved their position without long years of work or sacrifice'.[7]

Youth culture is a culture largely created by pop music. It has been the major carrier of social change during the past 30 years or so, the magic carpet which has floated from country to country and continent to continent as if national frontiers and iron curtains did not exist. With pop music to sweep them irresistably along, new attitudes to drugs, sex, dress, money, work, education, class and religion have tracked their way across the world at a pace which makes previous international movements of ideas seem elephantine by comparison.

Since the late 1950s, pop music has been the principal cultural diet of most teenagers throughout the world and, since teenagers unavoidably grow older, of a steadily increasing number of adults as well. It has become the focus of a complex youth sub-culture, determining values, ambitions, language and clothes. What pop musicians do, wear and say has become automatically desirable and right. Aiming at classlessness and universal appeal, they have proved to be one of the great divisive forces in our society, heroes to the young and monsters of idiocy and corruption to their elders.

Originally, but no longer, a form of protest, pop culture made a strong appeal to people who saw few opportunities for themselves in the kind of world which had produced and reared them. It has always been essentially adolescent, both in its rejection of tradition and in its awareness, sometimes wistful, sometimes savage, that it belongs to a stage in one's life which cannot last for ever.

The fact that the words sung, screamed, chattered and bawled by Elvis Presley and the lesser idols are repetitious clichés at best and gibberish at worst is a matter of no consequence, or rather a positive merit. The words and music together, the sheer noise, form a code understood only by teenagers, a protective barrier against the adult world.

What pop music has done – and, in such a short time, this is no mean achievement – is to make the use of connected, intelligible words seem

---

7   'Involvement in youth culture, academic achievement and conformity at school', *British Journal of Sociology*, June 1967, p. 158.

unimportant and even treasonable. Pop has always been hostile to the written word, insisting on the intrinsic superiority of what is spoken or sung. This is partly because what is set down on paper is permanent – and pop is against preserving the past or even referring to it – partly because reading and writing are solitary, individual activities – and pop culture is based on the shared experience. But pop is against literature for a different reason. It believes, as an article of faith, in the virtue of a deliberately impoverished vocabulary. Its own special language is colourless and impersonal, with vivid metaphors almost entirely absent from it. Those of its fans who have suffered the social misfortune of having been educated to use words well feel obliged to conceal the fact and to speak the basic English of the tribe. But this tribal language, wretched thing though it may be, is changing continuously, because it functions as a series of passwords and, as soon as the key words become known to the outside world, they must, as a matter of security and corporate pride, be replaced. The initiates, those who belong, alone know the correct, up-to-date words and meanings. Those outside the barriers are almost certain to get them wrong. They are always falling into the trap of using yesterday's in-language, without realizing that the real people are laughing at them for their ignorance.

There are those who believe, with some justice, that pop is not what it used to be, that what began as revolt has degenerated into mere surface manifestations, that each successive wave of pop music has appealed to an even younger and sillier age group than the one before. The Beatles became rich and secure enough to be able to laugh at it all. They were the aristocrats of pop and they could afford to have the aristocrat's privilege of mocking at the source of their wealth.

Ironically, pop culture, for all its scorn of the printed word, has, in fact, depended on magazines a great deal for its growth and cohesion. Publications like *Rolling Stone*, *Melody Maker* and *New Musical Express* are the pop music world's channels of communication. They have a large circulation, and the people who read them are by no means the same as the fans who go crazy at concerts. They are, to be more specific, rather older and they have more money. The people who buy these papers regularly constitute something which, strictly speaking, has no business to exist, a pop intelligentsia. Their part in the movement is to read and theorize about it and to listen to records in their own homes, leaving most of the up-front activity and the rough stuff to the coolies. Pop, like the USSR, may pride itself on its classless image, but it has its hierarchy and its elite none the less.

Most people are anxious to seem all of a piece. Having decided what their place and role in society are, they do their best to make sure that the way they look, sound and behave all contribute to the total effect. One should not dress, have one's hair done, eat, drink or talk in a style appropriate to the wrong age-group, social level, or cultural bracket. The public and one's friends should be provided with the right clues to the kind of person one is trying to be. The situation is in no way new, but the present manifestations can be bewildering to those whose standards were set some years ago.

The speaking and writing clues or, as I have chosen to call them, the language labels, are of three kinds. There are, first, the words and phrases which mark one off as belonging to a particular cultural group and which bind the members of that group to one another. Second, there are the ways of saying not only the special words, but the whole of the language one uses – the accent, the tune, the pauses, the projections, the throwaways, the playing-downs, the half-smile and, of great importance nowadays, the inverted commas in the voice. And, third, there are the words and phrases one takes care not to use, the pronunciations and stresses one avoids, the intonations which put one in the wrong social box. These labels, the things one does not do, are just as important as the other two kinds. One could perhaps call them the negative labels.

Labels of all kinds come and go, and one of the greatest difficulties which one generation faces in trying to communicate with another is the failure to realize that, with the passage of time, different concepts have become taboo or obscene and that yesterday's impossibilities are not only possible but normal. At one time, a song called 'The Chocolate Coloured Coon' raised no problems at all. Now, at least among the young, the use of the word 'coon' would be likely to produce a near riot and shouts of 'racist'. Equally, the older generation today finds the attitude of many, if not most of the young towards drugs, sex, violence and music largely incomprehensible. To be unfamiliar with the finer shades of meaning within the vocabulary which describes these activities is to confess to being a member of another tribe. Yet it would be foolish to pretend that everyone under 25 takes drugs, engages in street warfare, sleeps with the first comer and revels in loud pop music. Such a blanket categorization is simply not true. There are a great many so-called 'youth words' with which a substantial part of today's 'youth' is not familiar.

One can easily be led astray by superficial similarities, like jeans, Coke, beards, and long unkempt hair. But it is precisely because the uniform is so universal, because the person unfamiliar with sheep cannot tell one sheep from another, that the individual beneath the uniform has to be sought with great care. This is also true of what one might call uniform words. If one has only written evidence at one's disposal, the significant variation of tone and intention between one social group and generation and another are missed. It is especially for this reason that our notions of the English spoken in the past are bound to be unsatisfactory. Even with the most skilful interpretation, the written word tells only part of the story and our ancestors would certainly find many of our reconstructions and assumptions ludicrously wrong.

What one loses particularly if one has nothing more than print to rely on is the personal contribution, the pause before one utters the cliché, the deliberate mispronunciation, the degree of ridicule of habits which are not one's own. An extremely important element of the sub-culture which today is associated mainly with young people is what I call the Grandmother's Old Fur Coat Syndrome, making use of the objects from another age and another culture without identifying oneself with them. This is the secret weapon. For a number of years, many girls have taken to wearing a fur coat which belonged originally to their grandmother or, less frequently, to their mother. They would never have considered buying a fur coat for themselves, even if they had happened to have the money. A fur coat, bought new and of fashionable design, would be totally uncharacteristic of their lifestyle and philosophy. It would represent conspicuous expenditure, snobbery and an indifference to the sufferings of animals, all of which are likely to be just as repulsive and unthinkable to a member of the new generation as referring to black people as 'coons' or 'niggers'.

Paradoxically, however, one can best show one's revulsion, one's superiority to previous generations, by wearing this symbolic coat, rather than by not wearing it. To take it over and to be seen in it is not unlike putting a Dior dress on a scarecrow or a bonfire guy. 'I am wearing this coat in inverted commas and as a protest', a girl is saying in effect, 'and those with eyes to see will realize what I am doing and why I am doing it.'

This is very similar to what the more intelligent members of the anti-Establishment, anti-authority generation has been doing with the English langugage. They have taken over the language of the previous 'straight' decades and poked fun at it, by placing selected words and expressions within inverted commas, commas of which only they and those who think like them are aware. It is a situation with which the lexicographers cannot cope. Even with the help of their computers, their entry for the word 'chap' will provide no clue to the fact that many young people habitually use it in inverted commas. The dictionary-makers are prisoners of such value-terms as 'slang', 'taboo', 'obscene' and 'obsolete'. The overtones of contemporary English pass them by. Who would realize, with only a dictionary as a guide, that 'darling' has a completely different flavour, strength and effect, according to the age, social class and professional background of the person involved? Or that 'fool' and 'bastard' become steadily more insulting and more likely to provoke a breach of the peace as one moves down the social scale?

The Glossary

In the following pages I have excluded as far as possible those words, phrases and meanings which, although new or relatively new, have appeared in response to some general need which has been experienced by a wide section of the population, cutting through different age groups and social classes. Words of this kind – telly (television), blower (telephone), package (package tour), bird (girl) are examples – are of little or no value as labels, simply because they are used normally and naturally by so many otherwise distinct groups. There are, it is true, a very small number of people who at all times and in all circumstances say 'television', 'telephone', 'all-inclusive holiday', or 'girl', and it would be possible to bring them all together under the single heading of 'refusers', which would no doubt tell us quite a lot about them. Not to wear a label is in fact to wear a label which bears the inscription 'non-joiner'. But such a label could refer only to a person's non-joining habits so far as innovations in speech are concerned. In other respects – clothes, food, religious attitudes, accent – he or she might well be a confirmed and even passionate joiner.

None of the illustrations dates from earlier than 1950.

Six terms used in the course of definition and explanation

Alternative Lifestyle. The mode of life adopted by people, usually young, who have decided to turn their backs on capitalism, the profit motive, industrialism and conventional methods of making a living.

Alternative People. Advocates and practitioners of the Alternative Lifestyle.

Alternative Society. To begin with, a society within a society, composed of Alternative People practising Alternative Lifestyles. Then, as society moves steadily closer towards the Millenium, the new form of social organization which allows humanity to flourish and be happy for the first time since the Garden of Eden.

Hell's Angels. Groups of violent and entirely amoral young males who developed a vicious type of motorcyle-based culture in California in the 1950s and exported it widely during the 1960s. They display a total disregard of the law and the established order of society and an equal contempt for women.

People's Novelists. Writers belonging to a school of novel-writing, more or less flourishing from the early 1950s onwards, which drew its raw material from the more unfortunate, feckless and revolutionary-minded elements within British society. They are paralleled on the stage, in the film-world and on television by the manufacturers of kitchen-sink dramas.

Progressive Society. Nearly, but not quite the same as a society which is acceptable to Alternative People. Although vague, it is essentially socialist, in an idealistic way, and anti-capitalist, relying for its motivation on brotherly and sisterly goodwill, rather than on competition and greed. It is non-sexist, non-racist, and believes in putting the interests of the weak before those of the strong. Its advocates do not appear to worry very much about public finance, but, unlike the Alternative People, they are usually not against jobs and careers as such.

A

Ace. Very good. During World War I, 'flying ace' or sometimes just 'ace', in the sense of 'crack airman', was much used. It was a very officer-like word and most of the people to whom it referred were, in fact, officers, with a few sergeants thrown in to make up the numbers. In the 1920s and 1930s it fell into disuse, except in tennis and as an historical reference – 'a wartime flying ace' – mainly, no doubt, because there was nothing in peacetime for aces to do. With the outbreak of World War II in 1939, the word made a brief reappearance, but its days as a military noun were clearly over. Nobody talked about a Spitfire ace or a Hurricane ace. 'Fighter pilot' was the term with the prestige.

In the 1950s 'ace' came into widespread use, as part of the all-conquering march of pop music, but this time as an adjective. One could speak of an 'ace drummer' (*New Musical Express*, 27 July 1956), an 'ace recording engineer' (*Zigzag*, Feb 1973), and an 'ace band' (*Melody Maker*, 20 Jan 1979). It was also possible to say of a new song, 'the words are good to ace' (*Sounds*, 3 March 1979). It is still much used, but almost entirely within the worlds of sport, pop music and jazz. An 'ace goalkeeper' is just about possible nowadays, but nobody, except as a joke, refers to an 'ace fish and chip shop' or an 'ace undertaker'.

During the 1950s and 1960s an adjective, 'acey', was in limited use among teenagers and young adults – 'I met a real acey chick' (*Jackie*, 6 June 1964). It is never found today.

Acid. The drug, lysergic acid. This is the word used by people who take it or who view the taking of it sympathetically. So, 'I took what I thought was acid' (rock musician reported in *Zigzag*, March 1972). Those outside the drug world and those who are critical of it usually refer to LSD, not to acid. Journalists, whether drug-takers or not, who have reasons for wishing to appear knowledgeable and in the swim may well go for 'acid', not 'LSD', and write of, for instance, 'the old hash smoking and acid dropping Carnaby Street' (*Melody Maker*, 24 Jan 1981).

Adult. Pornographic. Essentially a word used by promoters and advertisers of pornography and found only in print. Nobody has yet been heard to ask in a newsagent's shop, 'Have you any adult magazines, please?', and nobody tells his friends that he collects 'adult photographs'. 'Unusual adult photo sets' (advert in *New Musical Express*, 18 July 1958) is the usual kind of context and shop window of the word.

Afterpunk. Pop music after about 1978, which is commonly reckoned to be the date by which the shock waves of original PUNK had died away. 'Afterpunk' could be described as a style which owes much to the rawness and energy of punk in its heyday, but which has a higher intellectual content. This is another way of saying that punk music has moved up the social scale and become more sophisticated, although not necessarily more likeable in the process. 'Afterpunk' is not, however, a word one finds used in ordinary conversation. It belongs to the world of pop journalism, on the higher and more analytical level. '1979 is the year of afterpunk' (*Melody Maker*, 31 March 1979) places the word in its market.

Ageism. 'Discrimination against the elderly' would be a very rough translation, but it misses the campaigning, join-our-struggle overtones of the word. 'Ageism is as insidious as sexism' (*Spare Rib*, Feb 1979). All -ism words need to be treated with great care, because, as elements in the language of polemic, they invariably contain a strong measure of exaggeration and iron out all the finer points in a situation. For those on the attack, there is never any time for qualifying details or for light and shade. The word 'but' does not exist for them. The plain truth is that nobody really knows exactly what 'ageism' is, least of all the people who use it regularly. But it sounds good, far better than 'treating old people unfairly' or 'not looking after them properly'. It is a word which can be used as a banner, and clearly labels the people who wave it. It is, incidentally, not part of the vocabulary of old people, most of whom have no idea of what it means.

Aggravation. In the sense of 'violence, quarrels, unpleasantness', this appears to have been first used in London in the 1950s and to have been confined for some time to working-class youths accustomed to gang fights and to not wholly undeserved trouble with the police. During the 1970s it was taken up much more widely by the pop/youth world and its London antecedents were largely forgotten. One then came across this type of usage: 'We've been getting heavy aggravation from things in our area' (Mandelkau: *Buttons*, 1971) and '. . . the aggravation and unpleasantness that developed' (rock musician, in *Zigzag*, June 1971). There was a parallel development of another meaning, 'hostile treatment by the police and by the law generally'. An example of this is 'You do get a lot of aggravation from the Old BILL.' (*New Society*, 26 June 1980)

In its various senses, 'aggravation' is a delightfully British euphemism and it feels like London through and through. One can well imagine Sam Weller and other working-class Dickensian characters using it. It remains, however, a word little used, except in inverted commas, by members of the middle class who are over 25.

Aggro, Agro. Aggressive, violent behaviour. A shortened form of AGGRAVATION, but with rather a different flavour to it. It was first used by London football fans – 'After some agro, they were let in free' (*Oz* 22 July 1969) – and in the 1970s passed into wider usage. Men teachers are quite fond of it – 'What's all the aggro in here then?' – and so are the police. However, among middle class adults it is not much heard and, in all classes, it has always been somewhat shunned by women and girls.

The compound noun, 'aggro merchant', meaning 'an aggressive person, a fighter', remains largely a journalists' word. 'A novel idea to deal with aggro merchants' (*Sounds*, 1 Dec 1979).

Airplay. A hearing on radio. A pop business/media/advertising word, never used in general conversation, except by people working within these industries, who have a language and style all their own. The pop music magazines have frequent references to 'airplay' – 'limited radio airplay' (*Rolling Stone*, 30 Nov 1978) and 'It's unlikely to get heavy airplay' (*Sounds*, 3 March 1979). With its echoes of 'airplane', the word still looks and feels American, which adds to its attractions for pop journalists, but acts as a barrier to its wider adoption in the UK.

Airspace. A block of time on radio. Almost, but not quite, same range of users as for 'airplay', but longer established. It had secured a firm foothold in the UK by the 1960s – 'He had enough money to win himself airspace' (Cohn: *Awopbop*, 1969) – and since then it has made a certain amount of progress outwards into the general conversation of the younger literate, although it is not always used completely seriously and one should listen hard for signs of possible irony in the voice.

Alkie. An alcoholic. A word almost confined to members of the drug and alcohol sub-culture, although it is used from time to time by those people, such as social workers and the police, whose work brings them into close contact with alcoholics. A friendly word, without overtones of reproach. 'The alkies embrace this new religion with hideous enthusiasm' (*Home Grown*, No. 3, 1978).

All that jazz. And all the rest of it, etcetera. A very dated left-over from the BEAT era, although it is still occasionally heard among younger members of the educated middle class, as a throwaway and a semi-quote. The following two examples are from the period when 'all that jazz' was getting a little long in the tooth, although behind the times as usual, journalists who catered for the adolescent market were no doubt under the impression that the phrases they were using were in the height of fashion. 'The domineering sex and all that jazz' (*Boyfriend Annual*, 1963) and 'If at first you don't succeed and all that jazz' (*Jackie*, 2 Jan 1965).

Alternologist. An expert on the ways and beliefs of what is known to its disciples as the Alternative Society, that is, a society motivated and organized quite differently from the one in which the rest of the community lives and existing parallel to it. The word is used, when it is used at all, almost entirely by the alternologists themselves, and then usually in print, because one can easily get tangled up when trying to say it. It can also be found in the writings of social scientists who have chosen to study the Alternative Society. 'Alternologists may easily have become victims of their own myth' (*Undercurrents*, July/Aug 1974).

Amazing. Outstanding, spectacular. The sense itself is of long standing in the language, being first recorded c.1700. It is included in the present Glossary only because, under the influence of the ad-men who earned a living from promoting pop music, it became one of the youth superlatives of the 1960s and 1970s and, in its ridiculous overuse and its intensity, something of a barrier between the generations. Heyday examples would be, 'The charity could organize amazing concerts' (*International Times*, 14 Oct 1966), and 'Amazing classics' (*Zigzag*, Aug 1972).

The absurdity of this usage was parodied in Kate Bush's 1979 pop song, *Wow!* – 'You're amazing/We think you're incredible'. But by then it was already declining in popularity.

Amp. (*i*) An amplifier used by pop musicians. 'They worked between great fortresses of amps' (Cohn: *Awopbop*, 1969).

(*ii*) To produce a great volume of sound. 'Amping it out like a hard-nosed animated juke-box' (*Sounds*, 3 March 1979).

'Amp', in both these senses, can be spoken as well as written, but only by people working in the pop music business and in the journalistic ventures associated with it.

Art. Pretentious, making unjustified claims to be serious or highbrow, as in 'There are a million uncomfortable art records this week' (*Sounds*, 21 July 1979). Used in this sense, 'art' is a term of abuse with which unashamedly lowbrow pop journalists attempt to undermine the position of those in the music business who show signs of forgetting that their sole function is to provide undemanding entertainment for the masses. A purely journalistic word when used seriously, but also adopted, within inverted commas, by bright and cynical people who are not pop journalists in order to poke gentle fun at those who are.

Artist. A practitioner, the field of operations being unimportant and with no suggestion of exceptional skill but nearly always with overtones of insincerity or dishonesty. Few educated people over 30 have it, with this meaning, as part of their active vocabulary but the age range is considerably wider among members of the working class. One can, as an example, 'explore the rip-off artists who kill many good talents under the guise of 'management'' (*Attila*, 23 Oct 1971). In this sense, 'artist' is a successor to the much longer established 'merchant'.

As it goes. As it happens. A throwaway expression, used mainly by teenagers in London and the South East of England, and very rarely found in print, even in magazines aimed at young people. A typical context is the following extract from a conversation overheard in a Brighton classroom (19 Nov 1979): *Teacher*: 'I expect it was in the drawer'. *16-year-old girl*: 'I suppose it was, as it goes'. It is as yet too early to decide whether the phrase is being carried into adulthood from adolescence, but there is some sign that this may in fact be so. The slightly truculent flavour of 'as it goes' adds to its attractions, especially in dealings with authority and with one's elders or social superiors.

Astral plane. Up with the stars, a different level of experience, such as that attained, or supposedly attained, by someone under the influence of drugs. In the 1960s this was an item in the extensive and widely used vocabulary of HIPPY mysticism. 'It buzzes you right into the astral plane' (*International Times*, 19 May 1967). Some of these expressions have seeped into the general language, often with a vague and weakened meaning or as fun words, but most of them are now period pieces.

A.T. Alternative Technology, simpler and essentially non-capitalist investment technology, judged to be particularly suited to the Third World and to plain-living communities everywhere, 'A.T.' is part of the semi-code language of Alternative Technologists. Nobody else uses the expression and most native English speakers, of whatever age, would be thoroughly mystified by it. One can therefore speak of an invention or a political initiative, '. . . which would open up A.T. to a lot more people' (*Undercurrents*, July/Aug 1974). *See* ALTERNOLOGIST.

Aware. Receptive to change, eager for a new world. During the 1960s and 1970s this was a key word among the Alternative People, those for whom the habits, structure and values of conventional society were an insult to humanity. As the hippy style of life gradually faded into mere freakishness and wilfulness, with little in the way of coherent philosophy to support and motivate it, gospel words like 'aware' degenerated into nothing more than tedious jargon. In their heyday, these words had punch and a certain dotty charm. 'Even those of us who are very very aware are still so unaware' (*International Times*, 19 May 1967).

Awareness. A changed state of mind, brought about by drugs. Like AWARE, this is hippy in origin, but it does not necessarily carry the same meaning. One can be permanently 'aware', without drugs ever having played a part in bringing about such a state, but 'awareness' passes as the potency of the drug wears off, although it is perfectly possible, and perhaps normal, for 'aware' people to cultivate 'awareness'. But, like 'aware', 'awareness' is very much an Alternative People's word. 'I'm concerned with awareness expansion'

(*International Times*, 31 Oct 1966) declares one of them, as a confession of faith.

Axe. An electric guitar. From the characteristic shape of such instruments of torture. The word is rarely used in conversation, being used mostly by pop music journalists, but with the addition of a few really dedicated and obsessive fans, who read every word of the music papers and regard them as Holy Writ. 'He wrenches run after run out of his axe' (*Melody Maker*, 20 Jan 1979). 'As a flashing axe, it takes some beating' (*Sounds*, 11 Dec 1982).

Axe work. Guitar playing. 'The axe work was supreme' (*Melody Maker*, 19 May 1979). It should be noted that the word is never applied to the classical guitar, played without benefit of amplifiers. Julian Bream is not an axe virtuoso.

B

Babe, baby. This American term of familiar address has never acquired British nationality, and it is rarely used here, except by worshippers of the American way of life and by those who have professional reasons for sounding American. When it does occur in the speech of what one might call normal people, there is nearly always an element of irony or parody present, the exact degree of which requires a practised ear and eye to detect. 'Well, who else, baby, who else?' (*International Times*, 14 July 1967) is a sentence for advanced students only, since not only does it parody the American usage, but it reflects the aggressive manner in which Americans frequently use the word.

Having said all this, one has to record, for the benefit of posterity, that 'baby' is sometimes used in the UK, absolutely straight, as a very intimate term of endearment.

Bad news. An unpleasant experience. Like the rest of the 'bad' compounds, this one is hippy in its origins. During the past five years, however, it has largely lost its old associations and become fairly widespread among the young and trendy. One finds, for instance: 'Being the daughter of her parents has', she says, 'never been bad news' (*Honey*, June 1979). The remark quoted here came from a girl who might be charitably described as a radio personality and in this context 'bad news' means little, if anything, more than 'disadvantage'. Nowadays, it is usually not a strong word at all.

Bad trip. Since the 1960s, this has had two meanings. The first, used in the drug world, is a frightening or confusing experience, resulting from taking a drug, usually LSD. The second, and now much more general, is any kind of unpleasant experience, without any drug connotation at all. However, the prestige of drug-taking, in certain circles, gives the second sense a vigour and acceptability which it would probably not otherwise possess. 'He looked like a man on a bad trip' (Cohn: *Awopbop*, 1969) shows the phrase in its first meaning, and '. . . except

8

for the Spaniards, man, they're a bad trip' (*Oz* 8 Jan 1968) in its second.

Bag. With the meaning of category, class, style, this was a much-favoured pop music word of the 1960s. It never passed into wider use and, even among the cognoscenti, it is little found today, although it would be incorrect to label it extinct or even obsolete, since it still seems to meet the occasional need. Two examples of 'bag' in its vigorous days are: 'We started at the same time as The Who, but no-one ever tried to put them into our bag' (*Friends*, No. 1, Jan 1969 – a pop singer talking), and 'Liverpool guitarist contemplates starting group in Floyd/Tomorrow bag' (advert in *International Times*, 31 Aug 1967).

Ball. To have sexual intercourse. An American expression which has never struck roots in the UK, at least in the spoken language, although certain journalists with their hearts in the USA have worked hard and devotedly on its behalf. Such efforts can be seen in 'It's music to ball to' (*Oz* 41, April/May 1972) and 'Hubert Plant brings the balling songs to perfection' (*Friends*, No. 1, Jan 1969).

Ball, have a. To enjoy oneself. American in its origins, and fairly obviously so – it feels thoroughly American – this expression has never made much of an impact elsewhere, although teenagers toyed with it for a few years in the 1960s and journalists dragged themselves along with it a little longer. 'Yesterday was fine. They had a ball' (*Jackie*, 26 Sep 1964) shows the determination of the writers of stories for teenagers not to be left behind in the chase after fashion, even if it was beginning to be a rather out-of-date fashion.

Ballgame. Area of operations, activity, responsibility. This essentially American word has crept into the everyday language of two kinds of people in the UK, the businessman, especially on the sales side, and the pop musician. These two have been the main carriers and importers of 'ballgame' which has, as yet, failed to pass into general use on this side of the Atlantic. 'I was letting him make the album, because it was his ballgame' (*Black Music*, Dec 1979) is typical of its field of use.

Balls. Courage, strength, nerve. Nothing is more British than 'balls' in its literal, sexual sense, but, curiously, this particular figurative use has caught on very little here, except among the trendier types of journalist, and even they have little to do with it nowadays. It remains stubbornly American. From its brief British flowering in the late 1960s and early 1970s we have 'The Olympia Press, all promises and no balls' (*International Times*, 5 Jan 1968), 'If CBS have the balls to promote this as a rock and roll record' (*Oz* 34, April 1971) and 'Not prissy folk, folk with balls' (*Zigzag*, April 1973).

'Balls', in the sense of 'nonsense, rubbish', is another matter. It is as British as steak and kidney pie, but until the 1960s it was always very much a male word. One of the triumphs of post-war feminism has been to make the expression unisex, although most women over 50 would still find tradition inhibiting them.

Ballsy. Direct, honest, strong. This word has had a similar history to BALLS. 'People are always trying to intellectualise rock music, but it's managed to stay very ballsy' (Pop musician in *Melody Maker*, 31 March 1979).

Bananas. Mad, excited, enthusiastic. There is no agreement as to whether this expression is of British or American origin, but the probability is that it was a British export to the USA during the 1950s and then returned late in the 1960s with a short second vowel and with its prestige greatly enhanced by its sojourn on the other side of the Atlantic. It is usually pronounced here in the British way, except in the pop music world, where the American style is just as frequently heard. One can do no more than make an intelligent guess at whether the following examples were spoken *à l'anglais* or *à l'américain*. 'I'd just go bananas' (interview with rock musician in *Zigzag*, 30 April 1973), 'How could you possibly say it had nothing to do with you, unless you were completely bananas?' (*Fanatic*, No. 5, 1977), and 'So I get back to discover the national Press have been going bananas over "Alien"' (*Sounds*, 21 July 1979).

Band. A body of instrumentalists playing music of a popular kind. Before about 1945 'band' was everybody's word, irrespective of age or class. One had brass bands, military bands, jazz bands, dance bands. After World War II the situation changed rapidly and radically. The new pop and rock music was always played by 'groups', not 'bands', partly to indicate the democratic, closely-knit nature of the performing unit – 'bands' had conductors, 'groups' never did – and partly, no doubt, because 'band' seemed too grand and pretentious to describe three or four people making music together. There was another important difference. Everyone in a 'band' could read music, whereas it was common, perhaps normal, for members of a 'group' not to be able to read a note.

So during the 1950s and 1960s, the young talked of 'groups' and their elders of 'bands'. From the early 1970s onwards, however, 'band' became increasingly used for small pop and rock groups, although not entirely seriously and with a strong flavour of pastiche. One has to be very sure of one's audience in order to be able to use the word on its own nowadays. According to its social context, it may or may not have elitist or old-fashioned overtones. 'Brass band', 'military band' and 'jazz band', fortunately, have never caused any trouble. We have always continued to have some firm ground under our feet. '. . . a chance to recognise what a fine band they've been all along' (*Oz* 33, Feb 1971); 'American band, *Cheap Tick*' (*New Musical Express*, 6 Jan 1979).

Barfly. A person, more often than not a woman, who frequents bars. It is strange that this useful American word is little found in the UK outside the world of journalists and novelists, to whom, of course, bars may mean more than they do to the rank and file of humanity. It should be noted that, in order to qualify as a barfly, a person must not simply flit from English pub to English pub. It is not synonymous with 'drinker' or 'alcoholic'. The barfly's bar must be, broadly speaking, of the American or hotel type, with stools on which the fly can conveniently settle, close to a bar on which it can rest its wings – '. . . a mutual acquaintance, an unhappy barfly' (*Sounds*, 24 March 1979).

Barnet. A hairstyle, less frequently, a head of hair. It is derived from the Cockney rhyming slang, 'Barnet Fair', meaning 'hair'. Now, in its shortened form, it is widely used and understood outside London, in the kind of circles indicated by the source of the following example. 'Westwood's barnet may not win prizes' (*New Musical Express*, 12 May 1979).

Bash. A lively, amateurish, loud, pop performance. An impromptu concert of the rock or pop variety. The first sense is illustrated by 'A house was chosen for the bash' (Mandelkau: *Buttons*, 1971) and the second by 'The Who's hastily arranged Rainbow bash' (*Melody Maker*, 12 May 1979). 'Bash' can also mean 'a party', but this sense is more common in the USA than in the UK.

All three of these uses are probably derived from the earlier expression, 'to have a bash', meaning to try, to have a go, but this has a much wider range of users than today's music-making or drinking 'bashes'.

Beat. A post–World War II word which has caused a lot of confusion in its time. One can distinguish three meanings.

(*i*) A style of pop music fashionable in the early Sixties, which is easy to illustrate but difficult to describe in words. It was an English phenomenon, different from rock and roll, and lay somewhere in the no-man's land between rock and ballads. Its heyday coincided with the emergence of the Beatles and for some time Beat and Beatles were inseparably connected. From this period come 'First a peek at the beat scene' (*Boyfriend Annual*, 1963) and 'Beat singing doesn't suit her' (*Melody Maker*, 24 Oct 1964).

(*ii*) A particular kind of personal appearance, unconventional and more than slightly unkempt. In this sense, the word, a considerably delayed and watered down derivation of BEATNIK, had a short life as part of teenage popular culture – 'It's chic to look beat in the daytime' (*Jackie*, 22 Feb 1964) – but it has survived as a possibly permanent term for a phrase which Western civilization passed through, 'the beat generation'. There is some overlap between 'beat', meaning 'beatnik' and 'beat' as an abbreviation of 'deadbeat', i.e. 'tired, exhausted'. Sense (*i*) 'beat' people did quite frequently cultivate a Sense (*ii*) 'beat' appearance and manner.

(*iii*) A philosophy and literary style associated with the Beats, young, bewildered American middle-class drop-outs and delinquents of the late 1950s and the 1960s. This is the meaning contained in 'Liberal idealism and beat mysticism will not save the sinking boat in time' (Nuttall: *Bomb Culture*, 1968).

Beatnik. A teenage bohemian, although the term was also applied to people in their early twenties who showed signs of wanting to remain teenagers for ever. In the 1950s in the USA and the early 1960s in the UK the young people who qualified for this label were scruffy, often downright dirty, and made much public show of their rejection of conventional ideals, morality and behaviour. So we find, within the classic beatnik period, 'Later in the evening she and her boyfriend are invited to a beatnik party' (*Boyfriend Annual*, 1963); 'Do other readers have problem brothers like mine, I wonder? He's a beatnik' (Letter to *Jackie*, 9 Jan 1965); and '. . . certain incidents involving

German beatniks' (*International Times*, 28 Nov 1966).

Not long afterwards, the general soap, scissors and respectability public was calling people of very similar appearance HIPPY, with much the same scornful and affronted overtones as for 'beatnik'.

Beaut. Something altogether exceptional in its class and richly deserving of admiration and respect. This not very elegant abbreviation of 'beauty', used both as a noun and a verb, seems to have originated in the USA in the 1860s and to have established itself in both the UK and Australia early in the 20th century although it was only very rarely heard in the UK during the period between World War I and World War II. Its new-found popularity among British teenagers in the 1950s and 1960s was almost certainly due to Australian, rather than American influence, with the Australian-inspired magazine, *Oz*, as a major factor in its adoption. While the fashion lasted – it waned long ago – one found an abundance of examples, 'He had some real beauts' and 'You can get in some beaut chords' (*Jackie*, 30 May 1964).

Beautiful. Just right, wonderful. A favourite superlative in the pop world during the 1970s – 'The B side is just beautiful' (*Zigzag*, June 1971) – it has since been supplanted by other and more up-to-date expressions. While it was in vogue, the combination with 'just' was so frequently found that one had the impression of listening to a compound noun.

Beautiful People, beautiful people. A term much used by the youth avant-garde in the 1960s and now obsolete. With the passage of time, the important difference between Beautiful People and beautiful people has been largely forgotten. The Beautiful People were rich, fashionable, trendy hippies. This is the reference in '. . . all the Beautiful People at a London discotheque, where super-powered sounds happen' (toothpaste advert in *Jackie*, 2 Sept 1967), and '. . . those god-like giants who stride amongst us in an aura of dazzling light – the Beautiful People' (*Oz*, 8 Jan 1968). It was not unknown for the Beautiful People to use the phrase about themselves, but more often it was an adulatory description from outside.

'beautiful people' was ironic and mildly derogatory. It carried the meaning of 'hippies or people dressing and behaving like them'. This would be a typical example. 'Beautiful people wanted for outdoor hippy production' (*International Times*, 5 Jan 1968).

Beeb. The British Broadcasting Corporation (BBC). A creation of the later 1970s, the inventor probably being the disc jockey, Kenny Everett. It was quickly taken up by journalists – 'Beeb slaps ban on sex' (*Daily Mirror*, 22 March 1979); '. . . the Beeb's latest response to widespread dissatisfaction with the unwieldy, remote 'local' radio station' (*Time Out*, 6 April 1979) – and is now in fairly general use, although almost entirely among the more educated sections of the population. It is rarely employed by people over the age of 40.

Beefcake. The cult of exposing the male chest. First noted in the USA in the late 1940s and now the common property of the English-speaking world, the word is, inevitably, particularly popular among homosexuals – 'Beefcake for Christmas? Revealing gloss photos of your favourite screen heroes' (*Gay News*, 9–22 Dec 1982). It can, however, be used in the more general sense of 'brawny, strutting masculinity' – 'What every beefcake on the street has got on his head' (*New Musical Express*, 7 March 1981).

Belting. Very good, clever, original. An expression that appeared from nowhere during the late 1950s. Its use by journalists catering for the teenage market may have given the impression that it was more popular than was actually the case – this danger is always present in literature which believes in the policy of holding a mirror up to its readers – but by the end of the 1960s it was little used. It was never an adult word, a typical context being 'I always thought it was a belting idea' (*Jackie*, 19 Dec 1964).

Bevvy. A drink. Originally Liverpool dialect, the word became much more widespread in the 1960s and 1970s, as a result of the prestige given by the Beatles to all things Liverpudlian. The People's Novelists were especially fond of it as a piece of democratic colour – 'We used to have a few bevvies in them days' (Hignett: *A Picture to Hang on the Wall*, 1966). So, too, **Bevvied up** means drunk.

Biggie. A big one, something very successful. The -ie ending is a fairly recent journalistic device for coining new nouns, for example oldie, NEWIE and FREEBIE. This class of words has, even so, shown distinct signs of popular appeal and examples from the list are often heard in conversation, especially among girls and younger women, who have always been fond of anything sounding like a diminutive. But a strongly journalistic flavour remains, although 'Dire Straits' chart biggie' (*Melody Maker*, 12 May 1979) does strain a little too much after effect.

Biker. A rocker, greaser, literally someone who rides a motorbike. The implication is always that the person in question is not one of society's more respectable or peaceful members – 'The bikers were there in force' (*New Society*, 24 May 1979) – and the word is much more likely to be used about the bikers than by the bikers themselves. Very much a British usage.

Bill. The police, a more widely heard euphemism being 'the old Bill'. During World War I 'Old Bill' was a veteran, an old soldier, who was usually depicted with heavy, drooping whiskers. The term is obsolete in this sense, but it was revived in the 1960s by anarchists, hippies, and others hostile to the notion and the forces of law and order, to mean their arch-enemy, the police. So, "Fite Dem Back' shifts the ground from the Bill to the Front' (*Sounds*, 24 March 1979). It is not a word used by the older or more law-abiding sections of the population.

Bins. Glasses, spectacles. This abbreviation of 'binoculars', not found in the USA, has been popular since the 1960s among British schoolchildren and older teenagers who have left school. It is rarely used by people over the age of 25 and, even then, almost exclusively by journalists, as in 'Ian Page's near-secret, near-sighted bins' (*Sounds*, 1 Dec 1979).

Biog. History, biography. The abbreviation, of very recent origin, is virtually confined to journalists and public relations people, usually with the implication that the work in question is a run-of-the-mill affair and not to be taken terribly seriously. It can be reported, for example, that a commercial concern intends 'to write their own record company biog' (*Sounds*, 24 Jan 1981), but the staff of *The Times Literary Supplement* would be most unlikely, even in the sanctity of the office, to refer to a new 'biog' of the Pope or Earl Mountbatten.

Biopic. A film biography. One could safely offer a large reward to anyone who heard this word used in ordinary conversation. It is a film critic's speciality, of recent growth, and there seems to be no particular reason to hope or expect that it will spread any further. 'A Hollywood biopic like 'Young Man with a Horn" (*The Guardian*, 13 March 1979) is essentially to be typed, not spoken, and then only by someone who gets paid for doing it.

Bit. Activity, way of behaving, act. The word implies cynicism and a lack of confidence in whatever the particular activity is. 'Bit' always contains a strong cliché element. A 'bit' is not really to be taken seriously. As examples of this usage, and of the attitude to life behind it, one can quote, 'In many ways the entire drug bit was a gigantic bore' (*International Times*, 27 Feb 1967); 'I was strolling past them doing my duchess bit' (letter to *Jackie*, 24 Feb 1968) and 'Please give up the Meditation bit – everyone else has' (letter to *Private Eye*, 8 March 1969). The expression feels distinctly passé today, but it fitted the philosophy of the nothing-lasts-long 1960s very well.

Bitch. This, in the sense of 'a lewd or fast woman', has been a widely used English expression since the 15th century. With the arrival of the infamous Hell's Angels on the social scene in the USA in the 1950s and in the UK in the 1960s, one had to reckon with a new shade of meaning. For the Angels and their admirers, 'bitch' became a synonym for any woman, since in their world view, the sole function of women is to be abused and exploited by men, to be mere sexual objects, chattels. 'Ernie came in with a black bitch who was his property' (Mandelkau: *Buttons*, 1971).

Black. Negro. For 30 years, this has been a most difficult word to use correctly and without causing trouble. In the 1960s, for a white person in the UK to call a negro 'black' was considered insulting, although negroes themselves were already making use of the word, as part of their campaign for racial equality. The intensity of feeling among young British whites on this issue was remarkable. For them, black people were sacred figures, and the slightest hint of what was taken to be racial prejudice was pounced on. 'Racist' was one of the most powerful and damning stigmas which could be attached to anyone and, to the young, most of their parents' generation were incurably and dangerously 'racist'.

Their parents, or some of them, took the point, acknowledged their crime, and began to refer to 'coloured' people. The climate then changed and, once again, they fell behind fashion, since during the 1970s it became acceptable to use 'black', instead of 'coloured' although the noun was still, for some curious reason, felt to be offensive and 'black people' was preferred, offering a close parallel with 'Jews' and 'Jewish people'. By this time, the blacks themselves strongly disliked being called 'coloured', since this placed them in the same social and ethnic compartment as Indians and Pakistanis, with whom they had no wish whatever to be confused. Black nationalism was very much in the air and those with brown skins had absolutely no part to play in that.

It is interesting to notice that it became normal to say 'black' earlier among pop musicians than in any other group. So far as the British population as a whole was concerned, 'There were opportunities for black musicians and writers' (*The Soul Book*, 1975) was ahead of its time. Four years later, however, the ordinary newspapers could write of 'harassing black people' (*Daily Mirror*, 22 March 1979) without any fear of causing a racial riot or of having the office windows smashed by a youthful mob.

Blag. To persuade, con, get something for nothing. This is an interesting case of an old-established word moving away from its low origins. In the 1920s and 1930s it was applied entirely to members of the criminal and semi-criminal classes, who earned a living by extracting money and goods from their gullible fellow citizens. During and after World War II, the dividing line between right and wrong, permitted and forbidden, became steadily vaguer and more shadowy and a rich crop of euphemisms was created in order to make illegal and antisocial acts appear normal and of no great consequence. 'Blag' was a handy word for just this purpose and it became much used by a new generation for which crude words like 'steal' and 'swindle' still had the power to produce a moral twinge.

We therefore discover that 'his cohorts blagged albums last Wednesday' (*Sounds*, 24 March 1979), meaning that these desirable articles were acquired for nothing, and that 'Joe is accosted by two teenage girls trying to blag tickets for one of the shows' (*Melody Maker*, 12 May 1979), meaning that two girls were using their wiles in order to extract a couple of free tickets out of Joe.

One also finds the noun **Blag**, 'rubbish, exaggerated talk', as a well-used word among teenagers and young adults from the mid-1960s onwards – 'It was all blag, of course' (Cohn: *Awopbop*, 1969). This succeeded 'blah', popular in both the UK and USA during the 1920s and 1930s.

Blam. To race. Very much a young person's word, it can refer either to people or to machines, but it always involves a lot of noise. It was not found before the 1970s. Among the aficionados, a motorcycle would be 'made to blam around a circuit at full bore' (*Superbike*, Sept 1978).

Bland. Mild, smooth, suave, soothing, gentle, not stimulating. In all these senses, 'bland' has been a part of Standard English for 300 years, usually but not always as a description of people or their behaviour. Since World War II, however, the meaning of the word has been widened in two directions. As food and drink have become increasingly tasteless, the need to discover a dignified synonym for 'possessing little or no taste' became of vital commercial importance and 'bland' appeared to fill the bill admirably. Anything which is 'bland' makes no demands on the palate or the judgement but there is no suggestion of inferiority in the term.

However, at the same time, 'bland' has moved into position as a term of criticism, often amounting to an insult. It is particularly favoured by those in the pop music world, whose livelihood depends on being different from their competitors. To be 'bland' here is to be dead. Bland coffee is one thing, but a bland singer is quite another. Two examples will make the point. 'Nobody likes doing articles on us anymore, 'cos we're so ordinary we're bland' (pop star interviewed in *Sounds*, 22 Dec 1979), and 'I'd rather be hated down the line than be bland' (*Sounds*, 24 Jan 1981).

Blandout. An excess of bland material, music, behaviour or whatever. One of the latest in a recent line of undesirable American exports with the -out suffix, the earliest probably being 'wipe-out'. This one has been favoured by pop music journalists and musicians, and by hardly anybody else. By looking in the right places, one finds such examples as 'The punters demonstrate their disillusionment with home-grown blandout' (*Sounds*, 24 March 1979).

Blocked. High on drugs. A friendly and uncritical word, uncommon before the 1970s, when one finds 'Jimmy rides out, blocked and happy, on his multi-coloured scooter' (*New Musical Express*, 12 May 1979). 'Blocked' is unlikely to be used by anyone unsympathetic to drug-taking.

Blow, have a. Smoke marijuana. An interesting extension of meaning, as one form of addiction came to replace another. A 'blow' was an ordinary tobacco-filled cigarette in the 1920s. In the new world of drug-taking, it is an addict's word – 'Yeah, I had a blow' (*New Society*, 26 June 1980).

'Blow' is also found as a verb, meaning to inhale a narcotic drug.

Blow it. To ruin, destroy, make a mess of something. A vague general term, used to begin with by members of the UNDERGROUND, but now more widely. The 'it' element of the expression can sometimes be translated by 'well-being', 'things going well'. 'We blew it this time, so let's try something different' (*Attila*, 13 Nov 1981) and 'They were just a boogie band. They had their shot and blew it' (*Melody Maker*, 19 May 1979) show the phrase in use. The modern 'blow it', one should emphasize, must not be confused with the expletive beloved by the Victorians, a favourite and nearly respectable euphemism for 'curse it'.

Blowout. Something excellent, immensely successful. An expression of American origin, confined to pop music fans and the journalists who serve them – 'Colosseum's new album "Valentine Suite" is a blowout' (advert in *Friends*, No. 3, Jan 1970). This meaning is paradoxical, since, in the case of tyres, fuses and oilwells, a blowout is far from being a token of success. But 'blow out', in the sense of a huge meal, one should note, is as British as steak and kidney pie, with a history that goes back to the days of William IV.

Blow out. (*i*) To snub. 'The TDS blew Maggot out and did a moonlight' (*Sounds*, 1 Dec 1979), and 'being blown out by these snotty little Leicester touts' (interview with rock group in *Zigzag*, Sept 1973).

(*ii*) To make a mess of things. 'That tour was blown out' (interview with rock musician in *Zigzag*, Aug 1972) and 'to avoid blowing the whole project out' (*Sounds*, 21 July 1979).

(*iii*) To greatly impress. 'It will always be people like Ray Charles who still blow me out' (interview with rock musician in *Zigzag*, Sept 1973).

It is not accidental that the examples given above all come from magazines closely associated with the world of rock and pop music. These are the people who need phrases of this slightly outrageous kind as much as they need the clothes and the hairstyles which stamp them as being not as other men. To sound and look bizarre is an essential part of the business, and to accomplish both these things in a way which is internationally acceptable is an art necessary for success. 'Blow out' is the kind of expression which meets its requirement to perfection. With one foot in the UK and the other in the USA, it is a perfect symbol of the universe which people like this inhabit.

Blow the mind. To impress, amaze, outrage. 'Blowing the mind' is usually, but not always, a fairly pleasant, although inevitably exhausting experience. It is a phrase brought into existence by drug-takers and hippies in the 1960s and much used by them, but now very common among the youthful and the recently ex-youthful. 'It's too easy to blow someone's mind. All we have to do is to go on stark naked or explode' (*Oz*, 21, June 1969). 'He enjoys blowing people's minds at hit gatherings by saying, "Actually I agree with Enoch Powell"' (*Schoolkids Oz*, April 1970).

Blue meanies. The police. The phrase gained wide currency as a result of the Beatles' cartoon film, *Yellow Submarine* (1968) which had spoil-sport characters called 'blue meanies'. The police are, of course, the men in blue and in the UK 'blue meanies' has echoes of 'bluebottle', which has been used since Shakespeare's time as a not over-polite name for 'beadle, policeman'. The use of 'blue meanies' has been confined for the most part to young people who are likely, for one reason or another, to find themselves in trouble with the law or who are, at the least, instinctively hostile to its representatives. 'If the blue meanies try to break it up' (*Attila*, 16 Oct 1971) provides a point of reference.

Bobby-soxer. A very young teenager, 'bobby-socks' or, rather, 'bobby-sox', being the short variety. Introduced into the UK from the USA in the early 1950s, the term was used almost exclusively by journalists who tried very hard to popularize it, but without any great success. Its American flavour and association were probably too strong to allow it easy access to the everyday speech of the young British. 'Frank excites the first bobby-soxers' (*New Musical Express*, 4 May 1956), when the phrase still had something of the freshness of youth. It is now a museum-piece.

Bod. A person of either sex. 'Bod' is a fairly warm, affectionate word, but it usually indicates a certain degree of cliquishness. 'Our bod can, and we tried him out on Carole, our typist' (*Jackie*, 8 Feb 1964) gives the modern flavour. This jocular abbreviation of 'body' is not new. It has been in use since the 18th century, but until recently it has always been considered rather low – it was a favourite among generations of medical students – and to be avoided by women. This is no longer the case. For 30 years at least, 'bod' has been issuing from middle-class mouths of all ages and both sexes.

Bogart. To keep a cannabis cigarette to oneself, to refuse to share it in company. Of American origin, the word was popularized by a song in the film *Easy Rider* containing the line, 'Don't Bogart that joint, my friend. Pass it over to me'. The reference is to the film actor, Humphrey Bogart (1899–1957), who was always to be seen with a cigarette hanging from his mouth. He never handled it and appeared to smoke it to the end without taking it from his lips. Those not personally involved in these matters are likely to find it difficult to translate. 'Help stamp out Bogarting, roll them longer with Esmeralda' (advert for cigarette papers in *Private Eye*, 23 Aug 1974), but initiates will experience no problems.

Boiler. A woman of loose habits, but not a prostitute. The exact degree of moral laxity is always vague, and in the theatrical/musical world it usually implies little more than 'tired, dishevelled troupers'. This is almost certainly what is to be understood by 'two boilers in various states of undress' (*New Musical Express*, 7 Oct 1978). The word, which seems to have appeared on both the American and the British scene in the late 1950s, is little found outside the entertainment world and its fringes.

Bollocks. Energy, vigour. In its literal sense of 'testicles', this is a very old word and certainly not one to use at a Royal Garden Party. The figurative meaning seen in, 'He thought it needed more bollocks' (*Sounds*, 24 Jan 1981), 'it' being a recording, is recent, however, and appears, as yet, to be fully at home only in the worlds of pop music and sport.

Bolthead. A very stupid person, a fathead. The adjective is associated with the appearance of Frankenstein, who has often been shown in films with a bolt through his neck and whose facial expression and body position suggest that his intelligence is minimal. Those who are addicted to Frankenstein films will probably understand the reference in '. . . any bolthead in the audience who's ready to ruck' (*Sounds*, 1 Dec 1979), but others may experience some difficulty.

Bomb. (*i*) To fail, go down badly. an American expression, used elsewhere almost exclusively in the entertainment world. A British student would not 'bomb', an American would. Typical British contexts are, 'She appeared at the Monterey Pop Festival, but bombed heavily and decided to call it a day' (*Oz* 33, Feb 1971), and 'What if 'Kiss Me Deadly' were to bomb?' (*Melody Maker*, 24 Jan 1981). **Bomb Out** is also found, with the same meaning. 'If my records bomb out . . .' (interview with funk musician in *New Musical Express*, 12 May 1979).

(*ii*) To rush around fast and noisily, usually on motorcycles, less frequently in old cars. 'At weekends they bombed up and down the coastline on their hotrods' (Cohn: *Awopbop*, 1969). An obsolescent youth-word, never used unsympathetically.

(*iii*) A lot of money. 'How many fat kids, fat kids who spend a bomb on the latest gear . . .' (*Sounds*, 24 March 1979). 'Bomb', in this sense, has been very widely used in the UK since the late 1950s. There must be very few people here who would be unable to translate 'He made a bomb out of it', but the majority of those who use the word regularly are probably under 50.

Bomb, go down a. Be a great success, receive a rapturous reception from an audience. 'The gig was fantastic – we went down a bomb' (*Pink*, 12 May 1979) is a modern example of an expression which has been in use on both sides of the Atlantic for 30 years, although, outside the more highly Americanized section of the entertainment world, the more grammatical, 'we went down like a bomb' is probably more common.

Boo-boo. A mistake, usually an embarrassing one. This rather coy term originated in the USA in the early 1950s and the British press was using it ten years later. It has remained entirely a journalist's word, mainly on *The Guardian* level, and, at least in the UK, one has never heard it used in conversation. 'We are bound to commit similar boo-boos' (*The Guardian*, 12 March 1979) has the authentic flavour.

Boob. (*i*) To make a mistake. Not American usage and, in the UK, no longer associated with any particular age-group or social class, although in the 1960s it had a teenager, young adult feel about it. So, 'I've boobed' (*Jackie*, 25 Jan 1964); 'The labelling machined boobed on just one copy' (*Sounds*, 3 March 1979).

(*ii*) A mistake, fluff. 'If you see someone making a boob on the box

. . .' (*My Guy*, 12 May 1979). Not used as widely in the USA as it is in the UK, although in the sense of 'a stupid person', the word is much more American than English.

(*iii*) Breast. This sense of the word certainly originated in the USA, but it was well entrenched in the UK by the 1960s, although with a rather different range of users. Here it belongs mainly to the middle class, especially its younger members, and one hears it more from men, which is not the American situation. One can therefore speak, without undue embarrassment, of 'sales ladies who maliciously shove my soft boobs into hard unnatural shapes' (letter to *Oz* 3, Aug 1967) and advise that 'a dab of dark blusher between your boobs will do wonders for your cleavage' (*Mates Annual*, 1979).

Boogie. Originally a type of dance music, a speciality of American blacks. Then, as a verb, to dance to such music. In the 1970s it acquired the additional senses of 'hurry', 'go', 'enjoy oneself', the last meaning often having strong sexual undertones. Among white British teenagers, however, it has mostly been a quiet word, with a relatively small element of excitement in it. 'Boogie on down the High Street and pick yourself up some trendy togs' (*Sounds* horoscope, 24 March 1979) is a trendy journalist's way of saying 'Hurry on down the High Street'. It is extremely doubtful, however, if many youngsters in the UK, white or black, have ever actually said, 'I'm going to boogie on down the High Street to pick myself up some trendy togs'. Some things are more easily written than spoken.

Boot, put in the. (*i*) Use violence, fight. Not American, and used much earlier in Australia than in the UK, in the specialized sense of 'kick an opponent when he's down'. This, the Australian meaning, probably arrived here as a result of the mingling of Australian and British troops during World War I. In the 1960s the expression gained a new lease of life, first among the rougher working-class elements, among adolescent boys and then, as an expression of group solidarity and vicarious living, among a much wider range of teenagers and young adults, journalists and novelists included. 'They didn't even turn off the transistors as they put the boot in' (Nuttall: *Bomb Culture*, 1968) belongs to this period.

The popularity of the phrase in its new existence was undoubtedly partly due to the habit of the young fighting-class of wearing heavy and aggressive boots. There was, and to some extent still is, a new boot-wearing class, accustomed to fight, maim and injure with its feet.

(*ii*) Make a point forcefully, step in, intervene, not necessarily physically. A journalist's usage for the most part – 'Put the boot in before it's too late' (*Private Eye*, 5 June 1970) – but it is also found more widely among those, such as young salesmen and businessmen, who cultivate an aggressive life-style.

Bootboy. A member of an aggressive, usually skinhead street gang – 'Punks, skins, bootboys' (*Sounds*, 24 Jan 1981). Purely British and part of the vocabulary of the boot culture, the word is used, not without pride, by the bootboys themselves, but also by those who admire them and by journalists with a toe in the teenage world. It is also employed, somewhat derisively and patronisingly, by non-violent and socially more desirable young people to indicate that they are familiar with the word and the type it represents, but that the boys are concerned are a lower order of humanity. It is a useful exercise to try to guess exactly what attitude is implied by '. . . no holds bootboy punk outfit' (*Sounds*, 3 March 1979) and 'beer-bellied Brentwood bootboy' (*Sounds*, 12 Jan 1979).

Bootleg. An illegal or pirated recording. This sense of a word long hallowed by the American alcohol industry is only found among the practitioners, journalists and exceptionally devoted fans of the pop music world. 'Can I get into trouble for buying bootlegs?' (letter to *Sounds*, 28 April 1979), and a note that a particular recording is 'only available on the 'Van the Man' bootleg' (*Sounds*, 3 March 1979) are a fair indication of the word's range of customers.

Bop. (*i*) To dance, clap, jump around to music. There is 'music for bopping and young love' (*The Soul Book*, 1975), and promoters have taken pains to 'make sure the crowd was bopping through the entire show' (*Sounds*, 3 May 1979).

(*ii*) To skip along. 'Robin comes bopping up' (Myers: *Fast Sam*, 1975).

(*iii*) Hit, attack, fight. In use in Victorian times as a good, solid British word, but revived recently, probably as a result of American influence. Lads with time and energy to spare have been in the habit, it appears, of 'setting fire to mansions early in the morning and bopping skinheads' (Mandelkau: *Buttons*, 1971).

This word, as the above examples indicate, has a curiously mixed history. Its career as a technical jazz term is beyond the scope of the present book. It is doubtful, however, if more than a tiny minority of white British teenagers, and an even smaller proportion of adults, have ever actually used 'bop', in the first sense given above, with any regularity. Journalists have virtually monopolized it. So far as the second sense is concerned, the number of non-journalist users has probably been rather higher. But, as part of anyone's active vocabulary and, in both meanings, 'bop' reached its peak of usage in the early or mid-1970s.

Bopper. An enthusiastic dancer, any young person. When the person referred to is very young, there is more than a suggestion of precocity and early sexual awareness. The word is always used by older people, not by the boppers themselves, and it belongs essentially to the world centred around pop music. So one finds 'teen black boppers' (*The Soul Book*, 1975), and a suggestion that one might 'try to lure some cute little bopper into the bushes' (*New Musical Express*, 12 May 1979).

Boring Old Fart. A boring person. This catch-phrase is associated particularly, if not exclusively, with middle-class trendies, especially those whose trendiness belongs to the recent past. It has slightly affectionate, rather than derogatory, overtones, rather as if one were referring to a once-popular old actor, who has had his day. It is not an easy phrase to translate accurately, as one can see from 'The anarchists of one year are the boring old farts of the next' Cohn: (*Awopbop*, 1969), and 'You might think I'm a boring old fart, but I'm really into Anthony Phillips' (advert in *Sounds*, 24 March 1979).

Bossa nova. A style of Brazilian music not unlike the samba. The term has been established in the pop world since the early 1960s and will presumably continue as long as the music itself survives – 'Most of their music is only feedback when they think it's bossa nova' (*Sounds*, 24 Jan 1981).

Bottle. (*i*) Nerve, daring, guts, strength. Originally, in the 1950s, a London expression, it moved into the pop music and media worlds during the late 1960s and then, through television and advertising, into general use in the mid-1970s. The widening of the market can be observed in 'He's got a lot of bottle' (interview with rock group in *Zigzag*, Sept 1973); 'Bad Company lost their collective bottle after a gruelling American tour' (*Melody Maker*, March 1979), and 'Even in a can, it's got bottle' (poster advertising McEwan's Export Beer, March 1979).

(*ii*)　Hit with a bottle. Part of the vocabulary of those who conduct their arguments in this fashion. 'I had an argument with a Hell's Angel and got bottled' (rock musician in *The Road to Rock*, 1974).

Boutique. A broad definition would be 'a small shop selling clothes', but this conceals the most interesting series of meanings and associations which the word has passed through during the last 30 years or so.

In the sense of 'a small shop, a booth', 'boutique' established itself in English in the mid-18th century, and it continued with this meaning until the mid-1920s, after which it almost vanished from view. It re-emerged, first in the USA, and soon afterwards in the UK, in the early 1950s, when, for the first time, it began to be associated only with clothes and accessories. As it was then used, a 'boutique' was a small shop or department within a store, selling fashionable, ready-made clothes and other dress and toiletry articles designed or commissioned by a couturier. By the mid-1960s a second kind of boutique was in evidence, with the young and trendy as its customers. It has now reverted entirely to its former up-market use. The Carnaby Street wave has passed over it and it is now once again an exclusive, expensive type of shop, run as a profitable sideline by one of the *haute couture* houses. The teenage takeover bid was highly successful while it lasted, but it proved to have no staying power. To the word's youthful slumming period belong 'Around the boutiques with Sam' (column heading in *Jackie*, 7 May 1966), 'The first psychedelic boutique busts in King's Road' (*International Times*, 14 Oct 1966), and 'Are you wearing the most way out clothes you could find in the boutique?' (*Jackie*, 4 Feb 1968).

Box. In the sense of 'television', 'box' is used by a wide range of people in the UK, but is probably heard more frequently among the under-40s. 'If you see someone making a boob on the box, let us know' (*My Guy*, 12 May 1979) is a typically colloquial context. 'Box', it is interesting to note, was being used in the early 1920s to mean 'gramophone', and by 1930 for 'wireless set'. As a synonym for 'television', it is doing no more than to bring a well-established tradition up-to-date.

With the meaning of 'head', however – another purely British usage – the market for the word is much more restricted. It belongs to the trendy and especially to those whose life-style has a hippy or pop flavour to it. 'They were stoned out of their boxes' (meaning high on drugs, *Sounds*, 3 March 1979).

Boy, boyfriend. (*i*) Male friend, boyfriend. English is, in this respect as in many others, a defective language. Even in Elizabethan times one found 'he-friend', 'she-friend', as clumsy equivalents for, say, the German *Freund*, *Freundin*. Throughout the 1920s and 1930s and for most of the 1940s, 'boy' was the usual term among the young and their parents for a sweetheart or lover. It continued to be used by working-class girls in the 1960s, by which time 'boyfriend' was being favoured among the middle classes. 'Let your boy make the decisions' (*Jackie*, 2 Oct 1965), and 'My boy – or should I say my ex-' (*Jackie*, 30 May 1961) illustrate this. With the young of all classes, 'boy' is now almost obsolete, although it is still used by older women about their daughters' boyfriends.

(*ii*) A general exclamation, with no particular meaning. 'Boy, does it hot up in summer' (*Mates Annual*, 1979) is a late example, since at this date it was no longer in use among the readers of *Mates Annual*. As so frequently happens, the journalists were running behind their public.

Bread. Money. 'Bread' was being widely used in this sense in the USA in the late 1940s. By the 1950s it had travelled abroad with the hip movement and then gained more extensive coverage as a result of the pop music explosion. During the early 1970s it passed into general use within the lower two thirds of the British social pyramid, although it continued to be fairly thoroughly shunned by the more refined sections of society, which regarded it as low. There are signs that it may now have passed its peak of popularity. The following examples belong to its heyday: 'The bread is there. You can earn up to 4000 dollars a gig' (musician in *Oz* 18, Feb 1969); 'Never made any bread from that particular manager – he just used us' (pop singer in *Friends*, No. 1, Jan 1969); 'A lot of people who really wanted to see Canned Heat couldn't through lack of bread' (*Attila*, 23 Oct 1971); 'He got straight bread instead of a percentage' (*Zigzag*, Aug 1972).

Breadhead. A person who pretends to have adopted an Alternative Lifestyle, but who in fact devotes much of his energy to the mainline pursuit of making money. The word originated in the USA in the late 1930s but it was certainly being used in hippy-style circles elsewhere by the late 1960s. 'They are what the Underground would call breadheads' (*The Listener*, 20 Aug 1970). Today it is little heard in any kinds of circles.

Breadless. Penniless, without money to buy bread. The word and the basic meaning have existed in English since the 14th century, but it has gained much wider currency in recent years with the popularity of the word BREAD. Nowadays, for this reason, it has a different flavour from the one which belonged to it for the first six centuries of its life. 'The breadless are the nastiest and most primitive beings in the city' (*Home Grown*, No. 2, 1977) conveys the modern, not the medieval or Victorian shade of meaning.

Break. To promote, publicize, make successful, get a break for. This sense of the word first appeared in the USA in the mid-1960s and within a short time it had crossed the Atlantic. Now, as throughout its career, it has been used almost exclusively in the entertainment, especially pop, music world. 'United Artists seem to have so many good bands, but they can't seem to break them' (*Zigzag*, April 1973), and 'I was just one they (the record company) were trying to break that year' (pop singer, reported in *Honey*, June 1979) set the word in its milieu.

Break big. To become a hit. '. . . mere weeks before "Roxanne" broke big' (*Sounds*, 24 Jan 1981).

Brill. An abbreviation of 'brilliant'. A catch-word current among British teenagers during the late 1970s, but not exported. 'Again are definitely on to something pretty brill' (*Melody Maker*, 19 May 1979) illustrates the field. The word was popularized by the British television comedians, Little and Large. The word is out of fashion among adults, but still used *ad nauseam* by children.

Bring down. A depressing experience, originally after a drug high, but later from any cause. An American HIPPY expression in the early 1960s, then quickly international in the English-speaking world. 'What makes all of this such a bring-down . . .' (Cohn: *Awopbop*, 1969) belongs to the period when the phrase had broken free from its drug-bonds. *See* BROUGHT DOWN.

Broad. A woman, usually of dubious reputation. There may possibly be a connection with the late-19th early-20th-century colloquialisms, 'broad', meaning 'wideawake, knowing', and 'broad in the beam' meaning 'broad-bottomed', but in the sense of 'a woman' the word is and always has been strongly American and rarely used in the UK, except by those with more than a toe in American culture. In 'The raw Texas broad made good in freaking San Francisco' (*Oz* 33, Feb 1971), the word is being deliberately and consciously used in a parody of the American idiom.

Brought down. Depressed. *See* BRING DOWN. Used originally by drug addicts and by those closely associated with them, it transferred naturally and quickly into the pop music world. 'That tour was blown out and we were very brought down' (rock musician, quoted in *Zigzag*, Aug 1972).

Brown tongue. An act of sycophancy, associated no doubt with the older-established 'arse-licking'. A phrase which ranks as coarse even in the pop music and entertainment worlds, which are not celebrated for refinement of taste and expression. Common in these fields since the early 1970s, it is little used outside them. 'He must have prompted more brown tongues than just about any other rock and roll artist ever' (*Sounds*, 3 March 1979) indicates the usage.

Brown-tongued. Sycophantic, grovelling. 'A somewhat brown-tongued expression of gratitude for their come-back.' (*Sounds*, 28 April 1979).

Brown wings. A decoration awarded to Hell's Angels on the occasion of their first homosexual intercourse. The expression originated in the USA in the 1960s and was soon being used wherever these unpleasant creatures existed. 'Most of the Frisco chapter earned their brown wings on this occasion' (Mandelkau: *Buttons*, 1971).

Bruce. Australian. The word can be used either as a noun or an adjective, and has an interesting history. It derives from Stanley Melbourne (1883–1967), who became Viscount Bruce of Melbourne and who was Prime Minister of Australia for much of the 1920s. The word is known in both the USA and the UK, but little used in the more respectable and middle-class layers of society. It appears to have established itself during World War II and to have moved soon afterwards into distinctly non-military fields, as evidenced by 'the basic Bruce' (*Sounds*, 3 March 1979).

B-side. An international pop music term for the reverse side of a recording, not the side for which the record is being chiefly publicized and sold. 'The B-side is just beautiful' (rock star, quoted in *Zigzag*, June 1971).

Bubblegum. Exceptionally banal teenage pop music. This Anglo–American term was used by 'thinking' rock musicians and journalists during the 1960s and early 1970s as a term of derision and contempt for particularly mindless Top Twenty music, at a time when pop was, incredibly, still thought to have some intellectual potential. 'The way to break the bubblegum market is simply to shout' (Cohn: *Awopbop*, 1969), and 'The fifth-rate bubblegum and mumsy pop music was discarded in favour of genuinely creative musical endeavours' (*Schoolkids Oz*, April 1970) belong to the word's vogue-period.

Buff. An expert, devotee, enthusiast. This American term, current in its present-day sense in the early 1950s, has not yet been fully absorbed into British English, even among people strongly sympathetic to the American way of life and to things American. Journalists have toiled long and hard to get it taken over and acclimatized, but, despite their sterling efforts, the word is nearly always spoken and written in fairly obvious inverted commas, to indicate its non-British origin and flavour. So, 'Jazz-buffs may find the evening light on scholarship' (*The Guardian*, 13 March 1979), and '. . . a blind dates buff' (*Jackie*, 22 Feb 1964).

Bug. To annoy, pester. An American meaning which, via pop music journalists, has made considerable inroads into the mental world inhabited by teenagers. Its 20-year popularity in Britain suggests that it may by now have become something of a fixture. 'The only answer is to bug hell out of the manager of your local hip bookshop' (*International Times*, 29 May 1967); 'She always criticises the way I dress or do my hair. It really bugs me' (letter to *Jackie*, 1 Sept 1979); 'They are particularly bugged by the arbitrary punishment meted out by some teachers' (*Schoolkids Oz*, April 1970).

Buggered. Physically exhausted. This once very non-drawing room word has lost much of its force during the past 20 or 30 years, largely as a result of being taken up and declassed by teenagers of both sexes. Australian influence has also been at work and this once powerful and beyond-the-pale word is now a mere shadow of its former self, an enfeebled metaphor. 'I was pretty buggered after the first year on the road' (rock singer, quoted in *Sounds*, 24 March 1979) illustrates the modern, unemotional usage, about which many older people still have misgivings.

Bullet. To do exceptionally well. Among American poker players, a bullet is an ace, and it was therefore natural in the pop music business to put a bullet sign on their sales charts against those records which have been particularly successful. 'The LP has bulleted on every chart this week' (advert in *Sounds*, 28 April 1979). As a verb and in this sense the word is not, however, in general use.

Bum. The two meanings of this word, one British, 'buttocks', and the other American, 'an idler, tramp, useless person', kept fairly strictly to their own sides of the Atlantic until after World War II. The British has continued to do so, but the American is now much more in favour as an export, largely as a result of its acceptance in musical and entertainment circles. In the UK, it should be noted, the noun is more censorious than the verb.

(*i*) A vagrant, drunkard, worthless individual. 'The bum took the bottle out of his mouth' (*Home Grown*, No. 3, 1978).

(*ii*) Of poor quality, trivial. 'She kept on trotting out on him in bum TV shows' (Cohn: *Awopbop*, 1969).

(*iii*) Badly played, mishit. '. . . finding his bum notes applauded as wildly as his very best solos' (Cohn: *Awopbop*, 1969).

(*iv*) To wander around, drift. It often implies begging. 'He spent a year bumming around the South of France' (Cohn: *Awopbop*, 1969).

Despite its fairly wide acceptance in Britain nowadays, 'bum', in all its senses, continues to have an American flavour and among older people in particular it is used much less in the UK than in the USA.

Bummer. A depressing or frightening experience. In both the UK and the USA it originally referred to a state of mind caused by drugs, but by the 1970s this specialized meaning had largely disappeared. For the past ten years it has been a great favourite in the pop music world. 'To be cut out in the middle of "Interstellar Overdrive" was a bummer' (*Zigzag*, Aug 1972), and 'For some time earlier in the year I was on a real bummer. I mean, I was really down for a while' (pop singer, reported in *Jackie*, 1 Sept 1979) represent the mainstream of present usage.

Bundle. A fight. An old-established sense of the word which, with the increased social prestige of violence, especially among the young, has gone up in the world, as one sees in 'The weekend bundles between mods and rockers in the summer of '64' (*Melody Maker*, 12 May 1979).

It retains its former working-class flavour, however, in '. . . more like to put you off bundling for keeps' (Cloggies cartoon in *Private Eye*, 12 Feb 1971).

Bundle, go a. In the 1920s and 1930s, a 'bundle' was a large sum of money, a fat wad of notes and, in the USA, 'to go a bundle on' meant to bet a large sum of money. By the 1950s, a new American figurative meaning, 'to be enthusiastic about', was beginning to cross the Atlantic and in the 1960s it had become a favourite among journalists writing for teenagers, although less popular among the teenagers themselves – '. . . go a bundle on those flowery sheets' (*Jackie*, 30 May 1964). Except in strongly Americanized circles, it has never really established itself in the UK.

Burn. (*i*) To swindle. Standard English in the 17th and 18th centuries, this meaning survived into the 20th century in dialect, and during the 1950s and 1960s it came into more general use via the international network of drug dealers. 'The promoter, who eventually burns them for 500 dollars . . .' (*Oz* 43, July/Aug 1972).

(*ii*) Swindling. 'I received some heavy complaints regarding burn artists and protection' (Mandelkau: *Buttons*, 1971).

Burn up. A stretch of very fast driving or riding. '. . . with burn-ups to the North Circular' (Mandelkau: *Buttons*, 1971). The Australian form is 'burn', without the 'up'. 'Rosie said she'd like a burn with me, if Bill didn't mind' (Mathers: *The Wort Papers*, 1972).

Bushed. Physically exhausted. The word has been used in this sense in North America since at least the 1870s. It came into the UK during the 1950s among social groups which were accustomed to freshening up their language with regular American imports. 'He gets back home, four in the morning, bushed and burned' (Cohn: *Awopbop*, 1969).

Bust. (*i*) To arrest, raid, prosecute, usually on a drug charge. The past participle is either 'bust' or 'busted'. 'Don't give them any excuse to bust you' (*International Times*, 30 June 1967), or 'Turkey is the worst country in the world to get busted in' (letter to *Oz* 15, July/Aug 1969).

(*ii*) A raid, arrest. 'A drug bust at Corpus Christi airport broke up the band' (*Melody Maker*, 24 Jan 1981).

(*iii*) To fight. 'I had strict principles about busting other groups who were wearing the colours' (Mandelkau: *Buttons*, 1971).

(*iv*) Exhausted, at the end of one's tether. 'She woke up broke and busted in Wallsend' (*Sounds*, 21 July 1979).

(*i*), (*ii*) and (*iv*) are all American in origin, (*iii*) is equally British or American. The use of 'bust' in all four senses is virtually confined to those who engage in the kind of activities which are likely to result in a bust or in being busted.

Buzz. (*i*) News, rumour. 'The buzz had got around that I was the guy to see' (rock musician, quoted in *Zigzag*, Nov 1972). This meaning existed in the UK in later Victorian times, but it became less frequently used during the 1920s and 1930s, only to surface again in the 1960s among the younger sections of society, possibly helped into fashion by (*ii*) and (*iii*) below.

(*ii*) Excitement resulting from drugs or other forms of stimulating experience. 'An orchestra had given me quite a buzz before' (rock musician quoted in *Zigzag*, April 1975); '. . . procaine and tetracaine. These two ought in theory to produce an amazing buzz' (*Home Grown*, No. 2, 1977).

(*iii*) To become excited. 'Bet you'll buzz for these' (*Jackie*, 25 Jan 1964). This is now obsolescent, or at least no longer in fashion among members of this age group. It never had any drug associations and its use was restricted to teenagers and to journalists operating in the teenage market.

C

Caff. The British have been taking pleasure in mispronouncing and mutilating French words since at least the time of Elizabeth I, and probably for much longer. 'Caff' was in existence as an abbreviation of 'café' in the early 1920s – it may well owe its origin to the presence of British troops in France and Belgium during World War I – but, among educated people, it has always been considered distinctly low. Outside the UK, it is used, consciously and slightly mockingly, as a quoted Britishism. Within the UK, it continues to be mainly working-class, but in recent years it has also been fairly widely used by young people with a middle-class background who are anxious to show how classless they are or, at the very least, to prove their solidarity with the working class. Writers have followed suit, observing individuals who are 'far too fastidious for the motorway caff' (Nuttall: *Bomb Culture*, 1968).

Camp. If they were prepared to be honest, a great many users of 'camp' would be hard pressed to say exactly what they meant by the word. As with so many fashionable expressions, to be vague is to be safe. One should, even so, make some attempt to separate out the several layers of meaning which have become associated with 'camp' over a period of three-quarters of a century.

Between about 1900 and 1910, it was in use, although not widely, in the sense of 'affected'. In the early 1930s, and still on a society level, it acquired the more markedly pejorative meanings of 'bogus, slightly disreputable or tarnished'. This was at a time when homosexuality was still a taboo subject. In the early 1940s one could begin to sense profound changes in what one might call the sexual climate of the UK and from that time onwards 'camp' was being used, among the fashionable and the intelligentsia, as a synonym for 'homosexual'.

Since then, the old and new meanings of the word have combined and intermingled to produce three distinguishable shades of meaning:

(*i*) Effeminate, self-caricaturing, in a sophisticated way. 'It's camp, of course, but funny and invigorating' (Cohn: *Awopbop*, 1969). With this is linked the use of 'camp' as a verb, in the sense of 'behave in an outrageous, self-parodying way, often with overtones of homosexuality'. 'Lester Young brought hip to a fine point in his last years by wearing ribbons in his hair and camping crazily around the bandstand' (Nuttall: *Bomb Culture*, 1968). '. . . seeks strong-minded camp type artist friends' (*Gay News*, 9–22 Dec 1982) probably belongs here although one should possibly use it as an example of (*iii*).

(*ii*) In the combination, **High camp**. Self-consciously bad taste, kitsch. 'It became high camp to read and collect comic books' (*International Times*, 29 May 1967).

(*iii*) Stylish. 'He's a nice boy. Real camp.' (*Sounds*, 24 Jan 1981). This has no pejorative overtones.

It is important to note that by the early 1960s 'camp' had moved unmistakably down-market. It had established itself on at least the upper levels of pop culture, although both then and now it is still used by the trendier type of intellectual, although much less so than ten years ago.

Carry. To possess illegal drugs. A meaning which is now, in the 1980s, fairly widely understood, but which is unlikely to be actually used by anyone who is not at least on the fringes of the drug world. This world, of course, includes the police. 'Anyone found pushing, carrying or fixing will be turned over to the police' (*Oz* 15, July/Aug 1969) illustrates how the word links those who enforce the law with those who break it.

Cat. A person, usually, but not always, male. In the UK this is still a conscious Americanism and, when used by any white people except the ultra-trendy and members of the pop music world, the inverted commas are fairly easily heard and felt. 'It's nice to have a young cat working with you' (*Friends*, No. 1, Jan 1969) and 'One cat came up to me the other day and said, "When are you going to play that old Tyrannosaurus music?"' (interview with pop star in *Cracker*, No. 1, 1972) indicate the word's customers. As a fashionable expression, it has long passed its peak.

Chair. A motorcycle sidecar. The use of the word is confined to those with a passion for motorcycles. Most people outside this particular magic circle would be totally baffled by 'I've just lost interest in chairs' (*Motor Cycle Weekly*, 31 Jan 1981).

Chap. This ancient synonym for 'man' – it has existed at least since the beginning of the 18th century – is traditionally a middle/upper-class word, and it is still used straight by both men and women belonging to these sections of British society. Since the 1950s, however, it has entered the vocabulary of younger working-class people, and of the *Private Eye* type of journalist, but always with slightly mocking overtones, indicating that public-school mateyness and team spirit are regarded as absurd and not to be taken seriously. The following examples show how 'chap' is viewed and used by what might perhaps be termed its secondary customers. 'So watch out, chaps' (*Private Eye*, 29 Jan 1971); 'This is spiffing wheeze music. Great ideas, chaps' (*Melody Maker*, 19 May 1979); 'Some public-spirited chap half-inched Noddy Holder's cherry-red Gibson' (*Sounds*, 24 March 1979).

Among members of the middle class, it is interesting to observe a significant difference between the way in which men and women, of all ages, use 'chap'. Many, perhaps most women of this class show a marked disinclination to refer to a 'man' and prefer the less obviously sexual 'chap'.

Chappie. A man. The word has an interesting social pedigree. A colloquialism in the 1820s, it became a society term in the 1880s and from then until the 1950s it continued in almost exclusively well-bred use, as a badge of the superior status of the speaker. Since then, however, it has moved some distance down the social scale, although, once away from its traditional owners, it is usually spoken and written in inverted commas, as one sees in 'I just could not seem to get through to these chappies' (*Private Eye*, 29 Jan 1971).

Charge. (*i*) To take marijuana. In the USA, 'charge' was used in this sense, both as a noun, 'a dose of marijuana', and as a verb, in the late 1920s. On the other side of the Atlantic, however, it was virtually unknown until the 1950s, when it seems to have moved into the UK via the West Indies and with the help and encouragement of the international drug trade. Very few people outside the drug world have ever used it in the UK 'Charging is as different from popping as liquor is' (MacInnes: *City of Spades*, 1957).

(*ii*) Marijuana – 'I saw you grow charge out there' (MacInnes: *City of Spades*, 1957).

Charisma. The personal power of an individual to impress others. This sense of 'charisma' has been in evidence since the mid-1940s. Since then it has become a trendy and tiresomely over-used word, once much favoured by intellectuals and pseudo-intellectuals, but now gradually passing out of esteem among these groups. When one does come across it today it has a dated feeling about it. By the late 1970s it had lost most of its vigour and had become largely meaningless, as one can see in '. . . a daily increasing quota of charisma' (*Sounds*, 3 March 1979).

Charming. How nice! The word is said with crushing or would-be crushing irony, about something which is the complete opposite of charming. This slightly up-market youth word was at the peak of its popularity in the 1960s and still has quite a lot of vigour left in it, although during the past ten years it has widened its age-range considerably, as its original users have grown progressively older and held on to at least some of the habits of their youth.

'Charming! He really had me worried there' (*Jackie*, 7 Feb 1981) represents a late blossoming among journalists supplying the teenage market.

Chart. To have a recording in the pop music charts. The noun is very widely used, in the sense of 'league table of current sales and popularity', but the verb is confined almost entirely to those earning a living of one kind or another in the pop music business. The verb-users are illustrated by 'One band of theirs, The Doll, who charted with 'Desire Me' in January . . .' (*Sounds*, 21 July 1979).

Chat up. To curry favour, talk to someone of the opposite sex with the aim of making a favourable impression. The first meaning has been widely current since the last decade of the 19th century, the second, although known previously, has found a large market within the youth world since the end of World War II. During this period it has remained very much a British expression, and part of the usual currency of journalists earning a living from teenagers – 'Don't smile when they chat you up' (*Jackie*, 29 Feb 1964), and 'I've been chatting him up for weeks now' (*Jackie*, 24 July 1965). The teenagers of the 1960s are the parents of teenagers today and they have carried 'chat up' along with them. It is certainly no longer only or even mainly a teenage word.

Cheapo. Cheap. The 'o' ending is added now to many adjectives by the young and trendy, but only before a noun or when the adjective is repeated. One can therefore refer to 'a cheapo holiday' or say that it was 'cheapo cheapo', but 'the holiday was cheapo' is not possible. There is probably Australian influence at work here, but there is as yet little sign, in either the UK or the USA, of the Australian habit of first abbreviating a noun and then adding an 'o' suffix to it – 'Salvo', for Salvation Army', for instance. Meanwhile, however, we have 'There's a cheapo compilation on RCA' (*Time Out*, 6 April 1979); 'Ring that cheapo package tours number' (*Pink*, 12 May 1979), and 'Broke? Then tart up the old gear the cheapo way' (*Mates Annual*, 1979).

Check out. Investigate. This American expression is increasingly used in the UK but still, for the most part, by pop culture and crime journalists and by others who readily identify themselves with the American way of life. So, 'on street corners groups of black youths check out the scene' (*Jackie*, 20 Dec 1969) and '. . . a band with promise, check them out' (*Jackie*, 9 Jan 1965).

Used intransitively, the verb has quite a different meaning, 'to be about to die'. One can say, as in the pop song, 'I'm checking out'.

Chew fat. Discuss, chat. 'Chew the fat' has been a not very elegant or well-bred British colloquialism since the 1880s, with the meaning 'grumble, brood over a grievance', and also, within the present century, 'tack, yarn'. Since the 1960s, the younger generation, in both the UK and USA, has played about with the expression, modifying it in small details, as in 'At that point appeared Will Birch to chew some fat' (*Sounds*, 28 April 1979).

Chic. Stylish, fashionable. This word has been used in the UK in reference to women's clothes and appearance since the mid-19th century. By the 1970s, however, it was being applied to a much wider range of objects and activities and had ceased to belong exclusively to the upper levels of society. Classless youth had made a successful takeover bid for it and in the process caused it to become almost unusable by those to whom social status was of prime importance. One now finds such examples as 'It's been chic this year, in the limited radical football circles, to talk about the remoteness of footballers from their community' (*Foul*, June 1974). Even 30 years ago, the thought of footballers being in any way chic would have seemed ludicrous.

Chick. A girl, usually young, physically attractive and fashionable. The word was first used in this sense in the USA in the late 1920s.

Nowadays, in the UK, it can be used by members of either sex, but it is more current among men. A magazine aimed at teenage girls can refer to 'a medium-sized chick named Sandra, with black hair' (*Jackie*, 4 June 1966), and a *Private Eye* advertisement announced that 'Two chicks want cash, anything legal' (5 April 1976). When used by girls, as it is in the last example, 'chick' carries a flavour of independence, of knowing what's what. But its life in the UK has been short and now, in the early 1980s, it is found less and less with each year that passes.

Chick-pic. A photograph of a girl, a pin-up. A word used by journalists and virtually no-one else. 'Check from the chick-pic on the next page' (*New Musical Express*, 20 July 1956) provides the market clues.

Choked. Disappointed, upset. Like 'choked off', 'choked' is used in this sense only in the UK and by pop music people and their hangers-on and admirers. 'Stones shake Carnegie Hall – but they're still choked' (*Melody Maker*, 27 June 1964). The expression has existed since the 1950s but it is much less used now than it was ten years ago.

Choked off. Disappointed, upset. For its range of users, see CHOKED. 'It was a very unpopular move. Everybody was choked off' (*Zigzag*, Aug 1972). This modern meaning should not be confused with the much older sense of the term, 'discouraged, told one was not wanted'.

Chopper. Motorcycle. A word much used by the rock/Hell's Angels fraternity ten years ago, but less in evidence today. In this sense, it is only British, although with the meaning 'helicopter', it is found on both sides of the Atlantic. The context usually allows one to judge if a person is travelling by helicopter or by motorcycle. 'British chanter Bob Halford arrives on stage astride a large chopper' (*Melody Maker*, 12 May 1971) leaves little room for ambiguity.

Chuck. To jilt, stop going out with. From the 1920s to the 1950s the expression was 'to give or get the chuck'. 'To chuck' then came on to the scene. It was used by British teenagers in connection with not very serious love affairs and by both sexes about both sexes. For some unexplained reason it became less popular between about 1968 and 1978, but now appears to be staging something of a comeback. 'This boy I chucked before keeps following and upsetting me' (letter to *Jackie*, 15 May 1965) illustrates the word in its first wave of popularity.

'Boys . . . if a better one came along, you chucked them' (*Spare Rib*, Feb 1979), and 'I chucked him because he was two-timing me' (*My Guy*, 1 Sept 1979) belong to the second wave.

Chum. Friend. A term which has gone down in the world. From c1680 until the beginning of the 19th century, it was almost entirely a university word. One had one's 'chums' at the university and nowhere else. It then passed fairly quickly into general use and continued as a widely acceptable synonym for 'friend', until shortly after World War II, when unpleasant things began to happen to it. Its present situation is approximately as follows:

(*i*) With the meaning, 'friend, constant companion'. Rarely used now, except in a pejorative sense, but still occasionally found among teenagers, meaning a 'good' friend, until the mid-1960s. In 'She makes fun of you from across the road with her gang of chums' (letter to *Jackie*, 23 May 1967), the use is clearly pejorative.

(*ii*) A business associate, member of a cosy clique or sinister cabal. Sometimes almost a synonym for 'accomplice'. The various shades of cosiness and nastiness are illustrated by 'years of businesslike, fast-moving committee-work with Arnold Wesker and chums' (Nuttall: *Bomb Culture*, 1968); 'Among the guests was not only the Grocer, an old sailing chum of Marley boss, Owen Aisher . . .' (*Private Eye*, 23 Aug 1974); '. . . sporting chums John Conteh, Bob Wilson' (*The Guardian*, 19 March 1979).

'Chum' was used in this 'bad' sense to mean 'suspect chum, a chum who was not all a chum should be', in the 18th century, although to a very limited extent. The ironical possibilities have always been there, as they have with 'friend' itself, but it is only in recent years and especially among the younger and more cynical intellectuals, that they have become the norm.

As a verb, meaning 'to be friends with someone', 'chum' has been fairly widely used since the 1880s. During the 1950s and 1960s this usage was popular among British teenagers – 'He chummed around with my brother' (letter to *Jackie*, 2 Oct 1965) – but it has long vanished from the language of the age-group.

Chunder. To vomit. This Australian term was popularized in the UK during the 1950s by the *Private Eye* cartoon, 'Barry Mackenzie', and was first taken up by *Private Eye* addicts who, like readers of *The Guardian*, are easy to recognize, but difficult to define. If one was to say that 'chunder' would be unlikely to be used by anyone not in sympathy with *Private Eye*, the point has probably been made as accurately as it can be.

Cinch. Something easy. The word originated in the USA in the 1880s, with the meaning of 'certainty'. It was fully naturalized in the UK by the 1920s and is still current with this meaning – 'A cinch for the sellers comes along on HMV per The Olympics' (*New Musical Express*, 9 Sept 1958).

The secondary meaning, 'something which causes no problems or is no trouble at all', is equally American and almost as old-established, but it was found only very occasionally in the UK until after World War II, when a new generation of teenagers took it up and put their stamp of approval on it – 'It's a cinch to keep neat' (*Jackie*, 25 Jan 1964).

Clapped out. Worn out, exhausted. Applied to both objects and people, this useful expression, first heard in the mid-1940s, became current among young people in the early 1950s and subsequently spread steadily up the age-groups, so that we have, for example, 'a clapped-out old judge' (*Private Eye*, 8 May 1979) and 'nothing but a clapped out old Ferrari' (*Home Grown*, No. 3, 1978).

For some reason, it is not found in the USA, except among members of that very restricted circle of people whose morale and prestige are improved by the use of British habits.

Class. Of good quality, professional, well above average. The adjective, 'classy', was well established in the UK by 1900, although it was little used by educated people. 'Class', a journalistic import from the USA, began to take over from 'classy' in the 1960s and, among media people, the process was complete by the end of the decade. These, the original and most devoted promoters of the expression, still use it straight, but among the more normal sections of the British population, it carries considerable irony and, for those who have ears to hear and eyes to perceive such important subtleties, is often a means of poking gentle fun at their fellow citizens who have adopted it as part of their normal, everyday vocabulary, people who would find nothing amusing or ridiculous in 'Ace lead guitar seeks class pro hard rock outfit' (*Melody Maker*, 20 Jan 1979), and 'This is a class field' (BBC TV commentary on 1979 European Indoor Athletics Championships).

Classic. Excellent, typical of the best of its kind, likely to be remembered and respected for a long time. In the UK, the word has had this sense, among others, for at least a century, but it has become a favourite word within pop culture, with special associations and shades of meaning, and it has been tediously overused by the trendy young during the 1960s and, even more, the 1970s, and by the media catering for their tastes. We have by now had more than enough of such things as 'a classic soul album' (*The Soul Book*, 1975); 'the classic drug movie of all time' (*Home Grown*, No. 3, 1978), and 'Lone Star were a classic band' (*Sounds*, 3 March 1979).

Clean. Free from incriminating evidence, especially concerning drugs. A meaning of ancient vintage among the police and members of the underworld. It was taken up during the 1950s by those involved in the underground drug culture and by those who liked to think of themselves as the associate members and fellow-travellers of such a culture and who took pride in knowing the right words. 'Both were clean, as were the majority of pop-groups that the police raided' (*International Times*, 2 June 1967).

Clobber. (*i*) Clothes. Used in this sense, the word has been common among Jewish people and Cockneys from the mid-19th century onwards and in Australia for a rather shorter time. It became a favourite teenage word in the UK during the 1950s and 1960s, but has since been replaced by 'gear' and now has a distinctly public school ring to it. 'I've been trying to persuade her to lend me her clobber' (letter to *Jackie*, 24 Feb 1968) is the word at the top of its wave of popularity. Nowadays it usually has a slightly derogatory sense – '. . . anyone turning up in 'Hard Times' clobber' (*Time Out*, 10–16 Dec 1982).

(*ii*) Possessions, baggage. Used in this sense by rather older people than those who, post-World War II, adopted (*i*). 'I'll give you a hand with all your clobber' (*Private Eye*, 5 June 1970) may quite possibly, in the usual *Private Eye* manner, be surrounding 'clobber' with faintly audible inverted commas, as a token of its love–hate relationship with the public schools and the upper classes of British society.

(*iii*) To say damaging things about someone or something. Derived from the more literal sense, 'to hit', which is, alone, common in the USA. This usage is found over a wide age-range, but continues to have a markedly middle- and upper-class flavour. In 'When in doubt, clobber the car' (12 March 1979), *The Guardian* has one foot in the middle classes and the other in supposedly classless youth, in typical *Guardian* style.

Cock-up. (*i*) A mistake. A British and, to a lesser extent, Australian usage which is not possible in the USA, owing to the very strong American taboo, observed by all classes, on the word 'cock', in all its senses. 'We've left out words and made other cock-ups' (*The Alternative*, No. 2, 1971), and 'The base player made a few cock-ups' (interview with rock musician in *Zigzag*, April 1973) cause no problems in the UK, but would be instinctively censored in the USA. The thought of 'rooster-up', as a possible American alternative, is not unattractive.

The expression has been common in the UK for at least a century, but before the 1950s it would bave been very unusual indeed for a woman to use it. Its transformation into a two-sex term is a mark of the success achieved by the feminist movement since World War II, although even now few women over 40 would probably feel entirely at ease if they were to say this or that had been 'a cock-up'.

(*ii*) To make a mistake or a series of mistakes with something. 'He had the audacity to cock up the opening' (*Melody Maker*, 24 Jan 1981). Feminine inhibitions and lack of inhibitions regarding the verb are approximately the same as for the noun, although many women who would feel able to say that something had been 'a cock-up', would stop short of saying that they had 'cocked something up'. As so often happens, the more literal and therefore more powerful associations linger longer with the verb.

Coke. Cocaine. The abbreviation has existed in the USA since the first decade of the present century, but it became an export only with the widespread increase in drug-taking after World War II, a phenomenon which coincided with the worldwide popularity of another symbol of American culture, Coca Cola. The fact that Coca Cola and cocaine share the same abbreviation, 'coke', with only a capital letter to distinguish them, and that only in writing, may have, on the one hand, given 'coke' – cocaine – a cosier and less dangerous image than it deserves and, on the other, allowed 'Coke' – Coca Cola – to enjoy a reputation for potency and daring which is certainly not justified by chemical analysis.

Considered in association, however, the two 'cokes' may well have made it possible for post-war youth culture and drug-culture to overlap more easily than would otherwise have been the case. The rock musician who said 'Coke is an addictive thing' (*The Road to Rock*, 1974) was, as it happened, referring to cocaine, but his remark would have applied with equal force to Coca Cola, and the same might be said of 'He was a coke freak' (*Oz*, Winter 1972).

It remains true, however, that although Coca Cola is, on the whole, a youthful taste – although the addition of forms of alcohol, such as rum, have moved the market into higher age-groups – an addiction to cocaine can produce euphoria and misery at any age. The situation is necessarily fluid, since yesterday's teenagers are growing older all the time and carry at least some of their habits, which include their linguistic usages, along through life with them. At the moment, however, in the early 1980s, it would probably be fair to say that, whereas 'Coke' is a word used by almost the whole British population, 'coke' is mostly confined to younger people and to those who, either as members of the drug world or as officials attempting to suppress it, are closely concerned with drugs in one way or another.

Collar. Hard work. This probably comes from the 19th century British colloquialism, 'collar-work', meaning heavy, laborious pulling for a horse. Used in this sense, 'collar' was little found before the mid-1970s and it is even now almost entirely restricted to the trendier sections of society, especially media people. 'The first Mrs. Sovereign who ever did a day's collar in her life' (*New Musical Express*, 7 March 1981) pinpoints the market with some accuracy.

Coloured. (*i*) Black, negro. Before the early 1960s, 'black' was felt to be an insulting term, if it came from a white person. 'Coloured' was the most widely employed euphemism. The situation now, in the 1980s, is quite different. After 30 years of the 'black rights' movement in the USA and its equivalent in other countries, 'black' is now used proudly and aggressively by the blacks themselves, and 'coloured' has been largely abandoned by white people, except among those getting on in years, where the old habit is rooted too deep. 'I've been impressed by the singing of a coloured American boy, called Bonnie Sattin' (*New Musical Express*, 2 Feb 1958), and 'The R. and B. attitude crept in after he heard coloured performers' (*Jackie*, 24 July 1965) reflect traditional feelings. 'I've been going out with my boyfriend for two months now. But the trouble is he's coloured' (letter to *My Guy*, 1 Sept 1979) is a surprisingly late example of the old usage. One has to suppose that the girl in question would so much like her boyfriend to be white that she uses 'coloured', in order to pretend to herself and to the world that he is less black than he really is.

(*ii*) A non-white person. In the UK, this is very rarely used as a noun nowadays, except when referring specifically to a South African of mixed blood. 'Got any records by coloureds?' (interview with pop singer in *Melody Maker*, 24 Oct 1964) would be possible today only if the speaker wished to be deliberately insulting to black people. *See* BLACK.

Combo. A jazz group. Making its first appearance in the USA about 1935, the word was used until the late 1950s, both among 'serious' jazz enthusiasts and as a HIP expression, to describe a small BAND. More recently, it has been kept alive by pop music journalists simply as a means of ringing the changes on the currently available words, of which there are never enough to make media people happy. So, '. . . his self-styled punk rock combo' (*Time Out*, 10–16 Dec 1982).

'Combos of booking clerks and quantity surveyors' assistants' (MacInnes, *Absolute Beginners*, 1959) shows the original use, while 'a mystery shrouded combo by the name of Doll by Doll' (*Melody Maker*, 31 March 1979) is merely a journalist indulging his fancy.

There has been a significant obstacle to the introduction of the term into Australia, since in that culture 'combo' already meant 'a white man living with an aboriginal woman'.

Come across. To dispense sexual favours. This is a recent and more specific extension of an existing British meaning, found soon after World War I, 'to be willing, pleasant'. It reflects the *Playboy*, male-orientated, all-women-are-for-one-thing-only attitude to sexual relationships, much affected by a certain type of journalist – 'Despite an evening of boozing with her, she wouldn't come across' (*Sounds*, 1 Dec 1979). The expression is, significantly, only used of women. A man, it should be noted, cannot 'come across'. He is assumed to be already there.

Come down. (*i*) The depressing period when the effects of a drug are wearing off. 'Whom did you murder on your last come down?' (*International Times*, 27 Feb 1967).

(*ii*) To emerge from a drugged stupour. 'He was coming down pretty hard' (Garner: *Monkey Grip*, 1977).

Both the noun and the verb are in use throughout the English-speaking world but, in this sense, only by drug-takers. The more innocent among us, who use sentences like, 'It was a terrible come-down', meaning loss of face or prestige, should beware of the danger of an embarrassing double-entendre.

Come on. A trendy expression of the 1960s and 1970s, with two distinct meanings, of which one does well to be aware.

(*i*) To act or behave, with a suggestion of pretence or affectation. 'They came on like space-age musical monsters' (Cohn: *Awopbop*, 1959), and 'This one comes on a bit more serious' (*Sounds*, 3 March 1979) give some guidance on this use of the term, which few people away from the more trendy end of the Alternative Society are likely to include in their vocabulary.

(*ii*) To put oneself forward, impose oneself. 'Hippies are a drag, too. They come on like nineteenth century colonialists' (*Friends*, No. 3, Jan 1970). The range of users is as for (*i*).

Come out. To openly declare one's homosexuality. Used by and about both male and female homosexuals, the expression has become fairly widely known with the increasing opportunities for homosexuals to present their world-view in print. 'After being spotted on the march by some of his pupils, John came out at school' (*Gay News*, 23 Feb 1978), and 'The Alex Dobkin come out show' (*Spare Rib*, Sept 1979) illustrate this meaning which, to the uninitiated, is all too easy to confuse with the earlier and more socially acceptable association of 'coming out' with debutantes. 'Lesbian mothers who decide to have children after they have come out' (*Gay News*, 9–22 Dec 1982).

It might, perhaps, be helpful to mention in passing that this series of come-plus-adverb compounds – come across, come down, come on, come out – can, for those who do not move in the appropriate circles, be nearly as perplexing and frightening as German compound verbs are to those whose acquaintance with the language is in its early stages. The fear of saying 'come on', when one really means 'come across' or 'come out' is enough to keep one well clear of the whole tribe.

Commie. Communist. The abbreviation, nearly always with a small letter, has been used, both in the UK and USA, from about 1940 onwards, by those well away from the political Left who have a strong dislike of Communism and all its works. 'Commie' users are mostly to be found in industry and commerce and among those with a limited formal education, but they also include better educated people who, for one reason or another, are anxious to stand well with the Right and with the Establishment. 'Anti-commie scorn' (*Daily Mirror*, 22 March

1979) is main line, but 'I'm not having commies on my staff' (alleged quote from Ian Trethowan, later Director-General of the BBC, in *Private Eye*, 8 May 1970) is something rather special.

Communication. Strictly speaking, understanding what other people mean and making oneself understood to others. It has, however, become a very vague and semi-mystical term, grossly overused by a wide range of people with pretentions to intellectual ability. One of many impressive-sounding and thought-preventing words borrowed from psychological and sociological jargon, 'communication' has itself become a barrier to communication, as one sees in such examples as 'Are you concerned with communication . . . just the realisation of human love reciprocated?' (*International Times*, 19 May 1967).

Communication, breakdown of. Gross, often wilful misunderstanding. A phrase much loved by politicians and fringe intellectuals, as a euphemism for the refusal of opposing parties to talk to one another or to discover what lies hidden in a dark forest of clichés. 'A breakdown of communication seems to have occurred' (*Sounds*, 3 March 1979) is almost certainly intended as a satire of official statements.

Community. A group of people, of whatever size, defined either by geographical limits or by identity of interests. A conveniently vague but impressive-sounding word, taken over from the social sciences for general consumption, and much used by politicians, journalists, estate agents and by those who dislike existing forms of social organization and yearn for something based more on the heart and less on the head. When one reads that '*Attila* is a paper for and about the community' (*Attila*, 6 Nov 1971), one immediately places oneself in the enemy camp by asking, 'What community?'

It is often a fraudulent, 'warm', 'caring' substitute for 'district, area, suburb' and is so used in 'situated in one of Toronto's most historic communities' (*Toronto Globe and Mail*, 31 Jan 1976), and 'The film is located in an attractive community' (*The Daily Telegraph*, 27 Nov 1975).

Concept album. An LP record consisting of several tracks linked by a common theme or treatment, and conceived as a whole. Among rock musicians, it has become almost a technical term, but it is sometimes used by outsiders, including fans and journalists, in a manner so vague as to be almost meaningless. '"I got to try it one time" is very much the concept album' (*The Soul Book*, 1975), and 'I'd like to do a concept album' (*Melody Maker*, 20 Jan 1979) may indicate clear thinking, but are just as likely to be woolly jargon.

Conceptual. Concerned more with the ideal than with the finished product. Originally used to describe an avant-garde approach to the visual arts, it has now become a fashionable and rather meaningless term in pop music circles. 'An arty band was being very conceptual' (*Sounds*, 3 March 1979) is probably a flattering and upstage way of saying that the band appeared to have some good ideas, but lacked the ability to put them into practice.

Consciousness. AWARENESS. A key word among hippies and their modern descendants, the 'awareness' being the result of drug experience. 'We enable individuals to expand their consciousness' (*Undercurrents*, Feb/March 1977) is a typical use of the term, which means nothing to those who lead an undrugged life.

Consciousness raising. Possessing the power of making people aware of their real situation, by means of carefully guided discussion or presentation of information. This has nothing to do with CONSCIOUSNESS as drug-takers know it. The term is used mainly by professional feminists and Left Wing political activists – 'This makes the play an illustration of a consciousness raising process which can happen in quite ordinary situations' (*Spare Rib*, Sept 1977).

Cool. (*i*) Cautious, reserved, fashionable, accepted. The limits of the meaning attached to the adjective are defined by the group which the user is trying to impress. 'Cool' in its modern colloquial senses and all the expressions associated with it started life as black American and spread across via the musical world. 'Play it cool for a while (*Jackie*, 18 Jan 1964) is so normal as to have become almost standard English, but 'Real cool, this get-up' (*Jackie*, 8 Feb 1964) is a little unusual, since 'real cool' was and is rarely used, except perhaps in inverted commas, by the average white teenager in Britain.

One's sensitivity to the various modern senses of 'cool' can be confused by the fact that, with other meanings, the words 'cool' and 'coolly' are old-established components of English as used in the UK. 'A cool customer', for instance, has been with us for at least a century. What we are concerned with here is the new wave of usage which entered the UK from the 1950s onwards, a wave exemplified by 'It isn't cool to rave about your own party' (*International Times*, 31 Oct 1966); 'I know kids who drank brasso because they thought it was a cool thing to do' (letter to *Oz* 21, June 1969), and 'Three cool cats met three cool chicks walking down the street' (interview with rock group in *Zigzag*, Sept 1973).

(*ii*) The manner or appearance of being at ease or of being in complete command of whatever the currently admired style happens to be. 'They spent the most part of their lives competing for cool' (Cohn: *Awopbop*, 1969).

(*iii*) Not smoking cannabis. 'Staying cool in Marrakesh would be like Alice not falling down the hole' (*Oz* 8, Feb 1969). To anyone not familiar with this drug-world term, the sentence would be completely unintelligible. The assumption would be, understandably, that the writer was referring to the temperature in North Africa.

Cool, blow or lose one's. To lose one's temper or self-control. 'He badly blew his cool by leaping nude aboard a policeman's back' (Cohn: *Awopbop*, 1969), and '. . . occasionally losing his cool to blast off about the suffering' (*International Times*, 28 Nov 1966) illustrate the usage of expressions which have made little headway in the UK outside circles in which the cult of things American is strong.

Coon. A black person. The word was in common use in the USA by the 1870s and in the UK about 20 years later. Like 'nigger', it caused little apparent trouble until the 1950s, when the negro problem began to be acute in both the USA and the UK and when even the traditional and much loved golliwog was seen as evidence of racism. Today, in the UK, 'coon' is used, sometimes patronizingly, sometimes defiantly and pugnaciously, by men – never women – with Right Wing leanings and clubman tastes. Alf Garnett, the famous working-class character in the BBC television series of the 1970s, was much given to referring to blacks, Indians and Pakistanis as 'coons', a habit which shared more recently with the fictional version of Mr Denis Thatcher, husband of the Prime Minister, in *Private Eye*'s highly successful 'Dear Bill' feature, where we find such examples as 'one poor Coon who had his whole bloody country pulled from under him during the celebrations' (14 Aug 1981).

Cop out. (*i*) To evade the issue. 'I asked why it was not shown and he copped out by saying it was too fragile' (*International Times*, 5 Oct 1967).

(*ii*) An evasion. The American sense of 'a failure to do what one promised' is rarely found in the UK, where the only meaning found with any frequency can be seen in 'Another quick cop-out is to say that it's not Women's Lib but People's Lib that counts' (*Attila*, 13 Nov 1971).

Both (*i*) and (*ii*) are of American origin and have certainly been in use in the UK since the early 1960s. They are still, however, mainly journalists' expressions, although with a certain trendy vogue among teenagers and younger adults, more particularly males. A *Guardian* word – 'The tactical necessity of ideological cop-outs' (*The Guardian*, 28 Sept 1982).

Copper. Policeman. First used in the 1850s, this is still, despite all the far-reaching social changes which have taken place since then, the most widely used term for 'policeman', among all classes and age-groups, a fact worth remembering when referring to the entries for FUZZ, BILL and other expressions for the agents of the law. The sheer stamina of the word is remarkable. The American abbreviation 'cop' is sometimes heard, but more often in the plural than the singular. '. . . just when I was on my way to making the coppers think I hadn't done the job after all' (Sillitoe: *The Loneliness of the Long Distance Runner*, 1959) and 'The burly 6 ft 4 ins copper' (*Daily Mirror*, 22 March 1979) are common property and intelligible to all.

Cornball. Corny, without originality. This clear-cut Americanism has never struck roots in the UK. It has been used here only by trendies and by those with a living to make in the pop world, and even among them its days seems past. '. . . a sultry-voiced lady – strictly cornball' (*The Soul Book*, 1975) represents the word at the peak of its use in the UK.

'Cos. Because. Since the early 1970s, this childish abbreviation has been much used in the UK by journalists catering for the teenage and pop market. Sometimes the apostrophe is used, sometimes not – 'cos the week-end looks like fun' (*Sounds*, 3 March 1979) can be set alongside 'For two years I rode around pillion 'cos we couldn't afford two bikes' (letter in *Motor Cycle Weekly*, 31 Jan 1981) and '. . . 'cos often they're just retreads of greatest hits cut at the Hammersmith Odeon' (*Time Out*, 10–16 Dec 1982). The writer of the *Motor Cycle Weekly* letter adds the information that she is 28, with a 6-year-old daughter. In her case, the distinctly twee 'cos' could possibly be a carry-over from her teenage days, but the fact that she sets it down on paper and in a letter presumably intended for publication, shows what a deep, permanent and nostalgic thing post-World War II teenage culture has been.

Cosmic. Earth-shattering, all-embracing. Originally used in the 1960s by hippies and by those engaged in the hippy-related cult of Meditation, the word passed into wider use as a slightly tongue-in-cheek superlative which was favoured during the 1960s and early 1970s by UNDERGROUND journalists. It is now obsolete, if not extinct, but, in its day, it allowed such extravagant assessments as 'The Exploding Galaxy Bird Ballet in cosmic dance drama' (*International Times*, 27 Oct 1967); '. . . the most cosmic singles' (Cohn: *Awopbop*, 1969) and 'The revolutionary cosmic band, Hawkwind' (*Oz*, Winter 1973).

Counterculture. Anti-Establishment culture. A word often used by 'normal' citizens as a synonym for alternative society. It is never, however, used by members of the Alternative Society themselves, or by advocates of it. "Woodstock', that 1970 valediction to counterculture' (*Sight and Sound*, Summer 1978) and '. . . counterculture schools with a radical tradition' (Corwin: *Education in Crisis*, 1974) both come from safe positions on the sidelines.

Coupla. Couple of. The barbarous American habit of abbreviating 'of' to 'a' and adding it to disyllabic words was anglicized very early in the present century, probably by 1905. 'Kinda' was one of the first and most consistently popular creations of this type. During the 1960s, the habit was given a new lease of life by journalists writing for teenage magazines, with results like 'He gave me a coupla pills' (*Jackie*, 18 Jan 1964). One comes across it much less often in this kind of publication today, at least in the UK, although it continues to feature in the tougher sort of fiction, where lazy, gangster-sounding speech has considerable prestige.

Cover. To record a version of an already popular song. 'Cover' is the only word in the pop music business which describes this process – 'For Brunswick, the four Aces have covered 'The World Outside" (*New Musical Express*, 5 Dec 1958). However, its use by the more enthusiastic and knowledgeable fans makes it a cult expression rather than merely a technical term.

It can also be used as a noun, meaning a recorded version of a song already popularized by another group or singer – 'The flip-side's one of their few covers' (*Sounds*, 21 July 1979) – and as an adjective, as in 'We were basically still a cover band' (*Melody Maker*, 12 May 1979).

Cowboy. A policeman. A teenagers' word in the 1950s, it is no longer used in this sense. '. . . his rapid disappearance at the approach of any cowboys' (MacInnes: *Absolute Beginners*, 1959) would be understood by very few people today.

With the meaning 'interloper, opportunist, non-professional verging on the criminal', 'cowboy' has now become almost standard English. One speaks and writes of 'cowboy lorry drivers', 'cowboy plumbers', and of undesirable operators in any field where the public is entitled to expect skill, training and legality, but is not infrequently disappointed. Pop music has its own good reasons for hating and fearing 'the cowboys' – 'After all the time we'd spent trying to break this band, these cowboys were going to ruin it all' (*Melody Maker*, 19 May 1979).

Cracker. A good-looking, interesting person, with sexual attractiveness particularly in mind. The word usually, but not always, refers to girls. Essentially a working-class teenager/young adult expression, it is not used in this sense outside the UK. 'I met Dawn on a blind date. My best mate fixed it up, telling me she was a cracker' (*Pink*, 12 May 1979) gives the flavour.

Crackers. Money. An American term, not much used in the UK outside *Melody Maker* type circles, where it is an accepted part of the currency. 'They fork out the crackers for their tickets' (*Melody Maker*, 1 Jan 1979) was not generally understood at that date, nor is it today. The word is not used in the USA in this sense, and in Australia only in the singular and as a negative expression – 'I walked into a country hotel in Queensland without a cracker' (Glassup: *We Were the Rats*, 1944).

Crap. (*i*) Rubbish, people, things or ideas of poor quality. 'It was spoiled for me because of the crap there' (*Melody Maker*, 24 Oct 1964); 'Our first L.P. in reality was crap' (*International Times*, 13 Feb 1967).

(*ii*) Deception, facade. 'Under the crap he was in real agony' (Cohn: *Awopbop*, 1969).

Despite its American feeling and associations, this is in fact a word of sound British origins, widely used since the 18th century, although not in polite circles, in the sense of 'defaecation'. The USA can, however, claim credit for the figurative use, which became firmly established in the UK in the 1950s, as a result of the two transatlantic bridges formed by hippydom and pop music.

The adoption here of 'crap' in its figurative sense was undoubtedly helped by the fact that 'crappy' was here already and had been since the 1840s, with the meaning, 'uninteresting, low-status, low-quality'. By the early 1970s, however, it had lost its 'low' associations, at least among the young, and had become classless and not particularly strong. In 'They make you work in crappy jobs' (*Attila*, 23 Oct 1971), 'crappy' could be translated fairly exactly by 'rotten' or 'lousy', which, although not precisely mild terms, are not guaranteed to seize the attention and imagination of the listener.

Crash. To sleep, especially, but not necessarily, after a drug bout. For the most part, a student, youth word, which was popular in the 1960s and 1970s, but has now had its day. 'There were six of them crashing on the floor' (*Brighton Voice*, Sept 1973) comes from the peak period.

Crash pad. A temporary place to sleep or live. The 'crash' part of the expression is post-World War II (*See* CRASH) but the ancestry of 'pad' goes back a very long way. A 'pad', in Elizabethan times, was a very basic bed, a bundle of straw on which one could lie. In Victorian England, a 'padding club' was a lodging house for tramps. The revival of 'pad' in the 1960s seems to have occurred first among students, who often experienced great difficulties in finding somewhere to live, and from there its extension to the world of the young drop-outs was natural and easy. Varying degrees of informality, comfort and decency are reflected in 'A list of crash pads in the city' (*China Cat Sunflower*, No. 1, Dec 1969); 'He took me immediately to his crashpad in the Mellah' (*Oz* 18, Feb 1969), and 'There's never enough hotels, so the Park operates a mass open-air crash pad' (*Home Grown*, No. 2, 1977).

It is interesting to observe how 'pad' has moved up socially during its second lease of life. Nowadays, it is often used by the English middle class in the sense of *pied-à-terre*, which would have been impossible 100, or indeed 50 years ago.

Crazy. (*i*) Amazing! How about that! Good! A catch-phrase of the 1950s, first used by jazz musicians and their hangers-on and which spread into a slightly wider field during the 1960s. As an exclamation, the word is now dead and most people today would probably misinterpret "And how is the car trade?', I continued. 'Don't tell a soul,' he said, looking round him, 'but it's prospering'. 'Crazy', I said.' (A teenager in MacInnes, *Absolute Beginners*, 1959), and "Does this look like something I will enjoy getting involved in?' 'Yes.' 'Crazy." (*International Times*, 1 March 1967).

   (*ii*) Exciting. 'It's really crazy down at one of the most popular boutiques of today in Guildford' (*Jackie*, 24 Feb 1968). A very popular teenage expression in its day, but now a mere shadow of itself.

Crazy mixed-up. Confused, muddled, with no aim or purpose. A catch-phrase which became an epidemic in the mid-1950s, after the birth of the teenage cult in the UK. It was very much used by the long-suffering parents of teenagers, especially in the phrase, 'Crazy mixed-up kid', which gave some sort of respectability to even the most outrageous and most irresponsible behaviour. If society had lost its direction and the old standards had been shattered, then there were always excuses for the individual. 'The whole crazy mixed-up world' (*New Musical Express*, 27 July 1956) makes the point.

Creep. A person with unpleasant characteristics, in use in the USA by the 1880s, but rare in the UK before the mid-1960s, when it became a general term of abuse and contempt among teenagers. It was and still is much favoured by girls when referring to boys. 'Boys can be gorgeous, witty, romantic, fun-loving creatures, but, as every girl knows, there's another type of boy around, too – The Creep' (*Jackie*, 12 May 1979).

Crombie boy. A sub-species of MOD. In the 1960s and early 1970s, certain very narcissistic Mods wore Crombie overcoats, as a badge of their membership of this special group. The cult had come to an end when we find 'Mods, suede heads and crombie boys' (*The Soul Book*, 1975).

Cruddy. Disgusting. Crud, an earlier form of Curd, goes back to medieval times, and in certain American and English dialects it came to mean 'sticky, encrusted dirt'. The adjective, common in the USA but so far confined almost entirely to youthful circles in the UK, is always used in its figurative sense, as in 'Those cruddy Nazi election leaflets dropping through your door' (*Sounds*, 28 April 1979). At the moment the word is showing no signs of spreading to other age-groups.

Cruise. To move about with the intention of picking up a man or woman, to approach someone with this in mind. Nowadays, the term is mainly confined to homosexuals – 'All those chosen have to do is to cruise each other on stage as though in a gay bar' (*Gay News*, 9–22 Dec 1982).

Cruiser. A person, usually a homosexual, who roams around with the aim of picking up a sexual partner – 'To the inveterate cruiser, bad weather is of no consequence' (*Gay News*, 9–22 Dec 1982).

Cruisy. Where CRUISERS are to be found – 'A cruisy American-style leather bar' (*Time Out*, 10–16 Dec 1982). Also *see* LEATHER.

Crumb. A person regarded as inferior and to be despised. In the 1950s and 1960s it was a mainly young working-class term of abuse, but it subsequently acquired something of a public school flavour. 'Shut up, crumb!' (Film version of Sillitoe: *The Loneliness of the Long Distance Runner*, 1962), and 'He must think I'm a real crumb, lying like that' (*Jackie*, 2 Oct 1965) come from the word's fresh and early days. It is much less used nowadays, although one still hears it.

Crumby, crummy. Inferior, unpleasant. In the 19th and early 20th centuries, it had only the meaning 'lousy', in the literal sense of the word. In the 1950s, both in the UK and the USA, it acquired the figurative meaning, 'of poor quality'. It is now mainly a teenage girls' word – 'No routine jobs! No crummy flat! We're really going to love and live' (*Mates Annual* 1979).

Crummo. A person of no consequence, someone who is ill-informed or not up-to-date – 'We dropped that suffix months ago, crummo' (*Time Out*, 10–16 Dec 1982). A trendy word, not found before the late 1970s.

Crumpet. Girls and women considered either individually or collectively and with a strong emphasis on their sexual attractiveness and possibilities. The expression has existed in the UK since the early 1880s, but until the 1950s it was always considered extremely low and the majority of well-bred people were unacquainted with it. Helped along by the new post-World War II attitude to sex, 'crumpet' then began to be used much more widely and it is now remarkably free of either age or class associations, although it is still used much more by men than by women. This situation seems to be changing, however, so that both men and women are being referred to by the opposite sex as 'crumpet'. The well-known broadcaster, Terry Wogan, for example, has been described, in 1982, as 'the thinking woman's crumpet'. The usage is almost exclusively British.

Cultural. Belonging to an ethnic minority. Mainly British and, in the UK, used chiefly by those white people who have a strong sympathy and empathy with their black fellow-citizens. Black people themselves are much less likely to use the term. The inverted commas in 'The In Crowd are in the enviable position of not being perceived as a 'cultural' group' (*Black Music*, Dec 1979) are significant.

Cunt. The vagina and the area immediately surrounding it, and hence, by association, a woman. This, the most common and, until recently, the most taboo of all sexual words has been in use since at least the 14th century. The only reason for including it is to draw attention to the marked weakening, if not breaking, of the taboo in the late 1950s. The Underground Press deliberately used the bluntest sexual terms in order to shock. This policy, whether effective or not, was designed to show how sexually liberated the users were. The headline 'Cunt Power Trials' (*Oz* 33, Feb 1971) would have been unthinkable 20 years earlier and might well have led to prosecution.

One should not exaggerate the extent to which the traditional barriers surrounding this word have broken down. In public, it still retains much of its old power, especially among women. It is still far from being a term which one can use lightly.

Cut. (*i*) To make a recording. 'The least commercial side that Humph has ever cut' (*New Musical Express*, 20 July 1956).

(*ii*) A recorded track. 'Hope-Evans' compositions are by no means filler cuts' (*Oz* 34, April 1971) and '. . . three cuts on the flip' (*Sounds*, 28 May 1979).

Both as a verb and a noun, this term is in the active vocabulary only of pop musicians and pop music writers, although it is understood by those fans and 'serious students' who devote time and energy to such matters.

Cut it. To make a successful appearance, be successful. From the pop music world, as illustrated by 'Would Kenny Jones cut it as a surrogate Keith Moon?' (*Melody Maker*, 12 May 1979). This question would probably be unintelligible to 95 per cent of the British public, irrespective of age.

Cut loose. (*i*) To begin, break out from what one was doing previously. 'Without preamble, the three piece band cut loose' (*New Musical Express*, 15 June 1956).

(*ii*) To let one's hair down, behave in an uninhibited fashion. 'Carla really cut loose with some righteous ringing' (*The Soul Book*, 1975).

This phrase had its origins among jazz musicians in the USA and it was found in similar circles in the UK by the early 1950s. From there, the transfer to a broader spectrum of trendy people was rapid, and the expression may now be on the point of passing into general use.

Cut out. To leave, especially in order to escape from something unpleasant. Of American origin, the phrase was in limited use in the UK by the early 1960s, among those whose culture was as much American as English, but since then it has not moved far outside its original circle of users and may now be fading away. 'Too much, so that cat is cutting out' (*International Times*, 5 Oct 1967) represents the expression in its heyday.

Cutesy. Cloying, sickly, sentimental. Applied particularly to pop music – 'The Motown sound was neither cutesy nor gimmicky' (*The Soul Book*, 1975) – this American word is fairly well understood by young people in the UK, but shows no signs of becoming a permanent feature of the language.

D

Damsel. A girl. In upper-crust English of the 1920s and 1930s, as immortalized by P.G. Wodehouse, and in university parlance of the same period, 'damsel' was a favourite term. After World War II, it moved downwards socially, often being used facetiously by pop hack journalists, as in '. . . the two young damsels, Sylvia and Jean' (*New Musical Express*, 20 July 1956).

This journalistic vogue coincided with the word's adoption by the Hippy class, which had a great fondness for expressions which sounded archaic, especially medieval. 'London inventor seeks hippie damsel in need of genuine relationship' (advert in *International Times*, 27 Oct 1967) is a typical example.

Dangler. A homosexual without the confidence to approach other men and doomed to masturbation – 'What I despise is being one of these solitary danglers' (*Gay News*, 9–22 Dec 1982).

Date. (*i*) A musical engagement or performance – 'The Pirates play their first British dates . . .' (*Sounds*, 3 March 1979). In the sense of 'a theatrical engagement', this word was in general use before World War I, but, curiously, it did not apply to musical performances until the mid-1940s, and then in the USA. It took four or five years to establish itself in the UK in this sense. Until the mid-1950s, its use was largely confined to the pop music world, but it has since become general currency.

(*ii*) A boy or girl friend. This has been normal American usage since the mid-1920s, but it has never struck such deep roots in the UK where it is used a good deal by advice columnists and other journalists, but less frequently by the boys and girls who actually have dates. 'Your date will be just as worried about the big night as you' (*Jackie*, 24 Feb 1968) illustrates the market and the customers.

(*iii*) To go out with a boy/girlfriend. Found in the USA very early in the 20th century, the verb has always sounded markedly and self-consciously American in the UK. It had a certain vogue among teenagers in the 1960s, but is little used today, except tongue-in-cheek.

58

'I've been dating Jim for about eight months now' (letter to *Jackie*, 15 May 1965) belongs very much to the past.

Deal. (*i*) To sell drugs. An expression little used outside the drug fraternity, but common enough there – 'The guy will get done for dealing, no doubt' (*Attila*, 23 Oct 1971).

(*ii*) An amount of drugs bought or sold. Another in-term, very likely to be misunderstood by those whose personal world does not include drugs. 'Your deals are underweight' (*Attila*, 16 Dec 1971) could sound entirely innocent to anyone not aware of its technical meaning.

Deejay, DJ. A disc jockey, a person who presents pop records, usually on radio. '. . . the deejay, Johnny La Guardia' (*Melody Maker*, 24 Jan 1981) is a recent example. The word first appeared in the USA in the mid-1950s. It came to the UK over the *Melody Maker* type of cultural bridge, but by the early 1960s it was in common use among pop fans and those who ministered to them.

Demo. (*i*) A public demonstration of protest. The abbreviation existed in the UK in the mid-1930s, but it had only a limited use, among professional protesters, until the 1960s, when a large number of young people began to adopt protest as a way of life, with the Campaign for Nuclear Disarmament (CND) and the Vietnam War as focal points of their activities. Since then it has passed into general use, although it is still more frequently found among those who favour demos and take part in them than among older people whose demo days are past. Broadly speaking, those who are not much given to demonstrations are more likely to use the full form of the word, whereas those to whom such activities are the breath of life will incline towards the abbreviation. It was therefore normal for the student paper, *Brighton Voice*, to refer to 'the Women's Lib demo' (Aug 1973).

(*ii*) A demonstration sample, a prototype. Used in the pop world in reference to recordings, this is not to be confused with (*i*) above. 'A demo tape' (*Rolling Stone*, 30 Nov 1978) is not a recording suitable for use during protest demonstrations.

Dep. To deputize. An abbreviation once favoured by pop music journalists, but much less seen and heard nowadays. 'Jimmy Nicol –

depping again' (*Melody Maker*, 27 June 1964) represents the word in the freshness of its youth.

Derivative. Unoriginal, an obvious copy or pastiche. A trendy term of abuse and scorn, much used by art critics and art students and common, too, in the musical world at its lower levels. 'Conceptually, they're anything but derivative' (*Sounds*, 21 July 1979) looks impressive, but probably means very little.

Diabolical. Very bad, regrettable. A word greatly liked by media people, especially those who earn a living in television. 'I think it was diabolical of Jimmy Hill to show it' (*Daily Mirror*, 9 April 1979) means that, in the writer's opinion, Mr Hill committed an error of judgement in including something or other in a sports programme.

Dig. (*i*) To like, enjoy. This is American in origin and dates from the late 1930s. Now international, it was found earliest and is still observed most frequently in jazz and pop music circles. 'An enjoyable record all round, but the rock fans won't dig it' (*New Musical Express*, 5 Dec 1958) and 'We'd dig to hear from you' (*Friends*, No. 3, Jan 1970) illustrates the usage.

(*ii*) To understand, take notice, pay attention. First noted in the USA in the mid-1930s, the word has BEATNIK associations and has been used almost entirely by those familiar with the pop/rock world. All other types of British user were always slightly self-conscious about it and tended to put it in inverted commas, although these were sometimes faint. It is found much less frequently now than it was ten years ago. "Dig this, Wiz!' I said to him' (MacInnes, *Absolute Beginners*, 1959), and 'Now dig what I'm saying' (*International Times*, 16 Jan 1967) belong to the word's period of popularity in the UK.

Dig that crazy. . . . Enjoy this exciting . . . . A catch phrase among the young of the 1950s and now completely dead. 'Dig that crazy pub' (*New Musical Express*, 14 Feb 1958).

Dig the scene. Understand. A youth expression of the 1950s and 1960s, now obsolete. MacInnes was quick to pick it up in 'Cool, please excuse me, but I don't quite dig the scene' (*Absolute Beginners*, 1959).

Disc. A record. The word was occasionally used in this sense in the UK in the late 1920s, but it came into its kingdom only in the 1950s, when it was the in-term among those employed in the pop music business and among pop music fans, although the older generation continued to refer to 'records'. So, 'This is a disc full of great tunes' (*New Musical Express*, 6 Jan 1956) and 'Select one of these fine discs now' (advert in *Sunday Times* colour supplement, 13 Jan 1973). Within the past five years, 'disc' has slipped from favour and 'record' has been widely heard again among the kind of people who would formerly have spoken almost automatically of 'discs'.

Disco. (*i*) A discotheque, a place where people dance to recorded music. The word was being used in this sense in the USA in the mid-1960s but was rare in the UK until about five years later, when discos began to take the place of the old-style dance halls, and 'The Starlight went over to almost 100% disco format' (*Attila*, 23 Sept 1971).

(*ii*) Mobile equipment used to play pop music for dancing. 'Mach Two Disco available' (advert in *Private Eye*, 1 Jan 1971).

(*iii*) A style of pop music emerging in the mid-1970s, which was particularly suitable for dancing to in discotheques. 'Disco' in this sense could mean either 'disco music' or 'disco dancing', which became a mania first in the USA and then worldwide after the success of the film *Saturday Night Fever*. 'You could still create massive sellers without being disco, punk or Paul McCartney' (*Melody Maker*, 12 May 1979), and 'Clearly then Pickett doesn't think disco's good music' (*Black Music*, Dec 1979) show the expression well established.

In its early days, 'disco' was used as an in-word only by the purveyors of discos and their youthful patrons, but it soon became universal, since there is no other word to describe this particular youth magnet.

Discography. A record bibliography, a complete list of recordings made by a particular performer – 'Membership brings you a discography' (*Sounds*, 3 March 1979). Apparently a British coinage, the word began to appear, in the *Melody Maker* in 1935, long before the days of pop, and in connection with jazz records. It has always, however, been a word for 'serious' collectors, and is hardly ever used by ordinary fans.

Disco queen. A striking-looking, exotic girl, often black, who can sing in the disco style and dance in the required spectacular fashion. There is consequently a never-ending demand for 'a girl to produce and promote as a disco queen' (*Sounds*, 21 July 1979).

Discotheque. A club for dancing to pop music recordings. In use in France, on the analogy of *bibliothèque*, from about 1950, and soon borrowed by the Anglo-Saxon world, although even in the late 1960s it was the full form of the word, rather than the abbreviated DISCO, which was normally found, as in 'New discotheque and club, 'Golden Cage'. Friends of mine running it' (*Jackie*, 2 Aug 1969).

Dish. A person, male or female, who is felt to be physically attractive. The word was used by Shakespeare in this sense (1599) and experienced a revival in the 1960s. 'Why, Kate, you're quite a dish' (*Jackie*, 2 Aug 1964) would have been perfectly intelligible to the author of *The Taming of the Shrew*.

Dishy. Attractive. Although the noun, 'dish', has a long history, the adjective is a modern creation. Popular in the 1960s and 1970s – 'When I tried on this blue poplin raincoat, I reckoned I looked dishy' (*Jackie*, 11 Jan 1964), and 'dishy would-be Labour Councillors' (*Brighton Voice*, July 1973) – it now has a slightly dated feel about it.

Disorientation. A feeling that one has lost one's bearing. Used as a technical term by psychiatrists in 1902, it became very popular during the 1960s and 1970s with the more intellectual drug-takers and with trendy admirers of sociological and psychological jargon, who were capable of referring to 'the seeking after that feeling of disorientation you get when reading film desirously' (*Sight and Sound*, Summer 1978).

Ditty. A 'light' pop song. An old word, nowadays reserved almost entirely for pop journalists, who have their own way of using it – 'This is a strolling-pace ditty with a spot-on commercial lyric' (*New Musical Express*, 26 Sept 1958).

Do. (*i*) To prosecute, charge, arrest, convict. A late 18th century British usage, which was regarded as distinctly low until after World War II, when attitudes to crime and criminals began to change, especially as a result of drug-taking, and the vocabulary which had hitherto been regarded as that of the criminal classes spread upwards and outwards through society. So, 'The guy will get done for dealing, no doubt' (*Attila*, 23 Oct 1971).

(*ii*) To take, often with a hint of excess. An insiders' word. 'He was doing the drugs' (*Zigzag*, Aug 1972).

Dodgy. (*i*) Unreliable, not to be trusted. A meaning found in the UK especially in London, from the 1890s onwards, but mainly among the working class. During the 1950s and 1960s, it moved upwards socially and is now widely understood, although not normally used by older members of the middle class. The pop world is very fond of it – 'My memory's a bit dodgy' (rock musician in *Zigzag*, July 1973), and 'The album sleeve makes them look a right dodgy bunch' (*Sounds*, 24 Jan 1981).

(*ii*) Suspect. 'When the meat was a bit dodgy, they used to curry it' (*Jackie*, 30 May 1964). The range of users is similar to that of (*i*).

(*iii*) Dangerous. 'Alcohol is still very dodgy' (musician in *The Road to Rock*, 1974). This meaning is not as common as (*i*) and (*ii*).

Doll. (*i*) A not very intelligent girl, made up and dressed to be sexually enticing. This British usage, first recorded in the 1770s, has fluctuated in popularity and social status. It has usually had scornful or patronizing overtones, but for a few years in the 1960s it had no pejorative sense among teenage girls, as evidenced by 'Any girl can be a doll' (*Jackie*, 11 Jan 1964).

(*ii*) A kind, generous person of either sex. This completely new meaning was first observed in the USA in about 1960 and spread rapidly overseas. In the 1960s it was popular, although not excessively so, among young people – 'You're quite a doll, Al' (*Jackie*, 4 June 1966) – but it is not greatly used in this sense today.

Dolly. A young, pretty girl. In this sense of the word – a British monopoly – the first recorded example is 1906. Used by men, it has slightly patronizing overtones. Used by women, it describes, less flatteringly, a particular kind of vacant, pretty-pretty girl. The two shades of meaning can be seen in 'Wanted, two dollies, twentyish, to look after two undomesticated blokes' (*International Times*, 28 April 1967), and 'Racey types move in circles that have dollies to match' (*Jackie*, 24 Feb 1968).

Since the 1960s, it has become, both for men and women, nearly always derogatory, indicating a pretty, silly, empty-headed creature. 'Dollies need not apply' (advert in *Private Eye*, 5 April 1974) makes the point.

Dolly bird. An attractive girl of fashionable appearance, usually unintelligent. A British expression, found from around 1960 onwards, and now widely used, although until the 1970s it tended to be mainly the property of young people. 'It's a mad mad tale of four dolly birds and their escapades in Swinging London' (film review in *Jackie*, 24 Feb 1968) reflects its first flush of popularity.

Doomy. Depressed, full of foreboding, miserable. A purely British expression, which originated as a noun in the RAF about 1945 – a 'doomy' was a prophet of doom – and became a popular youth-word of the 1960s, but always as an adjective – 'I was very doomy while we were making it' (rock musician in *Zigzag*, 30 April 1973), and 'The doomy side of his persona' (*New Musical Express*, 6 Jan 1979).

Dope. Drugs. First used in the USA about 1880, as a synonym for 'opium', it came into general use in the UK in the 1950s, when drug-taking was beginning to be a popular pastime among the nation's young. In the 1950s, it usually implied 'hard drugs' – 'a card-sharping dope addict' (*New Musical Express*, 13 Jan 1956) – but later it came to mean specifically marijuana and hashish, as in '*Home Grown* – Europe's first dope magazine' (*Home Grown*, No. 2, 1977), and 'I smoked dope since 1958' (*New Society*, 7 Feb 1980).

Dope fiend. A habitual drug-taker. The phrase, which is of American origin, at one time suggested enthusiasm and understanding – 'Have you dope fiends actually seen stuff like a good April sky?' (letter to *Oz* 21, June 1969) – but it can also be used ironically, as a way of poking fun at a person who is certainly not a dope fiend. Today, the expression is never used by people who take drugs.

Doper. A person who takes drugs. An in-word, used by drug people about drug people, as in 'Hollywood is offering a number of movies featuring dope and dopers' (*Home Grown*, No. 3, 1978).

Downbeat. (*i*) Low-key, depressed. The musical metaphor was being used in this sense in the USA by 1950 and was well established among British journalists five years or so later. Only very trendy people used it in speech, however, and it has a very faded appearance nowadays. 'Snap out of that downbeat mood' (*Jackie*, 8 Feb 1964), and '. . . a variety of situations concerning love and lust, most of them fairly downbeat' (*The Soul Book*, 1975) are typical journalistic contexts, at a time when the word was fashionable.

(*ii*) Understated, realistic. Also American in origin, this meaning of 'downbeat' has met with a wider acceptance than (*i*), but remains, even so, very much a media term – 'All war, all at sea, all Westerns, or all downbeat' (*Sunday Times* colour supplement, 3 Feb 1963).

Downer. (*i*) A depressing experience. Originally a drug-takers' word, in the USA it had, by the mid-1960s, come to mean any kind of depression, however caused, and was so used in the UK by the end of the same decade, especially in what one might call *Melody Maker* circles, where someone could be described as having 'a long history of downers' (*Melody Maker*, 20 Jan 1979). To avoid possible embarrassment, through innocence, it is as well to be aware of the phrase 'uppers and downers'. 'Uppers' are pep pills, such as amphetamines, and 'downers' are tranquillizers, like barbiturates.

(*ii*) Depressing. The adjective arrived slightly later than the noun. Found in such contexts as 'the downer side of life' (*Oz* 33, Feb 1971), it has not made much headway outside the fringes of intellectualism.

Do one's own thing. To behave in a completely individualistic manner, to go one's own way without any regard for the opinions of others. This formed a basic part of HIPPY philosophy in the 1950s and subsequently proved very attractive to young people the world over. Society often reacted unfavourably – 'By trying to do their own thing, the phenomena now described as underground pretty soon rediscovered the machinery of repression' (*Oz* 22, July 1969).

The expression has often been used by journalists as a light-hearted euphemism for sexual activity, as in 'Beautiful couples doing their own thing' (*Oz* 33, Feb 1971).

Drag. A bore, nuisance, problem. Known since the early 1920s, and as likely to have originated in the UK as in the USA, the expression, for the first 25 years of its existence, had strongly upper-class associations. In the late 1950s it suddenly blossomed out as a classless teenage expression, more likely to be used by males than by females. So, 'Spending holidays with my parents is a drag' (teenage girl in *Jackie*, 2 Jan 1965), and 'Flat hunting in London is, of course, one of the big drags' (*International Times*, 14 Oct 1966).

The adjective, 'draggy', which first appeared at about the same time as 'drag', is certainly of American origin, and has always been much less used in the UK.

Dread. A Rastafarian/Reggae/groovy type of black. The word has this specific meaning among blacks, but it is used more loosely and confusingly by white journalists and people in the pop music world, who like to give the impression that they are in the know, and whose professional world contains such people as 'the comfortingly familiar figure of Harrow Road dread, King Sounds, as host to the show' (*Sounds*, 24 March 1979).

Dreamboat. A man about whom teenage girls have romantic fantasies. The word came into use in the USA towards the end of World War I and had a certain vogue in the UK during the 1950s and 1960s – 'Just take a look at those stars – they may not be your dreamboats now, but they'll definitely be yours tomorrow' (*Boyfriend Annual*, 1963) – but it is now very dated.

Drop. To take drugs, especially LSD, by the mouth. 'Has never dropped acid and doesn't want to' (*Schoolkids Oz*, April 1970).

Drop in. To become conventional, to rejoin the Establishment. 'Drop out' is now standard English, but its opposite was a journalistic coinage, which never really caught on, possibly because the process it described was fairly rare. Such vogue as it had was during the late 1960s and early 1970s – 'To act as a nostalgic scrapbook for those who have now dropped in' (*Oz* 43, July/Aug 1972).

Drop out. (*i*) To reject conventional society. 'Stephen Williams, 17, tried dropping out in Morocco for a few months' (*Schoolkids Oz*, April 1970).

(*ii*) A person who rejects conventional society. 'The most incompetent and concerted set of drop-outs in Fleet Street' (*Private Eye*, 8 May 1970).

Both as a verb and a noun, the expression was trendy in the late 1960s and early 1970s, but soon became part of standard English. It is no longer identified with any particular age-group or social class.

Druggie. A person who takes drugs. A not unfriendly word, used by people who include drug-takers among their friends and acquaintances, but rarely by drug-takers themselves – 'The stereotype 1960s druggie' (*New Society*, March 1980).

Dude. Male person, fellow. A word with a long American pedigree, imported without great success in the 1960s by the more experimental and trendy kind of journalist – 'The dude came round every day and gave him his shot' (*Oz*, Winter, 1973). It is almost never used in conversation in the UK, except as a joke.

Duff. Of poor quality. The word was found in the 1880s in the sense of 'spurious'. In the 1930s it was being used in Glasgow with its modern meaning, and during World War II it became quite popular among members of the Services. From there, its adoption by the post-war young was easy and natural. It is applied only to things, not to people – '. . . some real duff seedy hotel' (pop singer in *Mates Annual*, 1979).

Duffo. Bad, inferior. The -o ending has been much used by the would-be vanguard section of British society from the mid-1970s onwards. The pop world is especially fond of it – '90 per cent of their songs are very good, the other half, well, duffo' (*Sounds*, 21 July 1979).

Dumb. Stupid. A meaning which has come full circle, beginning in England in the 16th century, or possibly earlier, revived in the USA in the mid-19th, and reimported to the UK in the 1920s. It was given a fresh lease of life by the new vogue for things and habits American which swept in during the 1950s as part of the teenage revolution, but it is still nothing like as widely used here as in the USA and one can easily look through half-a-dozen popular magazines without finding an example of it. 'They aren't that dumb' (*Undercurrents*, July/Aug 1974) is one of the exceptions.

Dumb-ass. Stupid. A pure Americanism, used in the UK only by those who feel close cultural links with the USA. Pop music journalists are such people and it is from them that we have 'dumb-ass fan letters' (*Sounds*, 3 March 1979).

Dumbo. A stupid person. This is a coinage from the early 1970s, with the '-o' ending much favoured by teenagers. It is still in fashion – 'Ever tried to explain a phone directory to a daft dumbo?' (letter to *Oh Boy!*, 19 Jan 1980).

Dyke, or Dike. A lesbian, usually of distinctly masculine appearance. This unflattering term appeared in the USA around 1940 and soon found its way to the UK, where it is rather more likely to be used by men than by women. Lesbians themselves find it offensive – 'He made the mistake of calling her a dyke' (*Spare Rib*, Jan 1979).

Dykey. Looking or acting like a lesbian. The adjective arrived considerably later than the noun and is much used by teenagers, especially by girls who are anxious to emphasise their own 100 per cent femininity – 'I am tired of dykey salesladies' (letter to *Oz* 3, Aug 1967).

Dynamite. Marvellous, exciting. This had a short spell of favour as an Anglo–American catch-phrase in the pop music world – 'What a dynamite photographer' (*Rolling Stone*, 26 Jan 1978), and 'The highest quality artists kick off the treadmill with one dynamite number' (*Sounds*, 21 July 1979). It is hardly ever found nowadays.

E

Eco. Ecology, ecological. The use of the abbreviation has so far been confined almost entirely to the trendier kind of academics and to those best described as eco-people, those who campaign for the protection of the ENVIRONMENT against the sinister forces which they believe, sometimes correctly, to threaten it. 'A Portuguese eco and anti-nuclear group' (*Undercurrents*, Oct/Nov 1978) would have its heart in the right place.

Ego-jockey. A person who organizes publicity for himself, usually to excess. A media expression, particularly common among pop music journalists. 'Tireless self-publicists and ego-jockeys' (*Sounds*, 21 July 1979) makes the same point twice over.

Ego-trip. Any form of activity which is calculated to flatter the ego and increase its size. In use since the late 1960s, this has always been mainly a journalist's word – 'the ego-trip of a politically aware bourgeois Englishman' (*Sounds*, 3 March 1979) – and 'It was just an ego-trip for them' (*Motor Cycle Weekly*, 30 Jan 1981), that is a chance to be lionised?

Ego-tripper. A person who is constantly trying to present a flattering image of himself. For the range of users, *see* EGO-TRIP. 'He doesn't think the ego-trippers take themselves as seriously as their TV counterparts' (*Foul*, Oct 1972).

Ego-tripping. Acting in a way calculated to flatter one's own vanity. Like EGO-TRIP and EGO-TRIPPER, the expression implies contempt. The disapproving overtones can be seen in 'a load of ego-tripping personality-cultist punks' (letter to *Attila*, 16 Oct 1971), and 'The superstar . . . his performance is based on ego-tripping, his music is aggressive' (*Spare Rib*, April 1975).

Elbow. Removal, exclusion. Not widely used outside the competitive atmosphere of the world of popular entertainment and even there somewhat low – 'After about a year he got a heavy elbow' (rock musician in *Zigzag*, July 1973).

Elitist. Manifesting a belief in the domination of one social group or class by another. First used in the early 1950s by sociologists and psychologists as a technical term, the word has subsequently become a term of abuse among left-wingers and militant feminists. In 'Librarianship is notorious for its elitist approach towards women workers' (*Spare Rib*, April 1975), all that is really meant is that women librarians are less likely to get the top jobs.

Energy. Life-force. Used a great deal by members of the UNDERGROUND Press during the 1960s and early 1970s, especially by those who were attracted by the hippy type of mysticism. In 'As in all marriages, the energy feedback remained a continual, occasionally terrifying two-way process' (*Oz*, Winter 1973), the word is probably not being used terribly seriously.

Environment. Surroundings. In its original scientific sense, 'physical context', the word had real meaning. During the 1960s, however, 'environment' became a vague crusading term, much loved by semi-intellectual hippies. It is now used *ad nauseam* by journalists, sociologists and the more earnest type of social campaigners, who regard a concern for something they call 'the environment' as evidence of political adulthood. This irritating, emotionally charged debasement of a useful, harmless word can be seen in 'allowing the spectator to control his environment, the centre being a tool for the discovery attitude towards life' (*International Times*, 13 Feb 1967), and 'A picture of life-styles and environments' (*The Guardian*, 13 Feb 1979). In the UK, the work of the Department of the Environment is greatly handicapped by its idiotic name.

Environmental. Relating to the environment, in the sense in which the word is used above in ENVIRONMENT. In 'a study of the railways to minimise the environmental impact of building sites' (*Undercurrents*, July/Aug 1974) it is clear that the writer is highly suspicious of the motives of planners and builders, possibly with good reason.

Environmentalist. A person vocally concerned about the quality of the ENVIRONMENT, a protester against bad town planning or the destruction of the countryside for commercial purposes. An environmentalist is usually a negative or conservative person, anxious to preserve the status quo against all attempts to change it. The positive environmentalist, someone who is attempting to create a pleasant environment, is not covered by the word. In certain circumstances, 'environmentalist' can be a term of abuse or contempt, as evidenced by 'cheap-minded environmentalists had been heard to mutter . . .' (*Undercurrents*, July/Aug 1974).

Epic. Outstandingly good, majestic, very impressive. 'Sunken and suffering, he was epic' (Cohn: *Awopbop*, 1969). A catchword of the 1960s, it is now obsolete.

Ethnic. (*i*) Inspired by a culture different from one's own. The word was first used in this sense in the USA, where one has had ethnic gardens, ethnic restaurants and ethnic grocers for many years, and began to establish itself in the UK very slowly in the 1960s, largely as a result of black, Indian and Pakistani immigration. Starting here as a sociological term – ethnic groups, ethnic minorities, and so on – it came to be used in a different way in the entertainment and art worlds, with faintly scornful and patronizing overtones, making it almost a synonym of 'folksy' – 'The Regulars have signed to CBS after a couple of ethnic singles for Greensleeves' (*Sounds*, 28 April 1979).
    (*ii*) A person whose taste in music, clothes, etc. leans towards the folksy, with elements lifted from strange cultures. It is this meaning which is implied in 'On one side there were the ethnics and on the other there were the commercials' (Cohn: *Awopbop*, 1969).

-ette. The suffix has been increasingly used during the past 25 years, in order to make:
    (*i*) A diminutive with a twee flavour – '. . . a muralette of Tahiti on the wall' (Terson: *Zigger Zagger*, 1967).
    (*ii*) A non-serious new female noun, as in 'the other glamourette' (*New Musical Express*, 21 Sept 1956), and 'a Neasden saunarette' (*Private Eye*, 17 July 1970). This usage originated in the USA, with such coinages as 'drum majorette', and became part of the *Private Eye* language fairly early in that magazine's career, in the late 1960s. The best known of the *Private Eye* -ette words is probably 'hackette', a woman journalist, which could possibly be able to be received into standard English.

Evil. Bad tempered, moody, malevolent. Current in the USA in the early 1960s, this meaning had crossed the Atlantic on the wings of pop music by the end of the decade and was fairly well established in the UK in the mid 1970s – 'I was pretty evil during the sessions' (rock musician in *Zigzag*, 30 April 1973).

Among the young, 'evil' has now almost entirely lost its moral and religious implications. One can now be 'evil' without being wicked or sinful, as indeed one always could when one was 'evil tempered'. The musician who complained of 'evil audiences' (Gold: *The Road to Rock*, 1976), was not accusing them of depravity or viciousness. They were simply hostile and ill-natured.

Ex. A former boyfriend or husband, less frequently former girlfriend or wife. This purely British expression first became common in the late 1950s and has shown remarkable staying power. Both the working class and upper levels of the middle class seem to be able to use it straight and without difficulty, but on the lower levels of the middle class it usually produces some degree of embarrassment, which is lessened, if not avoided, by surrounding it with audible inverted commas. In 'My boy – or should I say my ex?' (*Jackie*, 30 May 1964), and 'Try to stop thinking about your ex' (*Oh Boy!*, 19 Jan 1980), the social context is working class and no embarrassment is to be assumed.

F

Fab. Wonderful. This very British teenage abbreviation of 'fabulous' first appeared about 1960 and had a short life, its rise coinciding with that of the Beatles, 'the Fab Four', who were alleged to use it. 'He's gorgeous, he's super, he's fab' (*Jackie*, 11 Jan 1964), and 'The fab Beat Boot' (advert in *Melody Maker*, 6 Jan 1964) belong to the golden period.

The word has been used as an exclamation, as well as an adjective – '. . . all without leaving the building. Fab!' (*Jackie*, 4 June 1966).

It lingered on among journalists catering for teenagers longer than it did with teenagers themselves but, after largely disappearing from view in the early 1970s, it now seems to be staging something of a comeback – 'I think Lewis Collins is absolutely fab and I'd like to join his fan club' (letter to *Pink*, 12 May 1979), and 'YMO's fab 'Solid State Survivor'' (*Sounds*, 24 Jan 1981).

Fabbiest. Best, most wonderful. *See* FAB. 'We've found the fabbiest hat on the market' (*Jackie*, 2 Sept 1967).

Fabby. Wonderful. Another derivative of FAB which refuses to die. The teenage market remains oddly faithful to it, as one observes in 'But Pamela is feeling pretty happy to have this fabby forty-seven year-old for a hubby' (*Oh Boy!*, 19 Jan 1981).

Fable. Story, account of what happened. One of the tribal words of the BEAT/Jazz language used by the hippier British teenagers and their adored musicians of the 1950s and 1960s. Colin MacInnes was quick to pick it up. 'Hi! we all said and I asked Cool for the fable' (*Absolute Beginners*, 1959).

Fabulous. Wonderful. First noticed in the late 1950s, this was the superlative of the 1960s. It died of exhaustion half way through the 1970s, although it still appears as a ghost among those who were young 20 years ago. It began its life on the upper levels of British society and moved fairly rapidly downwards to a point somewhere near the middle of the middle class. Below that level, it tended to be replaced by FAB. 'Fabulous Spanish Mediterranean village' (advert in *Private Eye*, 22 May 1970) shows 'fabulous' still on the way down, but with not much further to go.

Faggot. A male homosexual. First observed in the USA about 1916, the expression became widespread in the UK during the 1960s, but subsequently lost ground, having failed to meet the challenge of the native 'queer'. It has always been very much an outsiders' word, little used by homosexuals themselves, except as an occasional mild joke. Some degree of contempt or amusement is usually noticeable, as in 'The faggots on the third floor were always trying to get to Ice' (*Oz*, Winter 1973).

Fagrag. A magazine for homosexuals. A word coined by journalists for journalists and seldom used by anyone else. '*Gay News*, the persistently excellent fagrag' (*Oz*, Winter 1973).

Fancy. To find someone sexually attractive. The word has been used in this sense since the 16th century and the reason for including it here is to draw attention to its changed social prestige in recent years. Throughout the 19th century and until the 1950s it was always considered rather low, by the middle and upper classes. Thereafter, like many other words, it moved rapidly towards classlessness, at least among the young. 'Don't wear this style unless you really fancy the guy' (*Jackie*, 15 Feb 1964) would have seemed a perfectly normal expression to a very wide range of teeangers at this date. Among older people, however, there is a marked social line, well down into the middle class, above which 'fancy' still produces working class, and therefore undesirable, echoes.

Fantastic. Wonderful, enormous. The successor to FABULOUS, the popularity of fantastic, as a youth culture word, peaked somewhere in the mid-1970s. 'There's a fantastic bloke travels on the same bus as me' (letter to *Jackie*, 24 Feb 1968), and 'We did that in a fantastic rush, didn't we?' (rock musician in *Zigzag*, July 1973) both belong to the word's good years. After something like a ten-year run, the nation was visibly tiring of it and the young looked for a replacement. Many of those who were young, or relatively young, in the 1970s have continued to use it, however, a practice which makes them sound, if not look their age.

Both as an attributive adjective – 'fantastic bloke' – and as an exclamation – 'Fantastic!' – the stress is usually on the second syllable, irrespective of the social class of the speaker, although different degrees of intensity are possible. But, among the better educated, especially those working for the media, there was an alternative stressing for the exclamation, with an almost equal emphasis on the first and second syllables and an appreciable pause between the two syllables. One still hears this sometimes among survivors of the 1970s.

Fanzine. A fan magazine. Created in the USA about 1949 and applied to begin with to magazines concerned with science fiction, the word quickly became caught up in the new international surge of pop music, where the number of fans could be reckoned in tens of millions, rather than tens of thousands, and was soon associated mainly with this kind of subject matter – 'Mark F. advised all his readers to start their own fanzines' (*New Musical Express*, 6 Jan 1979), and 'The fanzine is the only relevant form of free press today' (*Sounds*, 3 March 1979). Journalists have also produced an adjective – 'as seen through fanzine eyes' (*Sounds*, 24 Jan 1981).

Far out. Unconventional, outrageous, amazing, excellent. First found in the USA around 1954 and originally a HIPPY word, it had passed into more general use by the mid-1960s. Examples from its vintage period are 'A new magazine, *The Dick*, which is too far out to be printed' (*International Times*, 27 Feb 1967), and 'A very, very good far out record' (*Zigzag*, Aug 1972). It is now distinctly dated.

Fave. (*i*) Favourite. A short-lived teenage adjective of the mid-1960s, afterwards used ironically or mockingly. The early usage is seen in 'Her fave one is a thin strip of leather' (*Jackie*, 11 Jan 1964) and the later in 'Rupert's fave occupation is dancing the night away' (*Mates Annual*, 1979).

(*ii*) A favourite. *See* (*i*), but still on active service, as, for example, in 'It's got all your faves on it' (DJ on BBC Radio One, 4 April 1979) and '. . . a staple diet of dance-floor faves, flashy lights and snogging space' (*Time Out*, 10–16 Dec 1982).

Fave rave. Best, most exciting thing, favourite enthusiasm. Originally a DJ word, it was always a joke, and taken up as such by teenagers and those who cater for their tastes. 'I forgot to mention my fave rave of all time' (rock musician in *Zigzag*, April 1973), and 'When you've selected the album by your fave rave' (advert in *Sounds*, 28 April 1979).

Favourite. Good, nice. Part of the British teenage vocabulary in the 1960s, now a thing of the past. One could search for a week and not find anything resembling 'short skirts arc definitely favourite' (*Jackie*, 29 Feb 1964) today.

Fax. Facts. A print-only piece of Anglo–American nonsense favoured by pop journalists during the past ten years. 'Will Beatlemania never die? The fax as we have them are . . .' (*New Musical Express*, 12 May 1979), and '. . . no slouch himself at rock fax' (*Melody Maker*, 20 Jan 1979) will do as examples.

Faze. To confuse, amaze, distract. An American word, going back to at least the 1830s, which was wafted across the Atlantic in the 1950s by pop music and its journalists, but which has utterly failed to catch the imagination of anyone else here. 'Presley's deep Southern accent which fazes some Britishers' (*New Musical Express*, 15 June 1956) sounds as American and *outré* now as it did in 1956.

Feedback. Response, reaction, two-way communication. An electronics term, first noted in 1920, it was taken over by sociologists and media people in the 1950s. Nowadays, 'feedback' is sometimes obtained in a more or less scientific way by, for instance, market research specialists, but usually it means only 'observable response to what I/we are doing or saying'. 'We need all the feedback we can get' (*China Cat Sunflower*, No. 1, 1969), and 'We call ourselves the newspaper of the Brighton Tribe, but the amount of feedback is still minimal' (*Attila*, 23 Oct 1971) are examples of this vague usage.

Fella, Fellah. A young, trendy man. The spelling, 'fellow', indicates, in the UK, the traditional meaning, a male person of any age or type. 'Fellow' may be pronounced, among more educated people, more or less as it is spelt, or with a vague final syllable, corresponding to the spelling 'feller', reproducing the well-established habit of the lower orders. 'Fella' is sometimes pronounced as if it were spelt 'feller', but one also hears a broader sound, as if the speaker is mentally hearing the spelling 'fella'. Older people are not likely to be sensitive to the distinction between 'feller' and 'fella' but, in speech and in intention, 'fella' is the most common word for 'desirable man' among girls and young women in the UK. The authors of 'What with a dishy fella and super job, it's no wonder she's very happy' (*Jackie*, 18 Jan 1969), and 'Last week I met this fella that I've fancied for ages' (*Pink*, 12 May 1979) were sensitive to their public.

Femme. The more feminine half of a lesbian partnership – 'Femme seeks affectionate butch' (*Gay News*, 9–22 Dec 1982). A relatively modern word, not found before the mid-1970s, and rarely used by non-lesbians.

Filth. The police. This not very elegant term, which makes no secret of the speaker's hostility to the existence of law and order, seems to have first appeared at some time in the late 1960s. Its use has so far been confined to those elements among the male young for whom fighting, violence and anarchic behaviour are the breath of life. One such wrote, 'The filth are going to have one hellava time enforcing this particular law' (letter to *Superbike*, Sept 1978), although one suspects his letter may have been edited and made readable for publication.

Fink. Someone who lets one down, who behaves in a despicable or underhand manner. In the sense of 'informer' and, later, 'plain-clothes detective', 'fink' was in use among the criminal classes in the USA very early in the 20th century and by the 1940s it had also acquired the meaning 'a strike-breaker, a scab'. It has never been normal British usage among the members of any social group or class in any of these senses and even the latest and more general meaning given at the beginning of this entry is used in the UK only by those whose life-style owes a great deal to the USA, people such as the author of 'Miserable fink – just when I was looking forward to a good punch-up (*Undercurrents*, July/Aug 1974).

First wave. Original, pioneering. An in-term among pop musicians and the journalists associated with them – '. . . the only surviving first-wave punk band regularly working' (*Time Out*, 10–16 Dec 1982).

Fix. (*i*) Injection of a drug. 'He took a fix' (Nuttall: *Bomb Culture*, 1968).
(*ii*) To inject drugs. 'Watching someone fix' (Nuttall: *Bomb Culture*, 1968).
Both as a noun and a verb, 'fix' originated in the USA in the mid-

1930s. It moved to the UK 20 years later, when the drug habit was becoming international.

Flip. (*i*) To become very enthusiastic, excited. 'Why have the pop fans flipped?' (*New Musical Express*, 20 July 1956).

(*ii*) To have a strong liking or affection for something or someone – 'We can't all turn back somersaults to prove we've flipped' (*International Times*, 13 Feb 1967).

(*iii*) To become infatuated with a person – 'More 'n more girls are flipping these days for 18 year-old Tommy Quickly' (*Jackie*, 11 Jan 1964).

(*iv*) To play records – '. . . flipped a few discs (*Jackie*, 6 Jun 1964).

(*v*) The other, usually less important, side of a record – 'On the flip was 'Love Doctor'' (*The Soul Book*, 1976).

All the above senses of the word originated in the USA and were current there in the early 1950s. All of them entered the UK in the 1960s via the pop music world.

Flipped out. Unconventional, mad. In use in the USA in the mid-1950s and in trendy circles in the UK by the early 1960s, the expression is little heard nowadays. 'London 1967 is not ready for a completely flipped out newspaper' (*International Times*, 16 Jan 1967) illustrates the phrase in its heyday.

Flip one's lid. To become over-excited, hysterical. Originally American, the expression had a certain teenage vogue in the UK in the 1960s – 'I flipped my lid when I got to work' (*Jackie*, 2 March 1968) – but has now almost reached the inverted commas, parody stage.

Flip over. The reverse side of a record. Current among aficionados in both America and Britain in the 1950s – '. . . on the flip over' (*New Musical Express*, 13 Jan 1956) – it has been replaced by FLIPSIDE.

Flipside. The reverse side of a record. The present replacement of FLIP OVER among pop music fans and those professionally engaged in the business – 'The flipside is a re-recording' (*Sounds*, 3 March 1979).

Flower child. The original flower children flourished in California in the 1960s. They were so called from their habit of carrying or wearing flowers as a symbol of peace, love and tolerance of other people's peculiarities. They stood also for the non-violent rejection of existing customs and attitudes. They had withered away by the end of the decade, but while they were still blooming, one found such journalistic references as 'Editor . . . anxious to contact genuine and literate flower child' (advert in *International Times*, 31 Aug 1967).

Flunk. To fail a test or examination. An American word, which has achieved no success in the UK outside the usual America-breathing circles, exemplified by 'They all flunked out in both Music and English' (*New Musical Express*, 20 July 1956).

Folk. People. Except in compounds, 'folk' is American, 'people' is British, but 'folk', like FOLKS has been creeping in steadily and stealthily from the USA during the past 30 years, along the HIPPY/ entertainment world routes. So, 'Some folk forget all their beautiful ideas on sight of bread' (*International Times*, 2 June 1967).

Folkie, folky. A folk singer or folk singing enthusiast. This American word struck roots in the UK during the 1970s and is now firmly established here among musicians, singers and their fans. Its British history is summarized in 'I knew a lot of other folkies' (rock musician in *Zigzag*, May 1971); 'If all this makes him a folkie in your eyes, then so be it' (*Sounds*, 24 March 1979), and 'Big Al sounds like an old folkie' (*Sounds*, 24 Jan 1981).

Folknik. A self-conscious, untalented follower of folk music, possessing nothing but the trappings. Formed in imitation of BEATNIK, the word was around for a time in the 1960s, mainly among musical journalists – 'As for the commercials, they were folkniks, they were fakers' (Cohn: *Awopbop*, 1969) – but is now dead.

Folks. *See* FOLK. The word has a perfectly respectable British ancestry, but in recent times the all-powerful British class-system has been at work on it, so that there are now important differences between its usage in the USA and in the UK. In the USA, anybody, no matter what his social level, can refer to his 'folks', meaning his family and relatives, but in the UK this habit is confined to the working class and the lower middle class. Members of the upper and upper-middle class would take great pains to avoid it, as a vulgarism. In the sense of 'friends', 'good people', 'folks' is felt by nearly everyone in the UK to belong to the Americanized showbusiness world, although it has been widely used here for many years. Examples of the current British usage are:

(*i*) Parents, relatives. 'The folks practically turned into neurotic Purple People' (*Jackie*, 30 May 1964), and 'He was with his folks' (rock musician in *Zigzag*, Sept 1973).

(*ii*) People. 'Book now before it's too late, folks' (advert in *Private Eye*, 5 June 1970), and 'Don't forget the flowers and chocs, folks' (*Daily Mirror*, 22 March 1979).

Teenagers, most of whom feel they have a licence to move freely over the British class system, defy the rules outlined above. Those who come from above the middle line in society solve the 'folks' problem by projecting the word slightly, by speaking it with an American accent, or by cocooning it in a smile.

Force. A special protective power, supernatural guiding light. The film, *Star Wars* (1977), contained the sentence, 'May the force be with you', and this, with its hippy echoes, quickly became a catch-phrase among the young – 'You could see the force was with them' (*Sounds*, 3 March 1979). The force now appears to be spent.

Foul up. To ruin, make a mess of. The expression originated in the USA in 1945 and quickly installed itself in the UK among the young. During the 1960s it acquired general currency and there must now be few of any age who do not at least understand it. It is not yet as common as 'mess up', and 'mess things up', but it is still advancing and, with its somewhat stronger overtones, it may yet win the day. It is not necessary to specify what is fouled up. 'Every time a delivery gets fouled up' (*Jackie*, 19 Dec 1964), and 'Given his reputation for fouling up' (*Melody Maker*, 27 Jan 1979) are equally possible.

Freak. Of American origin, about 1965, in both the senses given below, 'freak' was soon taken up in the UK and now appears to be well established, although one has the impression that its users are mostly under 30.

(*i*) A hippy, a person subscribing to the ideals of the Alternative Society. 'The only other shops for the freak community are record shops and trendy boutiques' (*China Cat Sunflower*, No. 1, 1969) is a fairly early British example. 'UFO was already bulging to the walls with freaks' (*Zigzag*, Aug 1979) demonstrates that the word was flexible enough to survive and prosper in a post-hippy age.

(*ii*) An enthusiast. Once a hippy term, this is now very respectable and clearly meets a real need, at least in those sections of British society where strange passions are permitted. For those who are unfamiliar with this use of the word, it should be explained that 'freak', in its modern, hippy-derived sense, does not imply abnormality. The 'Harley Davidson freak' (*Superbike*, Sept 1978), and the 'Who-freak friend' (Gold: *The Road to Rock*, 1976) are, in this respect, entirely different from the bearded ladies, two-headed calves and other circus 'freaks' of the 1930s. No-one living before World War II could have produced an accurate translation of 'all the brown rice and vegetables a macro-freak could desire' (*Oz* 41, April/May 1972).

Freakess. A female FREAK – 'Wanted Poetic H.M. freakess for intelligent hippy-go-lucky freak' (advert in *Sounds*, 21 July 1979). The word has undoubted charm, but is little used, possibly because it is likely to produce accusations of sexism.

Freak out. Originally, in the USA in the late 1950s, it meant (*i*) an intense emotional experience resulting from drug-taking, or (*ii*) to have such an experience. In the early 1960s, again in the USA, the phrase lost its drug associations and became secularized. The new meanings were rapidly exported, so that one finds:

(*i*) To behave in an uninhibited way – 'Everyone was going to freak out regardless' (Cohn: *Awopbop*, 1969).

(*ii*) An occasion of uninhibited behaviour – 'Technicolour dreams, flashing light, wild fabulous freak-outs' (*Jackie*, 2 Sept 1967).

(*iii*) To become angry – 'I opened the sleeve and freaked out' (*Zigzag*, April 1973), and 'They both freaked out totally' (*Honey*, June 1979).

Freaked out. Outrageous, extremely unconventional. Its origins and subsequent development are the same as for FREAK OUT – 'Three chicks in LA, very freaked out; never seen anything like these' (musician in *Oz* 18, Feb 1969).

Freaky. Unusual, hippy-looking. Originally, in the USA in the early 1960s, one was 'freaky' as a result of drug-taking. This is no longer the sole or necessary cause of freakiness. By the mid-1960s, it was possible to be 'freaky' simply because one had decided to look or behave that way. Sometimes, as in 'UFO, the freaky club which I.T. has a share in' (*International Times*, 13 March 1967), it is not easy to decide exactly which kinds of freaks are involved.

Freebie. (*i*) Costing nothing – 'Lovable old lags in Wandsworth nick will be treated to a freebie concert' (*Sounds*, 1 Dec 1979), and 'Freebie badges' (*Sounds*, 28 April 1979).

(*ii*) A free gift, a present – 'Why didn't my copy contain the freebie?' (*Sounds*, 3 March 1979), and '. . . extracting the maximum amount of freebies from stingy relatives' (*Sounds*, 24 March 1979).

As both a noun and an adjective, 'freebie' originated in the USA in the early 1940s, but it was slow in finding a public in the UK. Until the late 1960s, it was little used here, even by journalists and public relations people, who have a virtual monopoly of both the word and the freebies.

Free school. An experimental school, not part of the state system, and run by people of avant-garde views, which include the rejection of authoritarian discipline. The name originated in the UK in the late 1960s, as part of the general educational ferment of the period, when many revolutionary-minded teachers had 'ambitious notions of founding a free school' (*Zigzag*, Aug 1972).

Frog. A French person. Used in the UK from the 1870s onwards, by members of the working class of all ages and by middle- and upper-class schoolboys. It was always, until recently, mildly insulting and by the 1950s it had become little used. In the late 1970s, however, after a long period during which words of this kind – Eyetie, Hun, wog, Chink, Jap, and all the other old favourites – were taboo among members of the new all-men-are-brothers generation, such words, purged of all their old associations, can now be used in a joking but friendly spirit, or so one assumes, and they are found in print in the trendier publications – 'He fined a French student £500. That'll teach the frogs to insult us' (*Time Out*, 6 April 1979).

Front. (*i*) To be the leader of a BAND – 'She fronts her own male outfit' (*New Musical Express*, 20 Jan 1956).

(*ii*) To perform with a band as what is intended to be the major attraction – 'a raucous wailing trio fronting a rock-soul band' (*The Soul Book*, 1975).

In the USA, the word was being used in both of these senses in the mid-1930s but it occurred in the UK only very infrequently until the 1950s, when it shared in the rising popularity of the new pop music.

Fuck. To have sexual intercourse. The word itself has been part of the

English language since the beginning of the 16th century, possibly earlier. What is new and indeed revolutionary is the extent to which this most taboo of all sexual terms has come out of the shadows during the last 30 years or so. It is now used with little, if any, hesitation or inhibition by the kind of people, especially women and girls, who would never have permitted themselves to utter it at one time.

In the process, it has almost certainly lost much of its former strength. It was, incidentally, always a considerably weaker and therefore less terrifying word in the USA than in the UK and it may be that something of the American attitude transferred itself to the UK since World War II, as part of the one-way cultural flow which was so important to the first real teenage generation.

Like the UNDERGROUND Press, feminist publications have deliberately used sexual terms which can be reckoned to offend the more conventional members of society, as part of their policy of total and unfeminine frankness in matters of sexuality. One therefore finds, as weapons in the campaign, sentences which would probably have brought a police prosecution in the 1950s and, certainly in the 1930s and 1940s, sentences such as 'Wendy, the 'easy' girl, without quite realising it, gets fucked at a party' (*Spare Rib*, April 1975).

The compounds of this all-purpose word are now both numerous and widely used. Ingenious new ones are being created all the time, mostly in the USA. Some of the more common are explained below.

Fuck film. A pornographic film – 'She made a living for herself and Ice by making fuck films' (*Oz*, Winter 1973).

Fuck music. Music which encourages moods and emotions likely to result in intercourse – '. . . fuck music for ex-hippies' (*Sounds*, 3 March 1979).

Fuck over. To create havoc, undermine, destroy – 'Fucking over the regime by forgery, bank raids, etc.' (*Oz* 44, Sept 1972).

Fucked up. Psychologically disturbed, neurotic – '. . . the fucked up vibes amongst long-hairs and straights alike' (*Attila*, 23 Oct 1971). A 'fuck up' is a 'mess' – 'I made a right fuck up of it' (*Sounds*, 24 Jan 1981).

Fuck one's mind. To disturb seriously, shake one's preconceptions to the roots – 'The MC 5 provide the definitive trip. They fuck your mind with a white poker' (*Oz* 18, Feb 1969).

Full frontal. (*i*) Completely naked and facing the front, displaying all – 'Full frontal nudity in the theatre' (*Private Eye*, 22 May 1970).

(*ii*) Full blooded, open, honest – 'A mighty slab of full frontal energy' (*Sounds*, 3 March 1979).

Originally, around 1890, an architectural term – a building as seen by someone directly facing it – 'full frontal' was in use by sculptors from about 1900. Exactly who extended the meaning to include the living human form is uncertain, but it seems to have happened in the 1960s and, in the atmosphere of the period, one or more art students may well have been responsible. The expression's real rise to fame was probably caused by the furore surrounding stage productions in the early 1970s, particularly *Hair*, and by the critics' need to find a non-hackneyed term for what their profession obliged them to witness.

Fun. Entertaining, amusing. 'Fun' has been sporadically used as an adjective since the middle of the 19th century, but it experienced a remarkable surge of popularity in the late 1960s and early 1970s, when times were easy and money plentiful and when it was fashionable not to take life to seriously. 'Amusing' was too upper-class to convey the prevailing mood – it had Noel Coward and debutante echoes – but 'fun' was as democratic as anything could be and fitted the bill to perfection. 'Fun furs', which in no way resembled the furs bought by previous generations, were a symbol of the mood. Even 'fun politics' were possible – 'Thirty years ago a Tory anarchist was a fun thing to be' (*Oz* 41, April/May 1972).

Funk. This originally meant, in the USA, 'the pungent odour given off by the sexually aroused female'. It then, in the 1950s, became a jazz term, describing dark, earthy, passionate, soulful music, but during the 1960s, in the pop music world, it was grossly overused and ceased to have any real meaning, as one can see from '. . . all the qualities of the gutsy, funk drumming that made his name' (*Oz* 18, Feb 1969); 'Funk attack drummer. Urgent for new original group going all the way' (advert in *Melody Maker*, 31 March 1979), and, silliest of all, 'The funk flows freely from each cut' (*Blues and Soul*, 1 Jan 1980).

Funky. Earthy, passionate, soulful. For its origins and subsequent career, *see* FUNK. It is better not to enquire too closely what is meant by 'Two more funky albums on Tamla' (*Jackie*, 2 Aug 1969), and 'Lacroix has a beefy, funky voice' (*Oz* 43, July/Aug 1972) but, for something totally and unarguably meaningless, one can surely do no better than 'A unique toothpowder that cleans the teeth and refreshes the breath in a natural funky way' (advert in *Private Eye*, 29 Jan 1971).

Fuzz. The police. First used in the USA In the 1920s, 'fuzz' became the most common word for 'police' in the 1950s and 1960s among drug-takers, hippies and other young Americans whose lifestyle included a hatred of the police. Similar types of people were using it in the UK soon after its American debut, but even after 20 years it has never become widely accepted and continues to have much the same size and kind of market here as when it was first imported – 'You should know how little you have to tell the fuzz' (*Oz* 15, July/Aug 1969); '. . . a lot of extra duty for the fuzz' (*Private Eye*, 12 Feb 1971), and 'Two fuzz appeared' (*Brighton Voice*, July 1973).

There are still those among the young, however, for whom the word is not fully acclimatized, as evidenced by the inverted commas in 'That's a trick in my good books for the 'fuzz'' (letter to *The Biker*, 7 Feb 1982).

G

Gear. Drugs. This splendid all-purpose word, with its basic meaning of 'equipment', has been used since the early 14th century to mean almost anything a human being has or could need, from clothes to tools, and from furniture to genitals. During the 1960s it added yet another meaning to its treasury, although as a symonyn for any kind of drugs, it has had only a very restricted use. Since its introduction, almost certainly from the USA, it has been entirely an in-expression, confined to the drug world. In 'No gear here', reads a notice in the entrance hall' (*The Listener*, 8 Aug 1970), the notice was for the benefit of the drug-taking fraternity. *The Listener* reporter was merely quoting.

Gig. (*i*) A public musical performance. The origins of 'gig', in this sense, are unknown. It was being used by the *Melody Maker* in the mid-1920s and it is as likely to have begun its life in the UK as in the USA. Until the 1950s it was used only by jazz and dance band musicians themselves and by fans whose keenness verged on professionalism. Thereafter, as pop music hit the English-speaking world with the force of a tidal wave, it became common currency, first among the young and then among the not-so-young. MacInnes, whose antennae were supersensitive to the habits of the young, was quick to notice the extension of the world's public – 'He was holding some auditions for an out-of-city gig' (*Absolute Beginners*, 1959) – and a few years later it had become a normal part of the teenage vocabulary – David finds it relaxing to drive home from one of the gigs where he's been playing' (*Jackie*, 26 Feb 1966).

(*ii*) Any job which is of short duration – 'The Fleet Street gig's the downright toughest assignment' (*Private Eye*, 1 Jan 1971). Nobody but a journalist has yet been known to use 'gig' in this way.

(*iii*) To perform at gigs – 'We gigged around' (rock musician in *Zigzag*, Aug 1972). The verb is nearly always compounded with 'around'. The expression, 'gig around' was first recorded in the late 1930s, in the USA. It was used only in musical circles.

Giggle. An amusing situation, a joke. A native British expression, 'giggle' was first used in this sense in the mid-1930s. It did not become common until the late 1950s, when the teenage world, and particularly the female part of it, took it up on a large scale – 'That would be a giggle' (pop group, in *Jackie*, 11 Jan 1964). It began to fall out of use in the early 1970s.

Ginchy. Attractive, sexy in a harmless way – 'Ginchy 18-year-old Tommy Quickly' (*Jackie*, 11 Jan 1964). A passing teenage fashion of unknown origin. Now obsolete.

Ginormous. A hybrid of 'gigantic' and 'enormous' – 'He's got this ginormous Georgian house' (pop musician in *Zigzag*, May 1971). Childish, absurd, purely British, and now mercifully dead.

Girlfriend. A female friend, a man's preferred female companion. The expression is much older than most people realize. It was in use in the USA in the 1850s and was occasionally found on this side of the Atlantic as well. For most of the 20th century, however, it has been much more American than British. Until the 1950s, the lack of 'girlfriend' or 'boyfriend' does not seem to have been greatly felt in the UK. One had a 'friend', one had a 'girl', one had a 'boy', and it was presumably felt that if one had a 'girl', she was friendly. In those innocent days of platonic friendships, it was not considered necessary to labour the point.

With the coming of the Permissive Society, the situation was no longer simple. Sexual relationships became more complicated and more subtle and nobody knew quite how to describe anybody any more. A 'girlfriend' was no longer simply and automatically a friend who was a girl. She might be, but she might also be the girl one happened to be living with. 'Friend', by itself, was not sufficient. By this time, homosexuality and lesbianism were officially admitted to exist, so that men had to emphasise their association with a 'girlfriend', and women with a 'boyfriend', to avoid all possible ambiguity, so far as the sex of the friend was concerned. On the other hand, 'girlfriend' and 'boyfriend' were immensely discreet terms, covering all possible shades of relationship between the parties.

'My girlfriend Paula' (*Jackie*), would have been just 'my friend Paula' 30 years earlier and, among the educated and the well-born, it still is.

Gives. Is going on. This American usage, in the combination 'What gives?' first appeared in the early 1940s and stayed safely in the USA for 20 years. In the early 1960s British teenagers began to like the sound of it – 'What gives?' (teenager in *Jackie*, 26 Sept 1964), and it has remained in the atmosphere as a slightly dashing expression ever since. 'What gives, chaps?' (*Sounds*, 28 April 1979) is interesting, in that it combines a conscious Americanism with an equally conscious piece of public-schoolery. Both have to be presented to the world in inverted commas, in order that the speaker can dissociate himself from them.

Glam. As a noun ('glamour'), an adjective ('glamorous'), and a verb ('glamorize'), this abbreviation belonged to the American film world from the mid-1930s until the mid-1950s, when it became a successful export. In the UK, the noun began as a teenage word – 'This has an extra zing of glam' (*Jackie*, 1 Feb 1961), and then moved upwards to become an upper-middle-class deb expression. The adjective has survived longest among music business journalists – 'Glam group Angel . . . (*Sounds*, 3 March 1979).

Glamour. Nude. A specialized use of the word, which is current among Anglo-American practitioners of pornographic photography – 'Want to be a glamour model?' (advert in *Private Eye*, 5 June 1970).

Glitz. Surface attraction. Probably New York Jewish in origin, this useful word was rare in the UK before the late 1970s. It is, even now, mainly confined to the world of show business and to the trendier kind of journalist – 'In among all that glitz and talk, there are many pop classics' (*Time Out*, 10–16 Dec 1982).

Goer. Someone with energy and high spirits. It became a youth-word in the early 1960s. When used by boys about girls, it implies that they are sexually active and probably promiscuous. 'A banger's a goer – a girl who'll do anything with anyone' (A 17-year-old boy, quoted by Willmot: *Adolescent Boys in East London*, 1966). 'Not much of a goer, is he?' (*My Guy*, 12 May 1979) means that the girl finds him lacking in drive, lethargic.

Gone. In an excited state. An American jazz musicians' word of the mid-1940s, taking up by Beat generation of the 1950s – 'Typical real-gone Jerry Lee Lewis' (*New Musical Express*, 11 April 1958) – and no longer used.

Gonna. Going to. In the 1960s, teenage and pop music magazines began, especially in their reports of interviews, to transcribe words as they were actually pronounced. In the case of certain contracted forms, this habit had the effect of making language look more American and therefore, in the UK, more 'democratic' and desirable, more authentic, the People's English – 'People were gonna sort of say anything' (rock musician in Gold: *The Road to Rock*, 1976), and 'They really want Maduer to be successful. It's gonna happen, and soon' (*Sounds*, 21 July 1979).

Goodies. In the 18th and 19th centuries, 'goodies' were sweetmeats, and this meaning continued into recent times, both in the UK and the USA. In the 1960s, the word became much used by middle-class trendies and students, to mean anything which gave pleasure or was desirable – 'This month's issue has got articles on cars, on free speech, and a whole lot of goodies' (*Attila*, 6 Nov 1971). It has recently been going down-market a little – 'Here we have a load of extra-special goodies for you! Like gorgeous pin-ups, pages of love stories . . .' (*Mates Annual*, 1979).

'Goodies' are sometimes the very opposite of good. Even drugs can be 'goodies' – 'Grooving about the city, enjoying the goodies' (*Home Grown*, No. 2, 1977).

Go with. Go out together. Among the young, this often has sexual implications, but since equally often it does not, one may have to make a guess at what the relations between a boy and a girl really are. In 'My pal knows a girl he used to go with' (letter to *Jackie*, 15 May 1965), the probability is, given the context, that no sexual activity is involved, but one cannot be sure.

Grab. Interest, catch one's attention, make an impression on. 'I was primarily interested in other guitarists – and some grabbed me, while others didn't' (Rock musician in *Zigzag*, Feb, 1973). American, in the music world in the early 1960s, the word was in the UK, among the same kind of people, in the late 1960s and soon afterwards passed into general use among the young – 'As my daughter puts it, "Life is whatever grabs you"' (*Daily Telegraph*, 18 Sept 1970).

Grabs. An informer. 'Grabs' began life in the UK in the 1950s as an underworld term for 'police informer'. More recently, its usage has widened to include anyone who passes on information, true or false, about other people. A schoolchild can now be a 'grabs'. 'Attention – a grabs named Joe, thick set with large head' (*International Times*, 2 June 1967) illustrates the original meaning.

Grass. Marijuana. It had this meaning in the USA in the early 1940s, and by the early 1960s it was being used in the UK, by consumers, traders and the police. Ten years later it had passed into wider circulation, as a word that all progressive people ought to know – 'The kid had been thrown out of school for selling grass' (*Oz* 4, Sept 1967).

Grease. The association is with GREASER.
   (*i*) Patronized or used by motorcycle enthusiasts – '. . . the all-night greasebar in Colmore Row' (*China Cat Sunflower*, No. 1, 1969).
   (*ii*) Made up of or associated with motorcycle enthusiasts – 'This gang was ordinary grease' (Mandelkau: *Buttons*, 1971).
   The word is not used as much today as it was in the late 1960s and early 1970s.

Greaser. The original greasers, long-haired motorcycle enthusiasts, belonged to California in the mid-1960s, and soon had their admirers and imitators in the UK. Later, the term was particularly associated with fanatics of the Hell's Angel variety, with greased hair, studded denim jackets and leathers. Greasers do not use the term about themselves, but they are not offended by it. The image is being continuously modified in minor details, but the first generation of greasers would recognize themselves in this recent description – 'Somehow I've become encircled by greasers – be-badged denims, Motorhead studs, that big-banded, big-bellied slouch' (*Melody Maker*, 12 May 1979).

Great. Very good, splendid. This sense of 'great' was imported into the UK from the USA in the early 1950s. The American flavour has almost disappeared among young people, among whom the word is fully naturalized, but the same is not true of the older generation. But, both in the UK and the USA, 'great' is certainly a word one can hear too often – 'Oh great, someone's doing something great here' (Paul McCartney, in *International Times*, 29 Jan 1967) and 'writing great songs and making great music' (*Melody Maker*, 24 Jan 1981).

Groove. The 'groove', in this case, is the spiral cut in a gramophone record which the needle or stylus follows. To 'groove', an expression which originated in the USA in the 1930s and spread much further afield during the 1950s and 1960s, was therefore to play jazz well or to enjoy dancing or listening to it. From this, in the 1950s, figurative meanings began to develop – to get on well with someone, to give pleasure, to make love. The 'groove' metaphor was important. The groove was the discipline, the prescribed way of doing something, from which it was important not to depart. One should enjoy oneself only in the knowledge of 'rightness', of being in the track admired by one's peers.

All these possibilities have to be reckoned with when one tries to interpret, for instance, 'If you don't know what grooving means, then you don't understand what's going on' (*International Times*, 13 March 1967), and 'Now we're talking and drinking and generally grooving' (rock singer in *Sounds*, 24 March 1979).

'Groove' can also be a noun, with the meaning 'interesting person or thing, within the approved limits'. 'He's a groove, he really is' (pop singer, in *Friends*, No. 1, Jan 1969) carries this meaning.

Groover. A fashionable, correctly aligned person, whose life revolves around excitement and pleasure – 'A new generation of groovers can't see what all the fuss is about' (*Oz*, Winter 1973).

Grooves. Fashionable characteristics or tricks, skilfully employed. In use in the UK since the mid-1970s, the word, in this sense, is not much found away from pop musicians and their hangers-on – 'Michael's own songs, while strong on grooves . . .' (*Time Out*, 10–16 Dec 1982).

Groovy. (*i*) Something which meets with approval, passes the tribal test of acceptability. This meaning came into mass circulation with the hippies. In the UK, it was well settled in by the mid-1960s, although with many of the original overtones (see (*ii*) and (*iii*) – 'He recently had a groovy record called 'Supergirl', which he wrote himself' (*Jackie*, 4 June 1966) – and continues to be much used – 'You just stand there while it's played and contrive to look ultra-groovy' (*Sounds*, 21 July 1979).

(*ii*) Pleasant, interesting – 'A moneyless society would be very groovy' (letter to *Oz* 18, Feb 1969).

(*iii*) Self-consciously up-to-date, modern – 'The Twisted Wheel

Club was the grooviest gig to play' (rock musician in *Zigzag*, Aug 1972).

Grossout. An excess of gross, crude behaviour, 'gross', as with other recent American exports beginning with the same adjective, giving the feeling of excess. 'So which brand of antipodean grossout is this?' (*Sounds*, 28 March 1979). It is a journalists' word in the UK.

Gross-out. A coarse, clumsy, ignorant person, usually, but not necessarily male. American in origin, it was little found in the UK before the early 1980s and is still mainly found in the pop music world – '. . . the more grotesquely blood-spattered gross-outs' (*Soundmaker*, 4 Dec 1982).

Grot. An unattractive person, usually male. Supposedly an abbreviation of 'grotesque', the noun is used by teenagers more than the adjective, 'grotty', which used to be very popular with this age-group in the 1960s – 'Ugh, you're not going out with that spotty grot, are you?' (*Mates*, 14 July 1979).

Grotty. This is British through and through. Since its introduction in the 1960s, its meaning has changed. The two stages have been:
　(*i*) Unpleasant, not meeting with approval. A teenage catchword in the 1960s – 'Everything in Batman is grotty, including them' (*Jackie*, 17 Sept 1966). 'Grotty', in this sense, has been used more by girls than by boys.
　(*ii*) Dirty, sordid. By the time the word had acquired this meaning, in the early 1970s, it was being used by a much wider age-range, as shown by 'We weren't around to defend their right to stay in their own grotty place' (social worker, quoted in *The Guardian*, 12 March 1979).

Group. A pop group. A British creation of the mid-1950s. Now largely replaced by BAND, which throughout the 1960s would have had impossibly old-fashioned associations with the 1930s, dinner jackets and saxophones. At the time, 'The group business is bigger than ever' (*Melody Maker*, 27 June 1964) was the only possibility.

Groupie, Groupy. (*i*) An American term, coined in the mid-1960s and soon found in the UK, for a girl who hangs around with pop groups and sleeps with them, for the status it brings her among her friends. 'Groupies leap about the stage with tambourines' (*International*

Times, 30 June 1967).

(*ii*) A hanger-on of any kind – 'Solicitors Rubinstein, Nash and Co., the celebrated firm of libel groupies' (*Private Eye*, 5 April 1974).

Guru. Spiritual mentor, leader, authority. The word was taken by American hippies from Indian religion and philosophy, exported as part of the hippy cult and then, having suffered considerable secularization, used much more widely. 'Your supercool guru of inner space reports from Nirvana' (cartoon in *Oz* 4, Sept 1967) ridicules the word in its hippy context. The religious associations have almost entirely disappeared when we come to 'R.D. Laing, guru to many young people' (*International Times*, 16 Jan 1977), and 'Every year Phil Birrell, a guru of TV programmes, examines the new schedule' (*New Musical Express*, 12 May 1979).

Guy. Man. In the UK, until World War II, 'guy' was always felt to be an Americanism. During the 1950s, however, the situation began to change, at least so far as young people were concerned, and 'guy' became much more widely used, especially by working-class girls, who welcomed yet another opportunity to avoid using the word 'man'. 'How to capture the ski-instructor, or any other guy you fancy' (*Jackie*, 9 Jan 1965), and 'What is awful is sleeping with a guy just for the sake of it' (answer on the problem page of *My Guy*, 1 Sept 1979).

'Nice guy' has become almost a compound noun during the past 20 years or so – '. . . as nice a guy off stage as he is on it' (*Daily Mirror*, 22 March 1979).

H

Habit. Drug dependency, habit of taking addictive drugs. A euphemism in the USA since the 1880s, when 'the habit' was a matter of visiting Chinese opium dens, it sprang out of hiding in the 1950s, when drug-taking became a popular pastime, first in the USA and then throughout the Western world. The use of the word is confined almost entirely to addicts and to journalists who wish to appear knowing – 'The story of someone seeking solace for the DTs and a habit' (*International Times*, 27 April 1967).

Hack. A journalist. The 18th-century meaning was less specialized, a writer who was prepared to do anything for money, and this had continued into our own times. In the early 1960s, however, the newly-founded satirical magazine, *Private Eye*, began to use 'hack' as its normal label for a journalist, with the implication that journalism was an essentially low craft and that, in order to earn a living, journalists would stop at nothing. From *Private Eye*, the word passed into general journalistic use – '. . . two quivering hacks' (*Sounds*, 24 Jan 81). It is very little used by the public at large.

Hairy. The word has had various colloquial senses since the 18th century. The two which follow are the latest in the series.
    (*i*) A person, usually but not necessarily male, with long, unkempt, hippy-style hair and attitudes to match. In circulation from the early 1960s until the mid-1970s, the word was used affectionately by hippies and with a certain amount of hostility and contempt by other people – 'Hairies had progressive (music)' (*The Soul Book*, 1975), and 'The hairies had to go to jail' (*Oz*, Winter 1973).
    (*ii*) Hair-raising, frightening. Used first in the USA, in the early 1960s, and in the UK, a few years later. Never much favoured by the over-30s but, among the young, normal currency with both sexes – '. . . competing in a number of races, I reckon it's going to be pretty hairy' (*Superbike*, Sept 1978).

Half-inch. To steal. The expression, Cockney rhyming slang for 'pinch', was widely used during World War I, but like many other items of rhyming slang, it experienced a strong revival with the rise of pop music in the UK and with the growth of a new lifestyle based on it. The youth-culture surrounding pop has always made a habit of borrowing Cockney expressions, possibly as an anti-Establishment gesture. So, 'It may seem a bit hard that someone else should half-inch the glory' (*New Musical Express*, 18 July 1958), and '. . . half-inch a couple of batteries' (*Sounds*, 3 March 1979).

Hang loose. An American phrase, used in the UK by the late 1960s. It has two senses.

(*i*) Nonchalantly to do nothing in particular – 'Groups of black youths check out the scene, hanging loose in shabby mail order overcoats' (*The Soul Book*, 1975).

(*ii*) To enjoy oneself, relax. 'There's still time for him to hang loose, 'cos he's only 46' (*Oh Boy!*, 19 Jan 1980).

Hang up. Of the many colloquial senses in which this phrase has been used, both as a noun and a verb, during the past 100 years, two first appeared during the formative years of the Permissive Society and are still with us. Both are worry-words, of which the Society, with its obsessions with states of mind and psychology, especially of the weirder kinds, has always had a rich supply.

(*i*) A problem, a worry – 'Now he has to spend another year in getting over all the legal hang-ups' (*International Times*, 14 Oct 1966).

(*ii*) To worry, make nervous or unhappy – 'Things like sound don't hang him up' (interview with rock group in *Zigzag*, Feb 1973).

See also HUNG UP.

Happening. A spontaneous or improvised theatrical event or entertainment. Beginning its life in the USA in the late 1950s, this meaning of 'happening' had a brief existence in the UK in the first half of the 1960s, but survived a little longer in a derogatory sense. 'The Stones' concert turned out to be more of a happening than a concert' (*International Times*, 14 Oct 1966). In the conventional press it was frequently used very vaguely, as a description of what were assumed to be hippy activities.

Hash. Hashish. The abbreviations first appeared in the USA in the mid-1950s and in the UK by 1960. It is used by connoisseurs to distinguish the resin product from GRASS, and by casual smokers as a general term for the drug. 'The vast tonnage of hash that was swept up from the floor' (*Zigzag*, Aug 1972).

Hassle, Hassel. Originally, in both the UK and the USA, a dialect word, it was brought out of obscurity by the American entertainment industry in the mid-1940s and taken up eagerly by the Californian hippies in the late 1950s. In the UK, it still has something of an American flavour, although it has been widely used here for many years, especially among musicians, students and media people. It can be either a noun or a verb.

(*i*) Problem, trouble, annoyance, confusion – 'We would be unaffected by the hassles of big profit margins' (*Oz* 9, Feb 1968), and 'There is a lack of bustle, flap and hassle' (*Pelham Pop Annual*, 1970).

(*ii*) To bother, irritate. '. . . hasseling with health inspectors' (*Brighton Voice*, July 1973), and 'You get hassled by the BBC' (rock group, interviewed in *Zigzag*, July 1973).

Head. All senses of 'head', in connection with drug-taking, originated in the USA – (*i*) below is pre-World War II – and rolled into the UK on the drug-wave of the 1960s.

(*i*) Someone who takes drugs. Used mainly by drug-takers and their associates, it can have a more general meaning, 'someone who subscribes to the attitudes of the Underground' 'Everyone from punchy old artists to vaguely smiling acid heads' (*International Times*, 14 Oct 1966).

(*ii*) Thoughts, state of mind. A favourite word among drug-takers, many of whom take a keen and almost professional interest in changes of consciousness. 'The only real parallel with the front-stage musician was the tightness of his head' (*Friends*, No. 1, Jan 1969).

(*iii*) Characteristic of hippy or drug culture – '. . . a little head music on 247 metres' (*Oz* 26, Feb 1970).

(*iv*) Members or sympathizers with the Alternative Society – 'Head psychologist offers help by post for any personal problems' (*Oz* 33, Feb 1971), and '. . . leaders of hippy communes and other prominent heads' (*The Listener*, 20 Aug 1970).

Headbanger. A pop music fan who likes to have his music loud and incessant, of the HEAVY METAL variety. The expression has been in use both in the USA, where it probably originated, and in the UK from the mid-1970s onwards – 'Their fans are long-haired headbangers' (*Melody Maker*, 31 March 1979).

Headbanging. Wild, enthusiastic headshaking, often carried to the point of actual physical and mental damage, usually performed to the accompaniment of suitable music. A form of ritualistic dottiness. 'This is where the fans keep in trim for concerts, practising the subtle art of headbanging' (*Melody Maker*, 19 June 1979).

Headshop. A shop selling soft drug accessories, such as pipes for hash smoking, papers for rolling cigarettes, cocaine spoons. It also caters for members of the Alternative Society in a more general way, providing such important items as incense, Indian clothes and foodstuffs grown in a philosophically acceptable manner – 'Mantra is the name of the latest headshop. They hope to be doing macrobiotic food soon' (*Attila*, 23 Oct 1971).

Heat. The police. Used first in the USA in the 1930s, where it could mean also 'pursuit by the police', the word still feels American in the UK. Its use is largely confined to members of the UNDERGROUND and to journalists. As a popular synonym for 'police', it is nowhere near the top of the table – 'If the heat does get too near, the boat is scuttled' (*Home Grown*, No. 3, 1978), and 'Imagine his chagrin when the local heat added insult to injury and arrested him' (*Musical Express*, 12 May 1979).

Heavy. For 200 years and more, 'heavy' has always had a number of colloquial senses, but its significance has changed since the 1940s with the new emphasis on spontaneity, classlessness, ease of manner, and freedom from restrictions. Anything or anyone which seemed to threaten these attitudes was 'heavy'. Within this context, one can distinguish these special senses of the word:
   (*i*) Serious, intense, intellectual, upstage. 'In the end you suffer from de-personalisation, loss of identity. It sounds heavy, but it does not happen like that' (musician, quoted in *Oz* 18, Feb 1969); 'Don't give us any of that Marxist heavy scene, man' (hippy, quoted in *Attila*, 16 Oct 1971); 'She has featured in the heavy press' (*The Guardian*, 19 March 1979).
   (*ii*) Loud, rather serious, in reference to rock music – '. . . plus catering, heavy music, an open-air market' (*Superbike*, Sept 1978).
   (*iii*) A heavy, depressed, brooding feeling, a sense of menace, hostility or violence – 'Our recent background of peace and goodwill left us ill-prepared for the heavies' (*Home Grown*, No. 2, 1977).
   (*iv*) To use physical violence, put up a show of power – 'Mark the

Yank who was with us, heavied them out' (*Home Grown*, No. 2, 1977).

Heavily. Seriously. 'He was really heavily into dope' (rock musician, in Gold: *The Road to Rock*, 1976).

Heavy duty. Impressively, shatteringly loud, in reference to pop music. 'Heavy duty' is an American phrase, meaning 'very strong, able to stand up to exceptional wear and tear'. It is commonly applied to clothing and machinery. 'His relentlessly heavy duty vocals' (*Sounds*, 3 March 1979) consequently contains more than a hint of irony.

Heavy metal. See also HM. A particular kind of loud, powerfully amplified rock music, popular in the late 1960s and again, after a respite, in the late 1970s – 'The Kiss band of recycled heavy metal' (*Rolling Stone*, 30 Nov 1978), and '. . . the shallow exploitation of old classics with heavy metal backings' (*Time Out*, 6 April 1979). A musician can be 'heavy metal' – '. . . heavy metal guitarist, Van Halen' (*Time Out*, 10–16 Dec 1982).

'Heavy metal' has its origin in military terminology, where it means 'heavy guns or heavy shot'. The musical meaning is therefore particularly apt, American coinage at its most creative.

Heel. A sly, deceiving, untrustworthy person, someone up to no good. From the beginning of the 20th century, 'heel' meant, in the jargon of the American criminal fraternity, 'double-crosser, petty thief, informer'. By the end of the 1940s, it had reached the UK with its present sense attached to it, and by the 1960s it was a popular item in the teenage vocabulary, especially among girls, the traditional prey of the heel type – 'I guess nearly every girl is a sucker for an attractive heel' (*Jackie*, 22 Feb 1964).

Hep. Up-to-date, stylish, knowledgeable. Established in the USA before World War I, it crossed to the UK in the 1950s with the West Indian immigration – 'Where can I get a shirt like that? It's hep' (MacInnes: City of Spades, 1957), but then began to lose ground fast to the alternative form, HIP, which, in the puritanical climate of the time, was felt to be more genuinely black, less polluted and corrupted by white influence.

Hep up. To modernize, make more exciting. Of music, to make faster, noisier, more lively – 'Colin may have hepped up his vocalising a bit' (*New Musical Express*, 14 Feb 1958).

Hierarchical. Arranged in order of power and influence. The type of democracy favoured by the Left Wing and the extreme feminists makes the notion of hierarchies anathema. For 20 years and more, they have always used the word with disgust and contempt – '. . . opportunity to work in a non-hierarchical, anti-competitive environment' (advert in *Spare Rib*, April 1975).

High. Under the influence of drugs or some other stimulant, usually with the suggestion of a pleasant experience. American from the early 1930s, British from the mid-1950s – 'Man, you're still high' (MacInnes: *City of Spades*, 1957). It is used both by the inhabitants of the drug scene and by those observing it from outside.

Hip. See also HEP. The word has a long history, beginning with American jazz and the black underworld. It has many shades of meaning, all linked to a central idea of exclusiveness, of being in the know, of high fashion.

(*i*) Fashionable and aware of being so, cool – 'They've improved enormously since then. Very, very hip indeed' (*Jackie*, 15 May 1965); 'People are willing to pay a lot for a hip product' (*Rolling Stone*, 30 Nov 1978).

(*ii*) Up-to-date, sensitive to advanced opinions – 'Your local hip bookshop' (*International Times*, 29 May 1967).

(*iii*) Smart, slick, fast – 'Lennon's hip, fierce rejoinder' (*Melody Maker*, 24 Sept 1964).

(*iv*) Trendy – 'A tragedy for the hip community' (*Zigzag*, Aug 1972) and 'London's hip fraternity were already on the case' (*Melody Maker*, 24 Jan 1981).

(*v*) The thing to do – 'In the Fifties, it seemed hip to like the more refined end of modern jazz' (Cohn: *Awopbop*, 1969).

Hippy, hippie. (*i*) A name, at first derogatory, which was given to non-violent young people of long-haired, uncared-for appearance and anti-Establishment opinions in California, where the movement started in the 1960s. Since the hippy way of life became unfashionable, the term has been used defensively by supporters of the hippy philosophy to describe an attitude based on tolerance, liking for mysticism, and withdrawal from the harsh realities of modern urban life. The exact meaning of 'hippy' can be decided only by considering the date. Broadly speaking, the genuine hippies were pre-1970, while their disciples and pale shadows belong to the period since 1970 – 'I am never going to love policemen, whatever the hippies might tell me' (*International Times*, 16 June 1967); 'Jimi Hendrix's career was sparked and nurtured by white hippies' (*The Soul Book*, 1975).

(*ii*) Associated with hippies, their philosophy and their way of life – '. . . its folklore apparently based on half-hearted hippy rumours' (*International Times*, 5 Jan 1968); 'Female Londoner seeks hippy-minded people' (*Sounds*, 3 Jan 1979).

Hipster. A smooth, sharp, city street, hip person, who knows how to survive. Originally, in the early 1940s, it described a smart, dandy type of black underworld character. Even in its diluted and vaguer white form, it still implies an element of sharp practice and street-awareness. In the UK it is often a term of abuse, used by Establishment-minded people – 'The 'hipster' movement in California seemed to be an outright rejection of accepted standards and values' (*The Lancet*, 15 July 1967).

Hip to. Aware of. 'Jerry is hip to the fact' (*Oz* 43, July/Aug 1972) is really a piece of journalistic showing off. Relatively few white English people of any age have ever used 'hip to', and *Oz* was, for all its pretences, a very white publication.

Hit. A swig of alcohol, an inhalation of a marijuana cigarette, occasionally a shot of another drug – 'It was cheap wine, which tasted like it had been fortified with anti-freeze. I paused, took another hit, and passed it back to him' (*Oz*, Winter 1973); 'Students who use drugs or alcohol while studying may do well to have a few hits before taking their exams' (*Home Grown*, No. 2, 1977).

Of American origin, 'hit', in this sense, was brought to the UK in the late 1960s, by the international drug movement.

Hitch. To travel by begging lifts. The word 'hitch-hike' first appeared in the USA in the late 1920s. The early hitch-hikers were mainly adults moving about the country in search of work, but since World War II the typical hitch-hiker has been the young person who is determined to go from one place to another, but is without the money to pay the fare by public transport.

'Hitch-hike' is now out of fashion. There is a generation gap here.

Older people still say 'hitch-hike', but the youth-word is now exclusively 'hitch' – 'Hitching around the Continent this summer?' (advert in *Private Eye*, 5 June 1970).

Hit parade. List of top-selling songs, musical items or records. First found in the USA in the mid-1930s and then the common property of the English-speaking world for nearly 40 years, 'hit parade', like 'hit record', is now very dated, although it does still appear from time to time.

HM. HEAVY METAL. Loud, deaf-making music. Only fervent fans would use this abbreviation – 'Why can't anyone like HM and punk? I do. I've learnt how to headbang and pogo at the same time' (letter to *Sounds*, 21 July 1979).

Hold. To carry drugs. Used in the USA since the mid-1930s, in the UK since the early 1960s – 'You can't get busted in a club if you're not holding (*International Times*, 2 June 1967).

Hols. Holidays. An abbreviation with a strong public school and upper-middle-class flavour, it was never in the British working-class vocabulary until the 1960s, when it began to be used tongue-in-cheek by young people with a very different background, as evidence that they had made a successful invasion of enemy territory – 'Head for Cornwall for your hols' (*Jackie*, 2 Aug 1969), and 'When we get back from our hols' (interview with rock group in *Zigzag*, July 1973).

Honky. An American expression, used in two distinct senses:
  (*i*) A white person, as seen by a black person, white people as a whole – 'Many blacks came to see it as a 'honky' conservative force' (*The Guardian*, 1 May 1971). In the UK, only a very exceptional white man would use this word straight and without inverted commas.
  (*ii*) An ignorant person, a country cousin – 'You're honkies, but at least act like you got some sense' (Mandelkau: *Buttons*, 1971); 'A honky kid from darkest redneck Mississippi' (*Oz* 44, Sept 1972).
  The word has not struck roots in the UK and is nowadays used very little, even by journalists and fiction writers.

Hood. Gangster. An abbreviation of 'hoodlum', current in the USA since the early 1930s. Mainly a journalists' and novelists' word in the UK – 'They were veritable hoods, anxious to demonstrate their power over respectable road-users by more than speed' (Nuttall: *Bomb Culture*, 1968); 'The Purple Gang – a notorious bunch of hoods who terrorised Detroit during Prohibition' (*Home Grown*, No. 3, 1978).

Hook. A catchy line of a melody in a pop song. The origin of the term is possibly the stroke on the stem of a musical note to indicate a time value shorter than a crotchet, and therefore something quicker and more lively. It may, on the other hand, mean 'a hook with which to catch the listener'. The expression seems to have appeared first in the USA in the late 1960s but, both there and in the UK, it is used only by pop/rock musicians and the journalists associated with them – 'I'd say I write good hooks (song writer in *Black Music*, Dec 1972), and 'The Aliens cough up a few slick hooks' (*New Musical Express*, 6 Jan 1979).

Hooked. Addicted to, obsessed by. An American drug-word in the 1920s, it was still being used there in the 1950s, in the sense of 'addicted to drugs'. It is now used only in a general sense – '. . . hooked on rock and roll' (*Rolling Stone*, 30 Nov 1978).

Hooker. A prostitute. This American term has not become popular in the UK, except among smart journalists and other people who find the American way of life immensely attractive at a distance – 'She has made a once moving song a hooker's dream' (*The Soul Book*, 1975), and 'Hookers smile sweet at Bella Donna' (*Sounds*, 24 March 1979).

Hookline. *See* HOOK – '. . . a dead catchy hookline' (*Sounds*, 24 Jan 1981).

Hooky. Attractive, ear-catching. Documented in the UK since the early 1970s – it originally came from the USA – it was for some years not much used except by journalists writing about pop music, but it has now been taken up by a rather wider public. There would be few British people under 30 who would not understand the meaning of 'a very hooky little number' (*Soundmaker*, 4 Dec 1982).

Hop. An informal dance. This pleasant little expression, which dates from the 1730s, died in the early 1970s, with the growth of DISCOTHEQUES as the main form of dancing among the young. It lingered longest among students, especially at the older universities – 'My friend Joan and I went to the college hop the other evening' (letter to *Jackie*, 24 Feb 1968).

Hopped, hopped up. An Americanism, with the basic meaning of 'stimulated'. It is used in three senses, all of which have crossed the Atlantic.

(*i*) Stimulated by a drug – 'Check Berry don't drink either, but he gets hopped' (*The Guardian*, 14 April 1973).

(*ii*) Exaggerated – 'The most hopped up tales you ever heard' (*New Musical Express*, 6 Jan 1956).

(*iii*) Tuned, given extra power – 'I had my machine hopped up' (*New Musical Express*, 6 Jan 1956).

Horse. Heroin. In use in both the USA and the UK in the early 1950s – 'We are working on a phase-shifter that will manifest horse and hashish direct' (*Home Grown*, No. 2, 1977).

Hubby. Husband. Since World War II, this usage has undergone an interesting transformation. It was in general British, but not American, use as a somewhat cosy abbreviation from the late 17th century until the late 1940s. During the latter part of this period it had a distinctly lower middle-class flavour. In the past 30 years it has been used in a slightly patronizing and unfriendly way, emphasizing the hen-pecked aspects of marriage and the less exciting features of domesticity and usually omitting such personalizing words as 'your' or 'her' – '. . . with hubby strumming a little guitar' (*New Musical Express*, 13 Jan 1956); 'Hubby sitting with eyeballs glued to the little screen' (*Private Eye*, 5 June 1970). Most despairing of all is the femininist/lesbian magazine, *Spare Rib*, – 'I saw the years ahead that they would spend with their hubbies' (Feb 1979).

Hung Up. Obsessed, disturbed. Widely used by young people, from the late 1960s onwards – 'How did I ever get so hung up on food?' (*Oz* 33, Feb 1971), and 'Jagger is just nasty and hung up' (*The Soul Book*, 1975).

Hump. The peak period of a drug experience – 'A normal acid hump is about 25–30 minutes' (rock musician quoted in Gold: *The Road to Rock*, 1976).

Hunk. A physically attractive man. An American word which came into use in the early 1960s among British journalists writing for teenagers and, to a lesser extent, among teenagers themselves. It is still with us and may well be a permanent fixture – 'She was left gasping at this dreamy hunk of manliness' (*Boyfriend Annual*, 1963); 'There are hundreds of hunks who look luscious, even though they've got a few wrinkles' (*Oh Boy!*, 19 Jan 1980). For homosexuals, it has a rather special significance, a man with the brawniness to attract and excite other men – '. . . a hunk in nothing but chains' (*Gay News*, 9–22 Dec 1982).

Hunky. Physically attractive (of a man). *See* HUNK. 'Tim and John Keane are two of the hunkiest fellows to hit Britain for ages' (*Pink*, 12 May 1979).

Hustle. Two American senses of the word have made themselves known in the UK during the 1960s and 1970s. They are:

(*i*) To press forcefully for something. This is used a good deal in the pop music business – 'Hustle for its re-release' (*Zigzag*, May 1971) and '. . . sufficient interest to hustle for the U.K. rights (*New Musical Express*, 6 Jan 1979).

(*ii*) To engage in some dubious transaction, especially drug sales – 'Dealers began hustling from doorways rather than the pavement' (*Home Grown*, No. 2, 1977).

The American term 'hustle' , meaning engage in prostitution', has never really become accepted in Britain, although it is widely understood here.

Hype. An American abbreviation of 'hyperbole', with three current senses, all of which have found their way to the UK during the past 20 years.

(*i*) Misleading publicity, promotional exaggeration – 'There's more hype, bullshit and hustling in the so-called progressive scene than anywhere else' (*Schoolkids Oz*, April 1970) and '. . . can't see the wood for the trees, hype for the style' (*Sounds*, 24 Jan 1981).

(*ii*) A person engaged in (*i*) – 'Man, you were the biggest hype of the twentieth century' (*Attila*, 16 Oct 1971).

(*iii*) To take in, delude, brainwash – 'Bogus alternatives are hyped into prominence and fortune with appalling ease' (*The Listener*, 15 April 1971).

I

Identikit. False, composed of stereotyped elements, utterly predictable. The original meaning, 'a face composed by experts from an assortment of components, in order to help with the location and identification of a person the police wished to interview', first came into existence in the USA in the late 1950s and was recorded in the UK in 1961. From there it was a short step to using the new word in a figurative and more general sense – 'Every soul artist interviewed seemed to have an identikit story' (*The Soul Book*, 1975). 'Identikit' was a perfect word for a generation which saw how strongly human beings were being typed by the society in which they lived and, at the same time, was terrified by the process which smoothed out and overwhelmed individually.

Idren. Brother. Originally a Rastafarian dialect word, 'idren' is now in more general use among white people anxious to emphasize their links and sympathy with blacks – '. . . him and his good idren, Roger' (*Sounds*, 24 Jan 1981).

Immaculate. A fashionable superlative, common in the pop entertainment world since the mid-1970s – 'Rafferty's immaculate album of last year' (*Melody Maker*, 12 May 1979). It should be noted that the word can be applied only to an object or a performance, not to a person.

In. Fashionable, part of the up-to-date culture of one's social group. British and classless from the beginning, this sense of 'in' entered the language as a youth-word in the early 1960s. For a year or two it was always printed with inverted commas, as evidence of its daring novelty – 'Casual styles are 'in'' (*Jackie*, 2 Oct 1965), but these were soon dropped.

-in. As the second element of a compound, this implies that a particular activity or protest has been organized as a proof of group solidarity. Originally used to describe black protests in the USA about

1960, it quickly became popular in the UK and elsewhere in the English-speaking world. Throughout the 1960s and 1970s, 'ins' were an essential part of student life, black protest, Left militancy and other assaults on the Establishment – 'What we need is hope-ins, be-ins and smoke-ins on a vast scale' (*Oz* 21, June 1969). The habit has probably now passed its peak, but as a permanent memento of a movement, SIT-IN seems to have become firmly established within Standard English.

Inbetweenie. Intermediate. It implies, in a rather cosy way, a middleperson or middlepersons of not very high prestige – '. . . their inbetweenie status' (*Sounds*, 24 Jan 1981) . The adjective, 'inbetweenie', appeared in the UK in the mid-1970s. The *Sounds* type of journalist introduced it from the USA and the *Sounds* type of journalist is still its main customer. In the USA, the noun, 'inbetweener', from which 'inbetweenie' was much later derived, goes back to about 1924. It never made any noticeable impression in the UK.

Incredible. Very good. A superlative much favoured in the 1970s, first in pop entertainment circles and then more generally among media people and the young – 'Shots' is an incredible visual experience' (*Oz* 43, July/Aug 1972), and 'That's incredible. Let's be involved in it' (rock musician in Gold: *The Road to Rock*, 1974) indicate the word's public in the days when it felt fresh and lively. It is now much faded.

Indie. An independent recording company not belonging to one of the big groups. The abbreviation was originally coined in the USA around 1940 to describe film companies. It was extended in the early 1960s, again in the USA, to include recording enterprises, and soon found its way to the UK – '. . . the first indie in England' (Cohn: *Awopbop*, 1969). Then and now it has been used only by those in and around the music business.

Info. Information. The abbreviation existed as a journalists' term in the USA before World War I. It passed into widespread use in the UK in the 1950s, mainly among those writing for the teenage and UNDERGROUND press, and seems set for a long career – '. . . all the inside info' (*Jackie*, 16 Jan 1964), 'Blinded by info, we stagger from one journal to another' (*Undercurrents*, Feb/March 1977). One would only rarely hear 'info' used in conversation, except as a joke.

Inner space. The working or sensations of the mind, the remoter parts of the mind. Much used by American beatniks in the late 1950s, the expression had a certain vogue among roughly similar people in the UK in the 1960s and early 1970s – 'We've gone from outer space to inner space' (rock group in *Zigzag*, July 1973). It is now obsolete.

Into. Involved in, enthusiastic about. Originally American, this sense of the word soon became a favourite with trendy people everywhere – 'If you like what we're into, please let us know (*China Cat Sunflower*, No. 1, 1969); 'Get stoned, get into each other and the vibe' (*Attila*, 23 Sept 1971). Now *passé*.

J

Jack up. Inject a drug – '. . . who have just jacked up an ounce of methedrine' (*New Musical Express*, 12 May 1979). Used in the USA in the 1960s, possibly earlier, 'jack up' is not recorded in the UK before the early 1970s.

Jay. The initial letter of JOINT, a cigarette containing cannabis – 'Another toke on the passing jay . . .' (*Attila*, 13 Nov 1971). A word confined to drug users.

Jazz around. To enjoy oneself – 'She sees her mates jazzing around, having a good time' (*Jackie*, 20 July 1968). A favourite youth phrase of the 1950s and 1960s in the UK, it is now obsolete within that age-group, but occasionally appears as a ghost from the past among older people.

Jerk. A stupid person. Purely American until the late 1940s, it made some small inroads among British media people in the 1950s and since then has had a limited currency as a youth word – 'I am an avid reader of *Honey*, and not one of those jerks that feels compelled to dash off lengthy missives' (*Honey*, June 1979).

Jive. To lie, exaggerate, deceive. 'I appreciate that he isn't jiving' (*New Musical Express*, 6 Jan 1979). The noun, 'jive', in the USA, is a word with a very wide range of meaning – black, especially Harlem, English, marijuana, jazz, and jitterbugging are some of them. However, neither the noun, meaning 'misleading talk', nor the verb, as here, are at all frequently found in the UK outside the field of jazz and pop music, musicians, and journalists, although the word has been used in this sense in the USA since the late 1920s.

Jock. A disc jockey. An American abbreviation of the late 1940s, 'jock' has so far been used in the UK only by the musical press and by disc jockeys themselves – '. . . the sharper club jocks . . .' (*Sounds*, 3

March 1979): '. . . featuring Russ and Richard, Brian Rae and lots of Guest-Jocks' (*Blues and Soul*, 1 Jan 1980).

Joint. (*i*) A place, building, room. In the USA, from about 1905 onwards, this meant 'a disreputable place', such as a low bar or night club, and it was normally used in this way in the UK as a very conscious Americanism, until the 1950s, when it no longer necessarily had a pejorative sense – 'We had to stop and leave the joint, because the joint didn't like what I was doing' (*International Times*, 2 Feb 1967).

(*ii*) A home-made cigarette containing cannabis. This usage was first found in the USA in the mid-1930s, but it was rare in the UK before the early 1960s. Now, however, it is the commonest word to describe this illegal article and the most widely understood outside the cannabis milieu – 'There we sit, grooving in our cosy pads to that well-worn stereo, friends in a circle, the odd joint passing around' (*Attila*, 23 Oct 1971): 'American students, toking on a more or less legal joint' (*Home Grown*, No. 2, 1977).

Junk. Any narcotic drug, most often heroin. Known in the USA since around 1925, 'junk' appears to have been little used in the UK before the late 1950s. Since then it has been mainly an habitués' word – 'I took drugs to go to sleep, drugs to get up. Then junk came along' (*International Times*, 28 March 1967).

Junk food. Processed food, of doubtful nutritive value and containing a high proportion of preservatives, colouring agents and other additives to increase its shelf life and superficial attractiveness. The term arose in the USA in the late 1960s and has since spread widely abroad, especially among environmentalists, Health Food enthusiasts, diet-conscious PROGRESSIVES and those with a mission to expose the greed and malpractices of the commercialized food trade – 'Body beautiful? It will be, if you take as much exercise as possible and cut out junk food' (*Mates Annual*, 1979).

Junkie. A narcotic addict, a consumer of junk. Of American origin, about 1923, the term was practically unknown in the UK before the late 1950s – 'If you have a friend who's a junkie . . .' (MacInnes: *Absolute Beginners*, 1959).

K

Karma. Destiny, fate. This is one of the many words taken by the Founding Fathers of American hippies from the vocabularies of Eastern religion and philosophy and later given a vaguer, more general and debased meaning.

For Buddhists, 'karma' is the total and essence of what a person has done during one of his successive states of existence, a totality which determines what is going to happen to him in his next state. Something of this meaning can be seen in 'Unless we can wipe out the menacing mountain of evil karma accumulated by the human race . . .' (*Oz* 9, Feb 1968), but it is a very filleted 'karma', which ignores the two essentials, that 'karma' is meaningless without the concept of successive states of existence, and that 'karma' can relate only to an individual. Group 'karma' is an impossible nonsense.

Keyboards. The whole gamut of instruments with keys which are the tools of a pop band. The term appeared more or less simultaneously in the UK and the USA about 1970. It is essentially a professional and journalistic word, although devoted and knowledgeable fans also use it – 'Composer, arranger, and keyboards player' (*Oz* 41, April/May 1972). It should be noted that keyboard instruments, such as the harpsichord and the pipe organ, which do not normally come under the hands of pop musicians, are not 'keyboards' in this technical sense.

Kick. (*i*) Interest, enthusiasm. 'Kick' was used in this sense in the 17th century, but was little used by the late 19th. It was revived, as a youth music word, in the 1950s – 'I went on an art kick' (*Jackie*, 28 Feb 1964). It can also be used in the plural – 'He liked singing purely for the kicks' (*New Musical Express*, 20 July 1956), and 'Yet there I am still getting the same kicks' (*International Times*, 13 Feb 1967).

(*ii*) To break free from drug addiction. In use in the USA about 1935, it remained an almost entirely American property until the early 1960s, when the international drug wave carried it abroad – 'Some of my friends have died in the course of their addiction, others have kicked' (*International Times*, 2 Feb 1967).

Kid. A child. The word has this meaning in the 16th century, but until the early 20th it was reckoned to smack of the lower orders. A well-bred woman would never refer to her 'kids', nor would she use the term in connection with the children of other well-bred women. By the 1930s there was strong evidence that 'kid' was moving up the social scale and by 1950, helped along no doubt by the democratizing experiences of World War II, almost any children could be 'kids'.

During the past 30 years, there have been certain subtle changes in 'kid' usage. It is now perfectly acceptable to refer to children as 'kids', even on quite formal occasions, if one is, for instance, a teacher, social worker or even politician. The use of the word by such people implies understanding and sympathy and a willingness to consider children as human beings with rights – 'I don't think I'd ever looked after kids before' (foster mother in *The Guardian*, 13 March 1979).

(*ii*) A young person, a teenager. This has been a common American usage since about 1880, but it was rare in the UK before the 1960s – 'The small seaside town was suddenly full of warring kids' (Nuttall: *Bomb Culture*, 1968). When the word is used by young people, the upper age limit for 'kids' can be considerably higher than when their elders are speaking. 'Kids' is used extensively by hippies and other community-minded people to emphasize group identity. The 'kids' are one's own people.

(*iii*) Supporters, followers, fans. Always in the plural – 'It's not the kids who are letting football down, it's the other way round' (*Foul*, June 1974); 'The worst thing is that the kids think we're breaking up' (interview with pop group in *Rolling Stone*, 30 Nov 1978).

Kiddo. A young person – 'You'll probably kill a few millions of us innocent kiddos in the process' (teenager in MacInnes: *Absolute Beginners*, 1959). The word appears to have originated in the UK in the 1890s. It had a brief teenage revival in the 1950s and early 1960s, and is used now only as a mildly humorous greeting, for example, 'Hello, kiddo'.

Kiddy. A young person. A faintly patronizing term. A 'kiddy' is an outsider, but one identifies oneself with a 'kiddo' – '. . . a serious-looking kiddy, with a pair of glasses' (MacInnes: *Absolute Beginners*, 1959).

Killer. Devastating, extremely good, sensational. First used in the USA about 1930, the adjective met with little favour in the UK before the late 1960s, when it began to enjoy a mild vogue, mainly among football and pop music journalists – 'The A-side's fine, but it's the flip that's the real killer' (*Black Music*, Dec 1979); 'That the band were going to deliver a killer set was evident' (*Melody Maker*, 12 May 1979).

Kinky. Sexually abnormal, perverted. The meaning 'odd, eccentric' existed in the USA in the 1860s and in the UK in the 1890s. In the 1920s, in the USA but not in the UK, it sometimes suggested some form of sexual deviation, especially sadism. In the late 1950s, the 'sexually perverted' overtones of the word suddenly hit the British young and the fashion trade, which saw a golden opportunity – ''Kinky' was a word very much in the air. Everywhere there were zippers, leathers, boots, PVC see-through plastics, male make-up' (Nuttall: *Bomb Culture*, 1968).

Since then, sexual abnormality has become normal and 'kinky' has largely lost its power to shock and excite. It survives among the young as an exclamation, spoken on rising tones.

Kinky boots. Knee-length leather boots which, with their associations of whips and torture, became a fashion for women in the mid-1960s. 'One might as well prosecute shops for selling kinky boots' (*International Times*, 14 Nov 1966). The long boots have continued successfully, but without the tag 'kinky', which, after a while, ceased to help sales.

Kookie. Unusual, eccentric, quirky, but not outrageous or offensive. The word was common among teenagers in the 1960s – 'Kookie type uniform supplied free' (*Jackie*, 1 Feb 19640, but is now dated.

L

Lads. Boys or men belonging to a close-knit, or supposedly close-knit group. 'It's the lads I'm thinking of' (Borstal governor referring to the inmates, in the film of *The Loneliness of the Long Distance Runner*, 1962); '1973–4 will go down as the season that the lads started coming on to the pitch' (*Foul*, June 1974); 'For all the lads, last year's performance in the final still rankles' (footballer in interview, *Daily Mirror*, 22 March 1979); 'It's how you see it, isn't it, lads?' (rock musician, talking to others, *Sounds*, 3 Feb 1981); 'A shop-steward added, "My lads couldn't take any more"' (*The Daily Telegraph*, 3 Feb 1981).

The use of 'lads' by, for example, trade union leaders or organizers is often tactical or political, suggesting a good deal more cohesion and unity of purpose than in fact exists. The intended effect is both to define and to cement the group. The word has been used for a long time in this sense, especially in the military world, but during the past 30 years it has acquired threatening overtones, as more and more social groups have identified their real or imagined enemies. The usage is purely British.

Lady. A woman. This is an exceedingly tricky word to use in the modern UK. Working-class females of all ages dislike being called 'women', although 'girl' is perfectly acceptable, even when applied to those well advanced in years. The reason for this curious attitude seems to be partly prudery – 'woman' is felt to be more biological and sexual than 'lady' – and partly a determination to bury the former distinction between 'women', who were working class, and 'ladies', who were middle and upper class.

So, to avoid giving offence and precipitating strikes and walkouts, it has to be 'tea-lady', 'cleaning-lady', and 'check-out lady'. However, when referring to one another 'woman' is preferred by the educated section of the middle and upper classes and female students are firmly 'women students' today, as they were 50 years ago. Among members of these groups, 'ladies' would be considered to be a bourgeois vulgarism.

In the late 1960s, 'lady' began to be widely used by young Americans as an everyday synonym for 'girl, woman', often with affectionate overtones and not at all tongue-in-cheek. It soon crossed the Atlantic in this packaged form, to become first part of the vocabulary of students and the super-hip and then of journalists. At this stage, its usage coalesced with the one described in the first paragraph above and it became a fully integrated member of British post World War II democracy.

But there are further complications and traps waiting for the innocent foreigner. Middle-class people, who nowadays would always use 'woman' when talking to others belonging to the same class as themselves, will often, perhaps normally, exchange this for 'lady' when the other person in the conversation is working-class. And, to confuse the issue still further, for all classes and social groups, a 'lady' becomes a 'woman' when one is annoyed with her or feels she has done something stupid.

So we have 'One sixteen year old lady I coupled up with was so good I let her stick around for a week' (Mandelkau: *Buttons*, 1971); 'An all-lady rock band' (*Superbike*, Sept 1978); 'Cleveland guy, 23, into Queen, Yes, Lizzy, Zep etc., seeks lady' (Advert in *Sounds*, 21 July 1979); 'Zane may be a hip lady who sends right on letters to the *Village Voice*' (*Spare Rib*, Sept 1979); 'When an old lady gives her hair a pink, blue, or even purple rinse . . .' (*Jackie*, 7 Feb 1981).

Laid back. (*i*) Relaxed. This expression originated in the USA in the 1960s. Much used in its early days by rock musicians and their associates, it spread abroad in the 1970s, by which time it was being applied to people, as well as to musical performances. Among those who use the term, to be 'laid back' is a quality to be greatly admired, immplying as it does that one is confident and totally in control of the situation – 'He plays a layed back organ' (*The Soul Book*, 1975); 'Laid-back it ain't. Hard, bright and flashy as diamonds' (*Sounds*, 28 April 1979); 'A beautiful country-tinged tune that suits Rafferty's laid-back style' (*Melody Maker*, 12 May 1979); 'Her cohorts seem somewhat more laid-back' (*Black Music*, Dec 1979).

(*ii*) Relaxed, because freed from anxiety and tension by drugs – 'I'm so laid-back, it doesn't bother me' (New York taxi-driver, referring to the city traffic, in *New Society*, 8 Aug 1979).

Lark. Fellow. Used briefly in rock and trendy circles in the UK, and only in the UK, during the late 1960s and early 1970s, and now defunct

– 'He's not a bad old lark, really' (rock musician, interviewed in *Zigzag*, May 1971).

Law. The police. So used in the USA from about 1925 onwards, it became popular among young people in the UK during the 1950s and 1960s – 'The law arrived in a radio-car and told everybody to disperse' (MacInnes: *Absolute Beginners*, 1959), and 'Look out, lads, it's the law' (cartoon in *Private Eye*, 8 May 1970). It is less commonly employed in this sense today.

Law shop. A police station. An alernative to the old-established 'Cop shop'. A youth word of the 1960s and 1970s – 'The John Street law shop' (*Brighton Voice*, July 1973) – it is much less popular today.

Lay. To have sexual intercourse with. An act of intercourse. A woman who is available for sexual intercourse. The expression originated in the USA in the mid-1930s and was in limited use in the UK soon afterwards – 'I'm marrying her for your sake, but I'm laying her for my own' (Greene: *Brighton Rock*, 1938).

The term is in common use among all classes of society in the USA but, for some unexplained reason, it has never been as widely accepted in the UK as in the country of its birth. The British working class has not really taken to it and the feminists, who rightly regard it as sexist, hate it. Men lay women, women do not lay men.

Lay down. (*i*) To play music, establish a certain beat. An expression much used and loved by jazz musicians since the 1950s – 'He laid down sound like someone playing at the bottom of the Cheddar Gorge' (Cohn: *Awopbop*, 1969); '. . . lay down a solid backing' (*Sounds*, 3 March 1979).

(*ii*) To make a recording – 'We laid down so many tunes around that time' (*Black Music*, Dec 1979).

Lay on. Three new senses of the word, all of American origin, entered the UK during the late 1960s. They should not be confused with the previous meaning, 'to provide', which has been Standard English for more than a century.

(*i*) To compel someone to accept something – 'The IRA are trying to lay something on the people of Northern Ireland' (*Attila*, 25 Nov 1971).

(*ii*) To lend, in the knowledge that the loan will probably not be returned. This sense of the word is used particuarly in connection with money and drugs – 'Someone lays a smoke on you. Crash out and miss a turn' (Game in *Attila*, 16 Dec 1971); 'You wouldn't maybe have a taste of something you could lay on me?' (*Oz*, Winter 1973).

(*iii*) To tell someone something in a forceful way – 'They went round to see him and laid various numbers on him' (*Zigzag*, July 1973).

In the UK, all three senses have remained very largely a journalistic monopoly, a badge of trendy people with more than one foot in the USA.

Leatherman. A homosexual who follows the cult of dressing in leather. To those unfamiliar with the world of homosexuals, the different categories are likely to be baffling and one can do little more than record their external characteristics – 'Mixed types, leathermen, stylists . . .' (*Time Out*, 10–16 Dec 1982)

Leave it out. To stop talking, playing or singing, to shut up. Originating in London in the late 1960s, it has made a certain amount of progress in pop music circles elsewhere – 'Don't ask me/to leave it out/to turn it up/or pack it in' (pop song, 'Don't Ask Me', by Ian Dury, 1979).

Lech, letch. A lecher. In the sense of 'strong sexual desire', 'lech' has existed since the late-18th century. With the meaning 'lecher', however, the abbreviation is much later, having been first observed in the early 1940s. It became popular with teenagers in the late 1960s, being used more frequently by girls than by boys, and, in general, by those with an above-average education. Journalists are fond of it – 'The other is just a young lech' (*Zigzag*, Sept 1973).

Lensman. Photographer, cameraman. An example of the tedious American journalistic device of adding '-man' to a noun in order to coin a new word. 'Lensman', first found in the late 1940s in the USA and about 1950 in the UK, has been entirely confined to journalists, on both sides of the Atlantic. The usage is satirized in 'The hapless Dowdneery and lensman were met at the landing-strip' (*Private Eye*, 5 April 1974), but it is straight in 'Well, all you amateur lensmen out there' (*Melody Maker*, 25 Jan 1979).

Les. A lesbian. First found about 1929 in the UK, 'les' is the most common abbreviation, although on the upper levels of society 'lessie' or 'lezzie' also exists. It is interesting to note that the full form, 'lesbian', is not included in *The Oxford English Dictionary*, mainly, no doubt, because the existence of lesbianism was not officially acknowledged until after World War II. The word appears to have entered the language as a colloquialism and did not become part of Standard English until the 1930s. By the 1950s, it had become possible to adopt a less outraged attitude towards sexual deviation and the shortened form, 'les', was evidence of this change of mood – 'Now Jill is a Les, and what is more, you may not believe this, a Les ponce' (MacInnes: *Absolute Beginners*, 1959).

Liberated. Freed from outside controls, conventions, traditions and authority, uninhibited. A word much used and much abused by the Left Wingers and feminists of the 1960s and 1970s – 'Hand to hand combat for liberated women' (*Spare Rib*, Sept 1979) – and not infrequently satirized – 'The dream of a new liberated movement, where monkeys could engage in significant dialogue with their keepers' (*Private Eyes*, 5 April 1974). The use of 'liberated' in this sense is nearly always evidence of over-seriousness. It would be difficult for anyone with a strong sense of humour to say that a particular recording contained 'some extremely liberated guitars' (*Sounds*, 3 March 1979).

Lick. A short musical, phrase, clever little piece of virtuoso flourish, usually on the guitar. The term existed among American jazz musicians in the 1930s, but was given much wider currency in the 1960s and 1970s by the huge army of pop and rock musicians and their journalist hangers-on. 'Somebody gets into a lick' (*Zigzag*, Sept 1973); 'The sound of stolen licks' (*New Musical Express*, 6 Jan 1978); 'I throw in a few licks when I get the chance' (*Melody Maker*, 31 March 1979).

Life-style. The complex of attitudes, behaviour, beliefs and possessions associated with a particular individual or social group. It should be noted that a way of living may demonstrate no cohesive style at all, and yet be judged worthy of the label 'life-style'. The phrase is not infrequently almost meaningless – 'We end up with a picture of life-styles and environments which are wide of the target' (*The Guardian*, 12 March 1979).

The term was created by Adfred Adler in 1929 and, as used by him and by other psychologists, it had a precise meaning, 'a person's basic characteristics, as established in early childhood', that is, the style unique to oneself, which one carries throughout life. In the 1950s, advertisers and journalists in th USA, always on the lookout for impressive sounding psychological and sociological jargon, hit on 'life-style', as a gift from heaven, and began to push it hard. It was somewhat slow to cross the Atlantic, but it eventually began to establish itself in the UK in the late 1960s, more particularly among fashion writers and advertisers. It is now evident – and Adler would turn in his grave – that, in the society created by Anglo-American advertisers during the post-World War II period, one's 'life-style' is rooted in one's possessions, in what one has, rather than in what one is and does. 'They encompass your whole life-style' (*New York Times*, 27 Sept 1981) summarizes the present situation of this unfortunate phrase, since the 'they' is a range of wallpapers and furnishing fabrics. Such debasement of a once stimulating intellectual concept makes 'life-style' a true child of our times.

Lig. (*i*) A free ride, something for nothing – 'Keith Richards went along for a drink and a lig' (*Melody Maker*, 12 May 1972)

(*ii*) To get whatever may be going free, to hang around doing nothing in particular – 'Avoid Steve Diggle and lig around' (*Sounds*, 21 July 1979), and 'Ligging their way through lavish freebies' (*Sounds*, 24 Jan 1981).

This is an interesting example of an old dialect word, a variant of 'lie', in the sense of 'lie around', which had fallen so far out of use as to be classified as 'obsolete' by the editors of *The Oxford English Dictionary*, but which was somehow rediscovered in the 1960s by the new pop culture, which liked the look and sound of it and gave it a new life.

Ligger. A hanger-on, parasite. Etymologically, this is a most interesting word. A 'ligger' is a pliable stake which holds down thatch and a hedge plant cut and laid horizontally. In both cases, it is a piece of wood which lies down, rather than stands up, and one can easily see how it came to have its modern figurative meaning, which is now well-established in the vocabulary of certain types of journalist, but not much found elsewhere. 'Apart from the usual droves of music biz liggers' (*Soundmaker*, 4 Dec 1982) indicates the market.

Line. A dose of cocaine, so called because, before being inhaled, it is arranged in a narrow line on some smooth surface, like a mirror –

'McKenny never did get his line' (*Home Grown*, No. 2, 1977). The term was imported into the UK from the USA in the 1970s.

Load. A job, performance. A pop music word of the 1970s and 1980s – 'We did a load at the Music Machine to help keep it open' (*Sounds*, 24 Jan 1981).

Lolly. Money, As an abbreviation of 'lollypop', this was in existence in Australia in the 1850s and in the UK not long afterwards. The new meaning, 'money', seems to have originated in London in the mid-1940s and it quickly became very widely used, especially among teenagers, for whom, in the new consumer society, money was the supreme sweetmeat, the source of all other goodies. 'The snag is lack of lolly' (*Jackie*, 2 Feb 1964).

Longhair. (*i*) A man with long hair and the habits and attitudes associated with it in the late 1960s, a HIPPY, a BEATNIK. The word originated in the USA, where it had echoes of 'longhorn cattle', but its transfer abroad was very rapid, as part of the migration of the hippy style – 'Chris Connelly is a longhair who's happiest painting pictures in his pad' (*Jackie*, 7 May 1965); 'The occasion attracted 5000 longhairs' (*Zigzag*, Aug 1972).
(*ii*) Associated with the longhaired breed – 'London's longhair haunts' (*Zigzag*, Aug 1972).

Loo. Lavatory. This socially divisive word was in very limited upper-class use in the late 1930s and most of the late 1940s. During the 1950s, 1960s and 1970s it moved steadily downwards through the various levels of the middle class, and as it descended it met the equally class-conscious term, 'toilet', on its way up. The two parties now seem to have agreed on an approximate frontier. Loo Land is, broadly speaking, inhabited by families whose children belong to the examination-passing class and Toilet Land by all the rest, which is much the same as saying that the boundary between the two lies somewhere within the lower-middle class. But there are important qualifications to be made. The North of England uses 'loo' less than the South, women everywhere favour the word more than men and, according to the company, social intermediaries, such as teachers and doctors, use sometimes one word and sometimes the other. 'Toilet'-class children will often use 'loo' as a joke, or to tease or please teacher, or simply to be uppish.

'Loo' is found in certain circles in the USA but, as yet, always as an obvious British export, with something of the same exotic cachet as Scottish knitwear or English china. In Australia it is difficult to use the word at all, because for nearly a century 'loo' has been the accepted abbreviation for Woolloomooloo, a suburb of Sydney.

Armed with all this information, one can attempt to fit 'Sophie skives off to the loo in lesson time' (*The Guardian*, 12 March 1979), and 'While we were in a camping shop, my little sister wanted to go to the loo' (letter to *Oh Boy!*, 19 Jan 1980) into the social pattern.

If one were to hazard a forecast, it would be that during the next ten years or so, 'loo' will be left in sole possession of the field, at least among young people. 'Toilet' already has something of a *passé* feel about it.

Loot. Money. A British Services word in the 1940s, usually with the meaning 'pay'. A favourite teenagers' expression during the 1950s and 1960s – 'As soon as I've made a bit of loot, I'm cutting out' (MacInnes: *Absolute Beginners*, 1959), it is now little used, except as a deliberate pastiche and by older people who know no better.

Love. Hippy shorthand for a whole philosophy of life, embracing peace, tolerance, sexual freedom, and self-awareness, with correspondingly unconventional social arrangements. A key word during the heyday of the American movement, it was exported to the world in the 1960s. It is not, and one cannot emphasise this too strongly, the same as 'love' in its usual dictionary sense. The following examples may or may not help – 'Two male American students urgently seek entrance into love community' (advert in *International Times*, 5 Oct 1967); 'That love scene was becoming a drag' (*Oz* 8, Jan 1968); 'The love crowd was perfect' (Cohn: *Awopbop*, 1969).

But the Underground itself was perfectly capable of poking gentle fun at the Love philosophy – 'Love is all you need . . . Could you lend me a fiver?' (cartoon in *Oz* 8, Jan 1968).

Lush. This word, both as a noun, meaning 'strong drink', and as an adjective, 'drunk', has an interesting history. It was in use in England by the beginning of the 19th century, but throughout Victorian times it was regarded as distinctly low. After World War I, it was very rarely heard in the UK but experienced something of a renaissance in the USA. In the late 1950s it returned to the UK as a successful American re-export, but this time it was no longer an ordinary working-man's word, a part of the youth-pop-drug scene – 'Where's the lush – hidden?' It's not. You help yourself from the sideboard' (MacInnes: *Absolute Beginners*, 1959).

The equally ancient meaning, 'someone who drinks heavily, a drunkard', returned at the same time – "I started out a lush, then started taking pot' (*International Times*, 28 April 1961).

M

Machine. Penis. 'Machine' was a fairly widely used colloquialism for either the male or the female parts throughout the Victorian period and until the early 1920s. During this first phase of its career it was always considered distinctly low, both in the UK and the USA. It began a new life in the USA with the motorcycle gangs of the 1950s, referring exclusively to the male organ, and it was adopted by similar groups in the UK in the mid-1960s. Its link with the aggressive masculinity of the other 'machine', the motorcycle, is obvious – 'He had black leather pants so tight that his machine showed through' (Cohn: *Awopbop*, 1969).

Machismo. The original Mexican-Spanish meaning, 'exaggerated masculine pride', has been increasingly replaced since about 1950, by 'mere sexual arrogance and swagger, usually of a rather brainless kind' – 'The faggots on the third floor were always trying to get to Ice. He had that kind of fast-gun machismo down to a fine art' (story in *Oz*, Winter 1973). It is associated especially with such outrageously male-dominated societies as those of Spain and Central and South America, the countries *par excellence* of the peacock, and, in the UK, it is used admiringly by those who envy the Spanish-style male his dominant and domineering position, and disparagingly by those, especially extreme feminists, who use 'machismo' almost as a synonym for 'male chauvinism'.

Macho. Confidently and aggressively masculine. It was in use in the USA in the early 1960s and became a very fashionable youth-word in the UK in the 1970s, often with derogatory or hostile overtones. 'Macho', it should be noted, can describe a person's state of mind, as well as his appearance – 'You really can look macho in colour co-ordinated combinations' (*Superbike*, Sept 1978); 'This was Moslem macho in action' (*Rolling Stone*, 11 Nov 1978); 'I don't like to be around diesel dykes or macho men' (pop singer, interviewed in *Sounds*, 24 March 1979); '. . . these tedious, dated and supremely irrelevant hunks of macho-strut' (*Sounds*, 28 March 1979); 'I'm trying to make a stand against the macho rock bit' (*Melody Maker*, 12 May 1979).

Among feminists and in journals aimed at women and girls, 'macho', like 'machismo', often means 'chauvinistic, aggressively masculine in an unpleasant way' – 'The double standards implicit in macho boozing, brawling, wife-beating and "chasing snatch"' (*Honey*, June 1979); 'Roller-disco couples, lurex transvestites, stiletto women, machos in leather' (*Honey*, June 1979); 'Caring goes against the male macho image' (*Spare Rib*, Sept 1979).

More recently, especially among young girls, 'macho' has come to mean little more than 'sexually attractive' – 'Just feast your peepers on these macho men' (*Oh Boy!*, 19 Jan 1980).

Mag. A magazine. The abbreviation was widely used by journalists and printers in the UK in the early 19th century and it has been an ordinary colloquial expression since mid-Victorian times, although it has always been carefully avoided by the well-bred. Today, with the British class system in a somewhat fluid and uncertain state, the flavour of 'mag' varies with the user. Run-of-the-mill teenage magazines, like teenagers of all classes themselves, use it straight, and so do the less exalted women's magazines and their readers – 'A few weeks ago in your mag' (letter to *Jackie*, 8 Feb 1964); '. . . the good news that the defunct mag, *Counterspy*, has been re-incarnated' (*Undercurrents*, Oct/Nov 1978).

If, however, the abbreviation is used in an up-market magazine – in a story, for instance – or in conversation by someone whose tastes are up-market, it will almost certainly carry patronizing overtones.

Magic. Wonderful. A universally applicable British superlative, popular since the early 1970s and favoured particularly by the young and the uneducated and by those who produce reading matter for them. It is much used by football fans and by the less elevated kind of football journalist – 'David's Still Magic' (headline in *Pink*, 12 May 1979).

Maiden. A girl. The word was much used by hippies in the 1960s but its vogue is long past. Hippies were extensive use of archaic language, sometimes seriously, sometimes as an in-joke. This habit was in keeping with their obsession with things medieval. 'Is there a sweet and gentle-natured maiden able to help me transcend the cloud of unknowing? (advert in *International Times*, 27 Oct 1967) may well, however, be a little tongue-in-cheek.

Mainline. (*i*) A large vein into which a drug can easily be injected.

(*ii*) To inject a drug into such a vein – '. . . whether you snort it or mainline it' (Gold: *The Road to Rock*, 1974).

In use in the USA in the mid-1930s, both the noun and the verb were established in the appropriate circles in the UK by the mid-1960s.

Make. To have sexual intercourse with. 'Make' was used in this sense in the USA from about 1918 and in the UK, sporadically and mainly among the educated, from about 1952. It was given a great boost by the American hippy culture of the 1960s and became popular among Alternative Society people in the UK at the same time – 'Dennis made his chick and kept her busy' (*Oz* 8 Jan 1968, as a parody of hippy language), and '. . . trying to make Steph, who doesn't want to know' (*New Musical Express*, 12 May 1979). The expression is less used today than it was ten years ago and one should beware of the risk of sounding old-fashioned.

Make it. To have sexual intercourse. See MAKE. For some unexplained reason, only males 'make it'. Females are apparently mere accessories. 'A teenager trying to make it in the front seat of his car' (*Rolling Stone*, 26 Jan 1978) is socially acceptable only if it is clearly understood that the teenager is a boy. The expression is used chiefly by young members of the working class.

Make love. If one had to select a simple clue-word for the Permissive Society, this would have to be it. Nowadays, among all classes and all age-groups, it is a polite synonym for 'have sexual intercourse', and it is used almost exclusively in this sense. Until the late 1960s, however, it was still possible, even among teenagers, for it to mean lovemaking with kisses, caresses and words, lovemaking which stopped short of actual intercourse, the traditional sense of the phrase. 'I don't think I'm in love with this boy, but the way he made love to me just swept me off my feet' (*Boyfriend Annual*, 1963) belongs to the old world of love and innocence. The sentence would be impossible today and the English language is poorer for the change.

Make the scene. To be part of hippy, trendy culture. Much used in the USA during the 1950s and 1960s, but in the UK only during the 1960s

– 'The "Tibetan Blue" is still going, but no longer makes the scene' (letter to *Oz* 18, Feb 1969). The expression is now extinct.

Make with. To get on with. This American beat/jazz expression of the 1940s and 1950s was never much used in the UK, although the teenage magazines did their best to popularize it – 'Mandy – she made it with the mirth' (*Jackie*, 11 Jan 1964), and 'How to make with the mountaintop stuff (i.e. yodelling') (*Jackie*, 6 June 1964). It is now dead.

Man. A general exclamation and form of address, used in the USA first by blacks and jazz musicians – the two were often the same – and then, in the 1950s and 1960s, by hippies. It seems to have entered the UK first with the black immigrants of the late 1940s and early 1950s – 'Man, you should ask' (MacInnes: *City of Spades*, 1957) – and it was powerfully reinforced by the new hippy/pop culture which began to arrive in the UK from the USA a little later. White teenagers here soon picked it up and during the late 1950s and early 1960s they were using it extensively and very consciously, in an attempt to sound 'beat', non-racist, and older than their years – 'Man, you seem to be in a black mood' (*Jackie*, 6 June 1964).

'Man' then became part of the general 'progressive' culture and nowadays seems to have lost much of its original flavour. One can often hear the quotation marks aound it, indicating the deliberate use of yesterday's speech. Sometimes parody is clearly intended, as a protest against the gross overuse of the word – 'A warning about that banana scene. It's a hoax, man! I ate 37 last week and just got very sick, man' (cartoon in *Oz* 4, Sept 1967).

Man, The. Always written, and spoken, with two capital letters. The boss, person in authority. An American, especially black, colloquialism from about 1918 onwards, it remained purely American until the 1960s, when it crossed the Atlantic as part of the international hippy culture – 'When The Man decides he wants you . . .' (*Oz* 22, July 1969), and 'Otic compromised with The Man' (*The Soul Book*, 1975). It is still not widely used.

Mandy. An abbreviation of Mandrax, a proprietary sedative which was first available in the UK in 1965. It was much taken as a sleeping pill by young people and was popularly supposed to have aphrodisiac effects. 'Another thing about Sandy/What often comes in handy/Was passing her a Mandy/She didn't half go bandy' ('Billericay Dickie', a pop song by Ian Dury, 1977).

Manic. Overactive, frenetic, mad. An instance of the specialist language of psychology being taken over and loosely used by the new 'PROGRESSIVE' generations of the 1960s and 1970s. The state has often been linked with drug-taking – 'Charged with manic speedfreak energy' (*Home Grown*, No. 2, 1977).

Manor. Urban territory. This made-in-Britain expression was first used in London during the 1920s by the criminal and sub-criminal classes, meaning 'police district'. It then became, during the 1930s and 1940s, 'part of a city within which a particular criminal operated' and afterwards, in the 1950s, 'the district where one felt at home and where one had power and influence – 'I'm happiest in my manor' (MacInnes: *Absolute Beginners*, 1969).

Marbles. Reason, common sense. 'To lose one's marbles' is 'to go mad, to act in an irrational manner'. First recorded in the early 1920s, it remained a mainly American expression until the 1960s, when it began to be used by the trendier members of the English middle class, encouraged no doubt by the fondness of P.G. Wodehouse, an Anglo-American, for the term. Since then it has found its way a little further down the British social scale, but not much – 'The lad hasn't lost his marbles after all' (*Time Out*, 6 April 1979).

Mate. Friend. This is now probably the most commonly used colloquialism for 'friend' among young people in the UK today, having pushed 'pal' and 'chum' far into the background. Before about 1960 it referred only to boys and men, but it is now unisex – 'She sees her mates jazzing around having a great time' (*Jackie*, 20 July 1968); 'A lot of my mates seemed to see only as far ahead as their white wedding' (*Spare Rib*, Feb 1979); 'It's a happy trip where people actually do go to see their mates' (*Sounds*, 21 July 1979).

Me. My. During the 1960s and early 1970s, teenage and pop journalists frequently made use of regional, semi-literate and traditionally working-class expressions in order to prove how democratic and how closely in touch they were – 'There I was, a year ago, in Glasgow Airport, returning from one of me boutique trips' (*Jackie*, 18 Jan 1969). This affectation has now fortunately passed.

Mean. First-class, excellent. This American usage, current since the 1920s, has been taken up in the UK by groups, such as rock musicians, which identify themselves strongly with the USA and things American – 'She writes a pretty mean column' (*Blues and Soul*, 1 Jan 1980). It has made little appeal among other kinds of people.

It is interesting to observe that other American uses of 'mean' – 'sharp', 'ruthless' – have not established themselves in the UK, even among the professonal worshippers of American culture.

Media. Methods by which information is communicated to the public. The word was coined by the American advertising industry in the 1920s and in the UK was used only in the phrase 'advertising media' until the 1950s, when the arrival of television as yet another 'mass media' brought a need to have a short general term to include television, radio, films and the press. Until that time, 'media' had been used as a singular only by the less distinguished kinds of journalists, but during the 1960s this ignorant usage spread upwards to more reputable people.

'Media' is now a well-established, almost indispensable word in the UK, but it is still mainly the property of the advertisers and public relations people, the trendier kind of intellectual and the media themselves. – '. . . or whatever the phrase is that media people currently use' (*Soundmaker*, 4 Dec 1982). The average citizen is not likely to chat much about 'media coverage', although he is familiar enough with the expression and realizes the extent to which it determines the style and values of life today.

Those whose livelihood depends on favourable treatment by the media will, however, constantly use the word as part of their professional and religious jargon – 'The media surrounding rock 'n roll' (interview with pop group in *Zigzag*, July 1973); 'The inchoate desire on the part of these critics to register this movie as a media event' (*Sight and Sound*, Summer 1978); 'The media's idea of beauty' (*The Guardian*, 19 March 1979).

Mediaman. A person employed in television, radio, publishing, etcetera. The word is used only by mediamen and mediawomen – 'Unsympathetic mediamen' (*The Soul Book*, 1975).

Mega-. Very large. This absurdly debased scientific prefix is a fairly recent arrival in the UK from the USA. It is little used outside the field of journalism, except by those who enjoy poking fun at journalists and their habits. It became popular suddenly during the Vietnam war, when the military machine produced the term 'megadeaths'. Nowadays, anything can be 'mega' – '550 and 600 lbs. of Jap megabike' (*Superbike*, Sept 1978); 'Yank imports playing the megahalls' (*Sounds*, 24 March 1979); '. . . a new shopping centre megastore' (*Sounds*, 21 July 1979).

'Mega' has also acquired the meanings, 'very important', 'very famous', replacing the previous favourite, 'super' – '. . . identifying the very thing that sets The Who above the other megabands' (*New Musical Express*, 12 May 1979).

In the pop world, 'megagroup' is even more superlative than its immediate predecessor, 'supergroup', a musical group made up of individual stars of extraordinary fame and talent – 'Latest Canadian Macho Megagroup, 'Triumph" (*Sounds*, 1 Dec 1979). It can also mean 'very exaggerated', as in 'Johnny Winter: a bad habit of mega-flash' (*New Musical Express*, 12 May 1979).

Mess up. To cause psychological disturbance. This is a specialized and recent use of an old-established colloquial expression, meaning 'disorganize, spoil'. It reflects the modern obsession with mental disorder and seems to have been first used in the UK in the early 1970s. It belongs essentially to the world of the semi-literate – 'That sort of uncertainty really messes me up' (pop singer, reported in *Sounds*, 21 July 1979).

Microcosm. A smaller version of something. During the 1960s and 1970s, this impressive-sounding, semi-scientific word, beloved of sociologists and politicians, filtered down to pretentious popular journalists and trendy intellectuals, some of whom seem unsure of what it means and of how to use it – 'TV screenings that serve as microcosms, ironic or otherwise, of the surrounding movie' (*Sight and Sound*, Summer 1978); 'It's like Grand Prix in microcosm' (*Superbike*, Sept 1978).

Mind-bending. Incredible, stupefying, capable of exercising a prodigious influence. The 1960s was the great decade for mind-bending, mind-blowing, mind-expanding and all the other wonderful results of drug-taking. In those days, drugs or the practice of techniques of meditation were valued especially for their power of influencing or altering the mind, and 'mind-bending' was consequently an important part of the hippy vocabulary. It has subsequently become a very vague term, used mainly by journalists who are anxious to show that their hearts beat in a progressive way – 'A kaleidoscope of mind-bending sound' (*The Age*, 20 March 1976), and 'Release, which has done such a lot to help those whose tastes in mind-bending lie in this direction' (*Melody Maker*, 29 Jan 1977).

Mind-blowing. Impressive, staggering, breathtakingly stimulating. This, like all the 'mind-' compounds, was first used by hippies and pop musicians and then more widely – 'Beautiful green pastures, mind-blowing mountains' (*Home Grown*, No. 2, 1977). It is now very dead.

Mind-expanding. See MIND-BENDING, MIND-BLOWING. A favourite expression among the hippies and their disciples. It refers, not to 'mind', in the sense of the intellect and of reasoning power, but to a vague state of increased 'awareness', such as is produced by psychedelic drugs – 'This gave primeval men their first indication of the mind-expanding vision' (*International Times*, 30 Jan 1967).

Mind-snapping. Extraordinary. A more recent alternative to the obsolescent, 'mind-blowing' – 'A mind-snapping discomix' (*Black Music*, Dec 1975).

Mixed up. Confused, uncertain of one's role or status. This phrase seems to have first appeared in the USA in the 1880s. Mark Twain belonged to the first generation to use it. After many years of peaceful, unremarkable existence, it enjoyed a great vogue in the 1950s and 1960s, with the emergence of the Teenager as an official species. Teenagers were necessarily mixed up and proud of it. 'Mixed-up kid' and 'mixed-up teenager' were virtually compound nouns. The adjective immediately suggested the noun, and vice-versa. But 'mixed-up teenager' took a little while to establish itself. For a time 'mixed-up adolescents' (*New Musical Express*, 20 July 1956) was possible, but by 1960 'adolescent' had become patronizing and offensive.

Mix It. To provoke an argument or a fight – 'They were unable to resist going out and mixing it' (*Home Grown*, No. 3, 1978).

Mixer. Troublemaker – 'You're a real mixer, aren't you?' (film of *The Loneliness of the Long Distance Runner*, 1962).

Mod. 'Mod' was one of the key words of the 1960s, but historians are likely to find it a source of considerable confusion, since it was used with three different meanings.

(*i*) Modern, up-to-date in clothes and fashion – 'They were all wearing kilts and we had on our mod dresses' (letter to *Jackie*, 2 Oct 1965).

(*ii*) Modern in attitude. 'After reading about a great mod teacher somebody got, I thought I would write and tell you about ours' (letter to *Jackie*, 7 May 1966).

(*iii*) A neat and tidy youngster of the 1960s, obsessed with clothes and not a little narcissistic. 'My first mod boyfriend owned a scooter' (letter to *Jackie*, 2 Sept 1967).

Monicker. A person's name. Originally Cockney, it achieved wide circulation among young people in the 1960s – 'These Merseysiders with the come-on monicker' (*Jackie*, 30 May 1964).

Monster. A great success – 'I think it'll be a monster' (musician, in *Zigzag*, May 1971).

MOR. Middle-of-the-road. A damning perjorative in pop circles – 'Truly hideous MOR instrumental' (*Sounds*, 24 March 1979).

Most. A general superlative for people, places and objects. First heard of in the USA in the early 1950s, it was in the UK by the end of the decade, but everywhere it had a short life and is no longer used. 'This ring is crazy – and the most' (*Jackie*, 24 July 1965).

Mother. Excellent, a winner. The curious expression, an abbreviation of mother fucker, originated in the USA in the 1960s. Abroad, it has always been felt to be very American and its use has been confined to those for whom its American flavour is an advantage – 'The Breaker Brothers 'Heavy Metal Be-Pop'. It's a mother' (advert for Arista records in *Rolling Stone*, 30 Nov 1978).

Movement. The Alternative Society, the Progressive Society – 'We also wish to publicise Movement events' (*Brighton Voice*, Sept 1973). In its day, the 'Movement' was used only by Movement people, never by outsiders. It has passed out of fashion.

Movie. A film. Although long used by the film world and by journalists, 'ordinary' British people of all ages still find it difficult to use this convenient American word naturally and without self-consciousness. George Bernard Shaw used it in 1918 and so did H.G. Wells in the 1920s, but, despite this encouragement from above, 'movie' has failed to acclimatize itself, even among the young and the revolutionary-minded, and it is interesting to wonder why. The range of users is much the same now as it was half a century ago – 'There have been many occasions when a play has been suitably transferred to the movie world' (*New Musical Express*, 11 April 1958); 'It is a movie that would seem to table the self-conscious technological preoccupation of much science fiction' (*Sight and Sound*, Summer 1978).

Mum. Mother. 'Mum' is a most difficult word for a British person to use correctly and well-nigh impossible for a foreigner. In general, it is a word which can be used easily and naturally only between parent and child, although it tends to be avoided, in favour of 'mother', by members of the upper and upper-middle class.

But the situation is much more complicated than that. To begin with, the sons and daughters of the non-mum classes can and do often use this socially perilous word in inverted commas, in such a way as to make clear that the amateur status of their own particular 'mum' remains intact and unchallenged, that their 'mum' is a strictly honorary one. A middle-class mother would find it perfectly possible to refer to 'all the mums' waiting outside the local primary school, but never to 'the mums' congregated for Harrow School Speech Day. 'Mum' is much favoured by journalists, especially headline writers, partly because it is so short and partly because of its cosy, democratic flavour. To use 'mum', rather than 'mother' is clear evidence that the paper's heart beats with the people. Even 'the Queen Mum' causes no offence, or so we are told.

It would hardly be an exaggeration to say that in the UK one could place a person socially with fair accuracy, if one were to study only his or her use or non-use of 'mum'. Two examples will illustrate how subtle an affair this can be.

'If you ask nicely, Mum will help you with any bits you find tricky (*Judy Annual for Girls*, 1968). *Judy Annual* is for young girls, not teenagers, and the use of 'Mum' here carries a hint of self-consciousness, a slightly patronizing air, which is combined wih a faintly embarrassing determination to be on easy and familiar terms with the girls. 'Your mother will help you' would not be the same.

'Foster mum Jeannette Roberts' (*The Guardian*, 13 March 1979).

Whether Jeannette Roberts would relish being described in this way, one simply does not know. *The Guardian*, in its anxiety to appear democratic and informal at all costs, obviously assumes she would.

Munchies. A craving for food. This American expression is used particularly to describe the longing for sweet food which is often experienced by cannabis smokers – 'I was at the time suffering from an acute attack of the screaming munchies' (*Black Music*, Dec 1979).

Muscle. High-powered, high-performance. This American adjective, which is often a synonym for 'strong', can be applied to almost anything that moves. It has become a special favourite of the international world of motorcycle enthusiasts, which can refer to 'a whole new breed of modern muscle bikes' (*Motor Cycle Weekly*, 31 Jan 1981). A policeman would not say of an offender, however, 'He was riding a muscle bike'.

Music centre. A radio, record-player and cassette-player/recorder in a single unit, usually with separate loudspeakers. This curious term first appeared in the mid-1970s, with the new fashion for stereophonic reproduction – 'Decca's Compact music centre' (*Gramophone*, 15 Jan 1974).

Muso. A music enthusiast, a pop musician. Of recent Australian origin, the term is used mainly by music journalists and by others earning a living in the pop music world, rarely by the enthusiasts themselves – 'Musos and students piled into the bar' (*Melody Maker*, 20 Jan 1979); 'Wanted keyboards, vocals, drummer, bass . . . dedicated musos only' (advert in *Melody Maker*, 19 May 1979).

N

'N. And. A particularly asinine American abbreviation, which became popular in the UK as a result of 'rock 'n roll'. Teenage magazines of the 1960s took to it like ducks to water – 'Here's a style that's soft 'n sweet' (*Jackie*, 26 Feb 1966). The fashion now seems well past.

Narc. A member of the police narcotic squad. This American abbreviation is used in the UK only by people personally involved in the drug culture – 'Narcs from 33 European and Middle Eastern countries are now banding together' (*Home Grown*, No. 3, 1978). 'Narc' should not be confused with its homophone, 'nark', an old-established term for a police informer.

Nasty. An unpleasant thing, experience, person. A British-born expression, which appeared about 1955 and is still with us – 'Here's a bit of a nasty' (BBC Radio 4, 'You and Yours', 31 March 1979).

Nause. Something that makes one feel sick or angry – 'It would be a bit of a nause for the people concerned' (interview with rock group in *Zigzag*, Dec 1978). A British expression, which surfaced in the early 1970s, and which is rarely heard from anyone over the age of 25.

Needle time. The number of minutes of music on gramophone records permitted to be broadcast within a given period. Purely British – '. . . the Musicians' Union needle time restrictions' (*Attila*, 28 Nov 1971). The expression is little used outside broadcasting and musical circles.

Negro. Black. In the UK 'negro' ceased to be the usual word for 'black', 'a black person', in the late 1960s. Before that time 'negro' was considered to be more polite, less offensive – '. . . prejudiced against negro performers' (*New Musical Express*, 21 Sept 1956); 'Chris sounds more like some negro singers than they do themselves' (*Jackie*, 7 May 1966). *See* BLACK.

Newie. Something new, especially a recording – 'Buzzcock's newie is a vast improvement' (*Sounds*, 3 March 1979). The expression was in use in the USA about 1945, and it has been regularly represented on the middle levels of British journalism ever since. It is also found among teenage pop fans.

News up. To give the news. An American beat phrase of the 1950s, popular with British teenagers then and in the 1960s – 'News up, please' (teenager in MacInnes: *Absolute Beginners*, 1959). Now extinct.

New wave. A type of rock music, similar to PUNK ROCK, which emerged about 1976. Among professionals, there are subtle differences between punk and new wave, but the word is used much more loosely by the average fan and by journalists – 'Hullo, girl, into new wave . . .' (*Sounds*, 3 March 1979); 'Bass guitarist for commercial post new wave band' (advert in *Melody Maker*, 31 March 1979). One should be careful to distinguish between New Wave – a form of rock music – New Wave (*Nouvelle Vague*) – a 1960s movement in the French cinema – and new wave – any artistic or political movement which marks a break with traditional ideas.

Nice. Interesting, stimulating. 'At first it was a nice scene' (rock group, interviewed in *Zigzag*, 1972); 'He made a nice noise' (Cohn: *Awopbop*, 1969). This modern meaning should not be confused with the more traditional senses, 'pleasant, subtle, precise', which belong to quite a different world.

Nigger. Black, negro. The friendly old nursery-rhyme days of 'Ten Little Nigger Boys' have long since disappeared. Nowadays 'nigger' is always, when used by whites, intentionally offensive – 'If you want a nigger neighbour, vote Labour, (National Front leaflet, 1970). Black people can and do use the word with reference to one another in an entirely warmhearted way and without the slightest expectation of trouble.

Nirvana. In Buddhism and Hinduism, the final stage of peace and blessedness, after the disappearance of all worldly desires and the absorption of the individual by the Deity. In psychoanalytic theory, Nirvana is the attraction felt by the psyche for a state of non-existence, something which Freud connected with the death-instinct. 'Nirvana' was one of the many hippy words borrowed from Eastern philosophy and religion and, under this influence, the word came to describe nothing more than a vague concept of heaven. 'The living theatre continued to wander in their own portable element of Nirvana' (*International Times*, 2 Oct 1967) is no more puzzling than most other examples of this period.

Nit. A fool. 'Nit' is usually an affectionate word. A product of Australia, it first appeared there in the early 1940s and in the UK in the 1950s. The average age of its users increased steadily during the 1960s and 1970s, probably because those who had acquired the nit-habit in their teens held on to it as they grew older, while new teenage recruits were no longer coming forward. In 'You silly little nit! Why didn't you tell me sooner?' (story in *Jackie*, 2 Jan 1965), 'nit' is still part of the teenage vocabulary.

Nitty-gritty. The core, the reality in the situation, what is really important. The expression was in being in the USA about 1960 and the British had taken it up by 1970 – 'When you get on that box, you're at the nitty-gritty' (Cohn: *Awopbop*, 1969). To begin with, it was almost an intellectuals' word, but businessmen and politicians soon took it up, in such contexts as 'It's time to get down to the nitty-gritty', and by the end of the 1970s it was dying from exhaustion, as a result of gross overuse.

Nod. Secret or privileged information. A fashionable police and underworld word, very little used elsewhere – 'A total of five police have now been suspended, following the Burt investigation, and the nod is they will soon be joined by four more' (*Time Out*, 6 April 1979).

Non-. Make believe, farcical, absurd. Traditionally, the prefix, 'non-', creates a word which has exactly the opposite meaning of the noun to which it is attached. A 'non-starter' is therefore a thing or a person which does not or will not start. In recent years, however, and especially since about 1960, 'non-' has been used in order to ridicule the noun, so that a 'non-event' is 'an event which deserves no attention', and a 'non-race' is a walkover. One uses 'non-' as a way of calling someone's bluff, of undermining a claim, of puncturing the Establishment view – 'Federal judges are now to appeal against the bizarre non-sentence' (*Sounds*, 1 Dec 1979).

Non-scene. Quiet, non-trendy, non-role-playing. With so many people anxious to be 'scene' nowadays, one can well understand the feelings of someone who 'seeks non-scene 25–35 year-old friend' (*Gay News*, 9–22 Dec 1982).

Nosh. (*i*) Food. Originally Yiddish, it was used more generally, first in New York and then elsewhere in the USA, in the late 1940s and early 1950s, and soon afterwards in the UK, where by the 1960s it had become a popular youth word – 'You can have a session from 12 to 3, have your nosh, then have your hair done' (*Jackie*, 4 June 1966).

(*ii*) To eat. The history is the same as for (*i*). 'There's Mick Jagger quietly noshing an alfresco meal in the board room' (*Pelham Pop Annual*, 1970); 'John Conteh takes time off from noshing back steak pies' (*Time Out*, 6 March 1979).

There are several compounds, of which **Nosh-up**, 'a meal', and **Nosh-bar**, 'a restaurant', are the most widely used.

No way. Certainly not, not at all, never. Found in the USA from about 1965 onwards, it became a much-used catch-phrase in the UK during the 1970s. Teenagers and the trendier journalists were very fond of it – 'No way have we tied up the hottest scoop in years' (*Superbike*, Sept 1978), and 'Is Robert Palmer the thinking man's Leo Sayer? No way' (*Sounds*, 1 Dec 1979). Its range of users has expanded as the original enthusiasts have grown older but, among young people, it is now felt to be dated.

Nuke. Nuclear power. An American abbreviation, dating from the late 1950s, and since used in the UK only by ecologists and anti-nuclear protesters – 'Eire's first big anti-nuke demo' (*Undercurrents*, Oct/Nov 1978).

O

-O. (*i*) A substitute for other adjectival endings, especially '-y' and 'ish'. This was a popular teenagers' trick in the 1950s and 1960s, with a strong Australian influence at the back of it – 'I asked this oafo brother of mine . . .' (MacInnes: *Absolute Beginners*, 1959).

(*ii*) A trendy journalists' device to change the flavour of the adjective to something lighter or less serious – '. . . none of that depressing sicko stuff' (*Melody Maker*, 19 May 1959).

O.D. Literally, 'overdose'. Used metaphorically and as either a noun or a verb, it means 'overdoing things' – 'Edmunds O.D.s on overdubs slightly less than usual' (*Melody Maker*, 19 May 1979). This has been American usage since about 1960, but is little found in the UK outside *Melody Maker* circles.

Oftimes. Often. Yet another example of the hippy use of archaic words and phrases, a habit which fitted into their nostalgia for what they considered to be the medieval period – 'He's not trying cynical bandwagon jumping as has been oftimes suggested' (*International Times*, 5 Oct 1967).

Oh boy! An exclamation with no particular meaning attached to it. In the UK, during the 1950s and 1960s, it always sounded very American high school and contrived to anyone who was not culturally more than half-way to the USA, but there were those who found no difficulty in using it straight – 'But boy, oh boy, Marty had made me sit up and take notice' (Letter to *New Musical Express*, 18 July 1958). Now, in the 1980s, one often hears a young person saying 'boy!' and 'oh boy!' tongue-in-cheek.

Old bill. The police. *See* BILL. 'Hordes of Old Bill materialised with dogs to put an end to it all' (*Sounds*, 1 Dec 1979). One of the less aggreeable aspects of the Permissive Society has been the hatred and scorn which so many young people appear to feel towards the police, the Enemy of the People, an attitude which contrasts strangely with the friendly relationship which existed 50 years ago. It is therefore ironical that such a generation should have selected, as one of its pet labels for the police, Bruce Bairnsfather's famous and popular cartoon character of World War I, the grumbling military veteran with the large moustache, Old Bill, who bore a close resemblance to the old style British policeman, gruff in manner, but kind at heart, totally incorruptible and carrying out his duty to the best of his limited ability. 'Old Bill' is a very sick joke, a Black Mass.

On the scene. In fashion, in the public eye. The phrase came from the USA in the late 1950s, had a brief run of teenage popularity – '. . . talking about Monkees, who are very much on the scene' (*Jackie*, 28 March 1967) – and then vanished.

Oriented. Directed towards, sympathetic to, concerned with. A piece of social-science jargon much used during the past 30 years by students, journalists and others who are anxious to display their allegiance to progressive views – 'They were much more booze oriented' (*Zigzag*, Aug 1972); 'There is also the Leboyer method, which is very child oriented' (*Spare Rib*, April 1975).

Out. Having publicly acknowledged one's sexual preferences, openly living the life of a homosexual or lesbian. The process of achieving this is called 'coming out', in the best debutante tradition. The expression is used almost entirely by the 'out' people themselves – 'The Bill would have appealed not only to people who are out . . .' (*Spare Rib*, Jan 1979). Current in the UK since about 1960.

Out of it. High on drugs, drunk. The expression has been current among addicts since about 1950 in the USA and since about 1960 in the UK – 'Old Tony would be a bit out of it' (rock group in *Zigzag*, Sept 1973), and 'I'm just like that, man, if I'm out of it' (musician, quoted in *Melody Maker*, 27 Jan 1979).

Out of one's head. Very high on drugs, drunk. Of American origin, the phrase has been used by addicts in the UK since about 1960 – 'Lying on my back one day, tripped out of my head . . .' (*Attila*, 23 Oct 1977).

Outrageous. Exceptionally good, really impressive. American for the time being, this word could well become a successful export within the next few years. At present it seems to be safely enclosed within pop territory, with a member of a black rock group telling his friends and colleagues in the UK that 'in New York you have to work very hard to get an outrageous response from the audience' (*Sounds*, 11 Dec 1982).

Own thing. One's personal field of interest, taste, inclination. The whole philosophy of the Permissive Society is based on the emphasis of 'doing one's own thing', implying, as it does, that everyone is a free agent and that social rules, precedents, traditions and values are irrelevant and unnecessary. Every person is unique and external controls are consequently dismissed. The point of being alive is to work out one's destiny and code of conduct for oneself. One should do what one wants to do, continuously freeing oneself from social pressures and limitations – 'You start out imitating and then you get your own thing' (*International Times*, 28 Nov 1966).

P

Pack. Packet. 'Pack' would have been considered indisputably American in the UK 20 years ago. The British had 'packets', the Americans had 'packs'. Then, about 1960, 'pack' began to be used here for cigarettes, and this usage became increasingly common among young people. 'Packet' has held its ground remarkably well, however, and observation suggests that very few people in the UK over 35 ever refer to 'packs' of anything, despite the constant efforts of advertisers to persuade them to buy 'the giant economy pack'. When 'pack' is used, even by young people, it is most likely to refer to cigarettes – 'Camels. I sent out for several packs of them' (Le Carré: *Tinker, Tailor, Soldier, Spy*, 1974).

Pad. Home, usually of someone young and in the fashion; any form of accommodation, especially of a temporary nature. In the language of the criminal classes, 'pad', in the sense of bed, has been used in the UK since the early 18th century. It still can have criminal associations – 'London D-Squad are active in the town. They have also searched several pads at the same time' (*Attila*, 23 Oct 1979), but for the most part the word has been more or less respectable since about 1960, although its raffish antecedents have probably helped to make it popular among the young, who are its principal users – 'Pad wanted for 3 or 4 people' (advert in *Private Eye*, 5 June 1970); 'Perfume your pad the dreamy way' (*International Times*, 31 Aug 1967).

During the 1970s, there is no doubt that 'pad' climbed a long way up the money ladder – 'He turned three little houses into a palatial pad for his family (*Woman's Own*, 13 Jan 1979). It should be noted, however, that the writer of this article was describing the dwelling of a pop star. The average reader of *Woman's Own* would be extremely unlikely to refer to her own home as her 'pad'.

Pal. A friend. This is a word to be used with great caution. The exact degree of friendship implied depends very much on the context and on the age and social class of the people involved. It was much more common 20 years ago among the British young than it is now, 'mate' having largely replaced it, except in the North of England, where it still retains much of its old flavour and popularity. In the South of England, if often has sarcastic or even hostile overtones nowadays.

'. . . an older brother, who sometimes brings his pals around' (*Jackie*, 15 Oct 1964) is the traditional usage, with 'pals' referring only to males. By the time one reaches 'Every time my pal and I go dancing, we get lumbered with various blokes' (letter to *Jackie*, 25 March 1967), 'pal' has become unisex, and in 'Grocer Heath and his pals' (caption to cartoon in *Private Eye*, 14 April 1970), the word is intended to suggest a public-school type of friendship, possibly with sinister implications, a cabal.

Paranoia. Medically, a form of schizophrenia which includes hallucinations and delusions. During the 1960s, what had previously been a useful scientific term became trivialized to mean 'any intense and unreasonable fear and obsession', and often just 'fear'. A high proportion of its customers since then have been trendy journalists, whose language does not stand up to close analysis – '. . . William's jangling nightmare of urban paranoia' (*Oz* 43, July/Aug 1972); 'The police got pressured into paranoia' (*Zigzag*, Aug 1977).

Paranoid. Displaying the symptoms of paranoia and, hence, through the process of popularization – *see* PARANOIA – suspicious, mistrustful – '*Street Press* has been much more successful. After two or three very paranoid and crappy issues, it's improved a lot' (*China Cat Sunflower*, No. 1, 1969).

Pash. Infatuation, excitement. This abbreviation of 'passion' was first recorded in the USA in 1914 and it was making its way in the UK in the early 1920s. During the 1930s and 1940s it was mostly used in three senses, 'a schoolgirl's infatuation for a teacher', 'a homosexual fondness for another boy' – this was public-school jargon – and, jokingly in the P.G. Wodehouse manner, as in 'the divine pash'.

With the arrival of pop idols in the 1950s, it was used for a while by journalists to mean, 'the kind of music calculated to produce uncontrollable excitement among teenage girls' – 'I guess there'll be plenty of swooning over this one, too. Real throbbing pash, ladled out relentlessly' (*New Musical Express*, 18 July 1958). The term is now fortunately extinct.

Payola. Bribe, bribery. Found first in the USA about 1938 and in the

UK in the mid-1950s, it has been used particularly in connection with the bribes given to disc jockeys and radio producers in order to ensure the frequent and favourable promotion of records – '. . . once the payola had been handed over' (*Zigzag*, Aug 1972), and 'In those days payola was very popular among black disc jockeys' (*Black Music*, Dec 1979).

Peachy keen. An American expression of the early 1960s, which has had some appeal in the UK, mostly among teenagers and those writing for them. It is used in two senses:

(*i*) Marvellous, cute – 'He thought that Sonny and Cher were peachy keen' (Cohn: *Awopbop*, 1969).

(*ii*) Happy, fond of one another – 'They seem to have resolved their squabbles and to be peachy-keen again' (*Jackie*, 24 Jan 1981, referring to a husband and wife).

Peasant. A barbarian, a person belonging to an alien culture, someone of uncivilized habits. 'Peasant', a popular catch-phrase among British teenagers in the late 1950s and during the 1960s, was a general term of derision, reserved for anyone outside the group to which the speaker belonged. It was first observed in Australia in 1943 and in the USA in 1947, and it may have come to the UK either directly from Australia or via the USA. '. . . the lady peasants who were using it to carry home their purchases' (MacInnes: *Absolute Beginners*, 1959), and '. . . those horrible peasants who ride motorbikes' (*Jackie*, 29 Feb 1964) indicate the possibilities.

Pen. To write either words or music. The music possibility is very recent, but there seems to be no good reason to object to it, since nowadays a writer of music is much more likely to use a pen than a writer of words is. Thomas Hardy was 'penning' in 1904, and this usage has been popular with journalists for half a century, although, except jokingly, with few others – '. . . the chap who penned the double-talk they call publicity' (*New Musical Express*, 27 July 1956).

Within the musical field it was only a short step from the words – 'Title song lyrics penned by Raymond' (*New Musical Express*, 18 July 1958) – to the music – '. . . 12 tracks penned by Nelson himself' (*New Musical Express*, 6 Jan 1979).

Person. One of the sillier words of our time, 'person' owes its current vogue mainly to the wish or necessity to avoid accusations of SEXISM.

Both in the USA and in the UK it is now illegal to confine job recruitment to people of a particular sex and advertisements must be worded accordingly. One cannot, therefore, ask for applications for a 'postman', unless one makes it clear that the 'postman' may be of either sex.

'Person' appeared to offer a way out of the difficulty, but some of the results – 'chairperson', 'boilerperson', 'cowperson' – of the two-pronged attempt to satisfy both the law and the feminists have been so absurd that caricature has been inevitable and journalists have had a field-day – 'Honda's spokesperson' (*Superbike*, Sept 1978); 'Our women TV persons' (*Daily Mirror*, 22 March 1979); 'Soundperson John Peel' (*Sounds*, 28 April 1979).

'I'm a Mediterranean person. I can't stand too much of Britain' (*Gay News*, 23 Feb 1978) follows the official feminist line – the writer could not consider herself 'a Mediterranean woman' – but it also indicates a rather trendy middle-class wish to be acknowledged as a type, with the approved attitudes and preferences, but without giving up one's right to be an individual. 'Type' would not achieve this result, but 'person' is perfect.

Phallocrat. A man who uses his sexual power in order to dominate others. A recent British word, first noted about 1977, which has so far been used only by a few smart and upstage journalists – '. . . the attractive phallocrat who has been sniffing around without success for some time' (*Sight and Sound*, Summer 1979).

Physio. A physiotherapist. The abbreviation appears to have originated in the UK in the early 1960s. It is particularly common in athletic, especially football, circles – '. . . when he was named as physio and reserve team boss at Falkirk' (*Shoot*, 31 Jan 1981).

Picker. A guitarist. Used in the USA since the early 1920s, 'picker' was very seldom found in the UK until the coming of pop music in the 1950s gave the guitar, in its electronic form, a prestige and importance it had never had before. As now used by pop journalists and performers, it suggests either an amateur standard of performance or a folk/country style – '. . . country pickers' (*The Soul Book*, 1975).

Pig. A policeman. This was a favourite word among criminals in Victorian times, in both the UK and the USA. It experienced an impressive revival in the 1960s, mainly as a result of the publicity given to the hippies and amateur revolutionaries of the period, for whom the police were the enemy of enemies – 'A pig comes into the park' (*Schoolkids Oz*, April 1971).

Pilled up. Under the influence of drugs, 'pill' being barbiturates or amphetamines. The expression dates from about 1963 in the USA and from about 1970 in the UK – '. . . some pilled up mod dancing around' (*International Times*, 13 Feb 1967); 'I figured he was pilled up to the eyeballs' (Mandelkau: *Buttons*, 1971).

Pillhead. A person addicted to drugs in tablet form, as distinct from a junkie who relies on injections. An American expression of the early 1960s, it has subsequently spread abroad, although it has remained mainly an addicts' word – 'The nearest Pablo has ever got to becoming a pillhead' (*Black Music*, Dec 1979).

Piss. Go very fast – 'Send the old bus pissing down the fast lane like a bat out of hell' (*Private Eye*, 5 April 1975). The whole 'piss' series of compounds is much used by the young, for example:

Piss Up. Make mess of something, ruin – 'It was me that always pissed it up' (*Friends*, No. 1, Dec 1969).

Piss Off. Annoy, depress. 'Did that piss you off at all?' (*Zigzag*, Sept 1973), and 'We were so pissed off with everybody' (*Sounds*, 3 March 1979).

Piss On. (*i*) Show oneself to be vastly superior – The Waller/Wood combination would have pissed on them' (*Zigzag*, June 1971). (*ii*) Make nonsense of – 'This pisses on her theories and intellectual arguments' (*Sounds*, 28 April 1974).

Piss-Take. Making fun of – 'A piss-take song about hippie chicks' (*Zigzag*, June 1971).

Plastic. Attractive on the surface, but with no originality or depth. This use of 'plastic' which, in both the UK and the USA, dates from the early 1960s, is a sad reflection on the quality of the plastic materials which were available at the time. 'Plastic' soon came to have the meaning 'inferior' – 'Hawaii, that plastic paradise' (*The Times*, 13 Feb 1970) and, somewhat later, it was discovered that people, too, could be 'plastic' – '. . . playing the part of plastic tearaway, Nicky' (*Melody Maker*, 24 Jan 1981).

Pomp. A full-bodied version or treatment, with nothing skimped or spared. This meaning, which originated in the USA, became current in pop music circles in the late 1970s – 'Lush, rolling hard rock/pomp' (*Sounds*, 24 Jan 1981).

Pompous. With the characteristics of POMP. 'The offering is sufficiently pompous and lavishly produced' (*Sounds*, 24 Jan 1981).

Popist. Related to, created by the world of pop music, with more than a suggestion of triviality and lack of seriousness. It is entirely a musical journalists' word – '. . . the popist myths of the British beat boom' (*New Musical Express*, 7 March 1981).

Poppy. 'Pop', in a patronizing and derogatory sense – 'We're not poppy in the same way as someone like the Moondogs are poppy' (*New Musical Express*, 7 March 1981).

Pot. Cannabis. The USA was using the word in 1938; the UK, always a statutory 15 years behind, had to wait until the mid-1950s for it. 'Pot' is the most respectable word for cannabis and the most widely understood. Probably because it passed quickly into general use, 'pot' had only a short life, except as a semi-joke, among people who actually took the drug. The different attitudes to the word can be seen in '. . . free concerts which refused to turn into orgiastic pot-freaked riots' (*Friends*, No. 1, Jan 1969); 'Pot is in the news again (yawn)' (*Oz* 34, April 1971); 'Smoking pot has its advantages over alcohol – it calms people down and they don't have to pee so much' (pop festival organizer, quoted in *Honey*, June 1979).

Pot-head. An habitual user of cannabis. HEADS, drug addicts, are subdivided into 'acid-heads', who take LSD, and 'pot-heads', who rely on cannabis. All three terms are American in origin. 'Head' itself goes back to the mid-1930s, 'pot-head' and 'acid-head' to the 1950s. All were in common use in the UK by the mid-1960s, mostly among drug-users or people closely associated with them – 'I had never met a schoolboy pot-head before' (Nuttall: *Bomb Culture*, 1968); 'My pothead husband . . .' (*New Society*, 30 Aug 1979).

Pouf, poof. A homosexual. There is nothing new about this word. It has been used in the UK since the middle of the 19th century, with its Australian variant, 'poofter'. Until the 1950s, however, few men were aware of it, and practically no women. Thereafter, with homosexuals and their activities receiving greatly more publicity than ever before, 'poofs' have become mentionable, although for older people the word presents certain problems since, in the UK, it also means, usually with the spelling 'pouffe', a padded stool, not unlike a stuffed elephant's foot, for drawing-room sitting.

Homosexuals themselves never use the term and regard it as insulting. For the rest of the population it is consequently derogatory – 'Some of the city's top poof raves . . .' (MacInnes: *Absolute Beginners*, 1959); 'She heard the Master of Ceremonies make a reference to 'poufs in the Union bar'. People went up to the University bar to demand an apology' (*Gay News*, 9–22 Dec 1982).

The plural is generally 'poufs' or 'poofs', but occasionally, on the analogy of 'hoof', 'pooves' – 'You bloody pooves make me sick' (Forsyth: *Day of the Jackal*, 1971). A verb is also possible – 'They pooed around a little' (*Melody Maker*, 5 Dec 1971).

Powerpoppy. Confidently, aggressively played pop music, usually of a not very distinguished kind (*see* POPPY) – '. . . powerpoppy, with slickish singing thrown in' (*Sounds*, 24 Jan 1981).

Prat. A pretentious person. A general term of abuse or contempt, often applied to people of another social class or to those claiming to belong to another class – '. . . fat ruling class prat, Henry VIII' (*Sounds*, 28 April 1979); 'Being prats, they take themselves very seriously' (*Sounds*, 24 March 1979).

In 19th century criminals' language, the 'prat' was the backside. This has continued into modern times, although the range of users is now much wider – it is still not a drawing-room word – together with the equally old-established meaning, 'an incomplete or ineffectual person'. The present sense dates from about 1968. In the UK, it is particularly common among people who display a strong dislike of the status quo.

Pressie, prezzie. A present. From the Australian, where the more usual spelling is 'prezzie'. In the UK, but not in Australia, 'pressie' is mainly a young people's word and more common among girls than boys – 'When my sister's birthday came and she opened her pressie from Gran . . .' (*Mates*, 11 Aug 1979).

Pressing. A gramophone record, a batch of records made at the same time. First introduced in the mid-1950s, this has always been a journalists' word – 'her latest Columbia pressing' (*New Musical Express*, 20 July 1956), and 'It's a beautiful pressing' (*Attila*, 1 Nov 1971). Even the most enthusiastic of amateur collectors is unlikely to want to discuss his 'pressings'.

Print. A recording. Entirely a music journalists' word – 'Reg. Owne's print of 'Flamenco Love' . . .' (*New Musical Express*, 13 July 1956).

Progressive. A kind of sophisticated and often pretentious and arty rock music which developed in the mid-1960s and has now faded away. It featured electronic equipment, the use of Eastern instruments and other non-standard techniques, and it aimed at an audience which was more 'thinking' than the average. Its devotees had a very serious, even intellectual attitude to music – 'Girl required to sing for progressive band with strong Eastern influence' (*Friends*, No. 1, Jan 1969).

Promo. Promotional material, advertising. The abbreviation was first used in the USA about 1960 and then moved quickly into the UK – 'There was a refreshing absence of promo garbage within the envelope' (*Oz* 34, April 1971); 'He's his own promo man' (*Sounds*, 1 Dec 1979).

   In the UK, the word has been used mainly by the pop music business, where it can be used either adjectivally, as above, or as a noun – '. . . making a Sound of Music parody promo' (*Soundmaker*, 4 Dec 1982).

Provo. (*i*) A member of a group of Dutch anarchists in the mid-1960s, specializing in political 'happenings' in public places. The term later spread to other countries, including the UK – 'A provo happening in London would mean a lot of things' (*International Times*, 14 Oct 1966).

   (*ii*) The act of protest itself – 'Provo was a rebellion without obvious cause' (Neville: *Playpower*, 1970).

   The term 'Provo' was Dutch. The original movement has disappeared, but its rise coincided with that of the IRA in Ireland, when the members of the Provisional IRA (Irish Republican Army) have been known as the Provos.

Pseud. Pretentious. 'Present-day trendsetters, as pseud as they come'

(*The Spectator*, 26 Sept 1962). Also a pretentious person – '. . . a middle-class pseud' (*Sounds*, 24 March 1979). 'Pseud' was not invented by *Private Eye*, although the magazine, born in 1961, was undoubtedly a powerful force in popularizing it.

Pseudo. Pretending to be, bogus. Found in the UK from the mid-1940s onwards, 'pseudo' soon became a cult word among young intellectuals, who used it as a means of undermining and scoffing at people and ideas of which they did not approve, such as '. . . pseudo-liberated hippies' (*The Soul Book*, 1975).

Psych. An abbreviation of 'psychoanalyse', first used in the USA in the mid-1960s, it means 'make someone feel uneasy, put him off his stroke, by deliberate and carefully planned tactics'. It is used particularly in sport – '. . . showing off, swearing, bitching at the umpire, why? She's trying to psych you out of the game' (*Honey*, June 1971).

Psychedelia, psychodelia. The culture surround MIND-EXPANDING drugs. The word appeared in both the UK and the USA in the mid-1960s – '. . . the soft Southern encroachment of dope and psychodelia' (*The Soul Book*, 1975).

Psychedelic, psychodelic. (*i*) Using drugs, produced by drugs – 'Was the Last Supper a psychedelic orgy?' (*Private Eye*, 22 May 1970).

(*ii*) Anyone associated with LSD and the culture surrounding it – 'The San Francisco psychedelic eruption' (*Zigzag*, Aug 1972).

(*iii*) The swirling, neon-coloured style of decor and dress which was the commercial expression of psychodelia – 'First psychodelic boutique bursts in King's Road' (*International Times*, 14 Oct 1966); 'Bright colours became the permanent thing in psychedelic dress' (*Oz* 4, Sept 1967).

(*iv*) Mad, crazy, in a figurative sense – 'The latest weirdest club to hit the London scene, full of psychedelic fun and fab music' (*Jackie*, 2 Sept 1967).

For the origins of psychedelic', *see* PSYCHEDELIA. Its heyday was the 1960s, 'the psychedelic 60s'. It is much less used today, but when it does surface the meaning is often very uncertain. 'When critics talked misleadingly of a psychedelic revival' (*Melody Maker*, 24 Jan 1981) could be any of the four senses.

Psycho. A mad, wild, violent person. This abbreviation of 'psychopath' was first used in the USA in the early 1940s and in the UK soon after the end of World War II. '. . . the same kind of hatred psychos have for Jews or foreigners of coloureds' (MacInnes: *Absolute Beginners*, 1959); '. . . an unreformed woman-beating junkie psycho' (*Sounds*, 28 April 1979).

Psych out. To act in a way calculated to disturb someone, put him off his game. The usual intransitive form of PSYCH, more common in the USA than in the UK – 'Years ago no player would deliberately set out to put another player out of the game. This happens now – whether it's psyching out or going over the top' (footballer, interviewed in *New Musical Express*, 12 May 1979).

Psych up. To prepare oneself mentally – 'Psyching myself up on the strength of their title-track hit single . . .' (*Sounds*, 21 July 1979). A trendy verb, brought in from the USA in the early 1970s and now used in the UK chiefly in the upper levels of sport and pop music and by journalists with a special interest in these matters.

Punk. An abbreviation of PUNK ROCK, 'punk rocker'. In the USA it has had several meanings during Victorian times and the 20th century – 'touchwood', 'rubbish', 'a passive male homosexual', 'a showbusiness apprentice'. The 'touchwood' meaning came to the UK with the American army during World War I, both as a noun and an adjective, the latter having the sense of 'rotten, inferior'. It continued to be used in this way on both sides of the Atlantic, and in Australia, until the mid-1970s. There was also a late-1960s meaning, 'raw, unappealingly unsophisticated' – 'I'm not interested in what some hippie punk kid has to say' (*Oz* 43, July/Aug 1972).

'Punk' acquired another sense about 1976, in connection with a new style of pop music – 'punk rock' – and the bizarre dress and hairstyles which went with it. The early devotees of punk rock were given to wearing absurd articles, such as razor-blades and safety pins as personal adornments and, later, emphasis was placed on eccentric styles of cutting and colouring the hair. Outrage was and is the name of the game – 'Punk to me was always for taking the piss out of people' (interview with punk musician in *New Musical Express*, 12 May 1979).

'Punk' is the attitude of mind, the style, the activity, and a 'punk' is also a person involved in it all – 'Girl punk wants to meet Clash freaks' (advert in *Sounds*, 21 July 1979).

Punkette. A young female punk. The word is generally used in a slightly patronizing way by people who are past the punkette age – 'The Buzzcocks have denied any involvement in the affair of the three punkettes who disappeared' (*Sounds*, 1 Dec 1979).

Punk rock. A type of loud, fast, aggressive, outrageous rock music, popular during the mid-and late 1970s. The term is first recorded in both the USA and the UK about 1972 – 'The art of punk rock poetry' (*Oz* 43, July/Aug 1972).

Punky. Anything related to PUNK ROCK and its accompanying style – 'From Delta Five the punky delivery is even more interesting, as the singers are women' (*Spare Rib*, Sept 1979).

Punter. Formerly 'a gambler', the word is now used to describe an amateur, hanger-on, customer, client, average enthusiast in any form of activity. Since about 1970 it has been very common in the entertainment business and in sport. The music papers use it with slight overtones of condescension and superiority – 'It doesn't matter if your act isn't up to much, as long as you give the punters a good show' (*Time Out*, 6 April 1979). 'An audience which is a peculiar mixture of people from the record companies and the media, plus a contingent of ultra-keen young punters' (*Melody Maker*, 12 May 1979); '. . . as soon as a punter mentions 125' (*The Biker*, 7 Feb 1981).

Push. To sell drugs illegally. First recorded in the USA in the 1930s, together with the noun 'Pusher', it was being in the UK by the mid-1950s. Until the late 1960s, it was confined mainly to people personally concerned with drugs and the drug trade, but it is now so widely used that it can be considered Standard English – 'All the dubious ghetto chic of pimps and pushers' (*The Soul Book*, 1975).

Put down. To record. The phrase was being used in the USA, in the sense of 'to play music', 'to establish a rhythm', about 1944. The secondary meaning, 'record', came later, in 1965. It is now widely used by pop musicians everywhere – '. . . during a break between putting down tracks for their latest album' (*Pelham Pop Annual*, 1970); 'They're going to put down three or four new songs' (*Melody Maker*, 20 Jan 1979).

Q

Queen, quean. A male homosexual of effeminate appearance. Originally spelt 'quean', the word was fairly common in the 19th and early 20th centuries, although for much of this time the existence of Queen Victoria caused certain problems with its use. Except in Australia, it seemed to disappear into the background between World Wars I and II, but returned with increased strength in the 1950s, when the new public tolerance of homosexuality brought with it the need for a vocabulary with which to describe and discuss previously hidden practices – '. . . being a poof is a full-time occupation for so many of the dear old queens' (A young homosexual, in MacInnes: *Absolute Beginners*, 1959); '. . . a gang of washed-out old queens' (*Private Eye*, 5 June 1970).

Queer. (*i*) Displaying or possessing homosexual characteristics. An American expression, dating from the early 1920s, it was in use in the UK by the early 1930s. Very rarely used by homosexuals themselves, except as a joke, it is the word most commonly used by the general public – 'Everybody keeps giving me strange looks, thinking I'm a queer' (*Daily Mirror*, 22 March 1979).

(*ii*) A male homosexual. The history and limitations of the noun are the same as for the adjective – 'There's a couple of queers who run a hotel . . .' (*Zigzag*, Sept 1973).

R

Raise consciousness. To make politically conscious, more aware of one's legitimate grievances. The phrase, used particularly by feminists and left-wingers, originated in the USA in the early 1960s with the hippy movement – 'A Leeds teacher told us how she is helping to raise consciousness among her pupils' (*Spare Rib*, Feb 1979).

Randy. Sexually aroused, desirous. First noted in the late 18th century, this word, until the 1950s, was nearly always used with reference to men, although in the USA the situation was rather different. It is a mark of social change since World War II that it is now used indifferently by and about both men and women, at least as far as young people are concerned. Older women, especially of the middle-class, still find the word difficult to use, although they know perfectly well what it means. It can cause certain problems in the USA, where the Christian name Randy is very common, but in the UK the difficulty rarely arises – '. . . the randy cat at the far end of the blower' (MacInnes: *Absolute Beginners*, 1959); 'Here I am, a healthy, randy male' (*International Times*, 13 Feb 1967); 'I bought a lot of brandy/ when I was courting Sandy/With the aim to make her randy/When all I had was shandy' (pop song, 'Billericay Dickie', by Ian Dury, 1977).

Rap. In all the senses mentioned below, 'rap' represents American usage, exported to the UK during the 1950s, but still understood only in certain circles, more especially those connected with jazz and pop music and those in which black people are prominent. It is found much more frequently among journalists than their readers.

(*i*) To talk, chat, with a suggestion of enthusiasm and skilled repartee – 'I and the people I rap with think it important . . .' (*Oz* 21, June 1969); '. . . goodly people to rap to . . .' (*Attila*, 23 Oct 1971); '. . . rapping with the band' (*Melody Maker*, 27 Jan 1979).

(*ii*) A talk, usually long, involving a carefully cultivated art of repartee – 'In the second part of his fascinating rap with me' (*Black Music*, Dec 1979).

(*iii*) A criminal charge – '. . . the first obscenity rap against the

152

underground press' (*Oz* 43, July/Aug 1972), and 'Boxie's murder rap gets her not only freedom . . .' (*Time Out*, 8 April 1979).

(*iv*) To extemporize, play music or sing as a conversation piece – 'All I know how to do is rap' (*Sounds*, 11 Dec 1982).

(*v*) Achieved in a coasting manner, with only a small expenditure of energy – 'It was just a rap record' (*Sounds*, 11 Dec 1982).

Raunchy. An American word with a very wide and confusing range of meanings – dirty, mean, incompetent, bawdy, earthy, sexually provocative, exciting. Not all of these have crossed the Atlantic with success. Two are now fairly widely understood and used by young people in the UK.

(*i*) Basic, earthy. This is often applied to the style of certain pop singers – '. . . his alternately caressing and raunchy style' (*The Soul Book*, 1975); "Days of Rage', raunchy and angry both' (*Sounds*, 3 March 1979); '. . . a slick, yankee-rock style, with chunky, raunchy vocals' (*Sounds*, 24 Jan 1981).

(*ii*) Pleasant, exciting – 'I'm being smothered in a lot of teenage adulation. It's quite raunchy, really' (pop star, quoted in *Cracker*, 1972).

Rave. Modern, desirable, exciting. Only the adjective, used in these senses, is recent. The verb and the noun are much older and are well understood by both young and old. 'Rave guys love it' (*Jackie*, 25 Jan 1964), and 'They have a rave three piece suit' (*Jackie*, 7 May 1966) illustrate this sense of the word at its peak. It is now dated and no longer used by the young.

Raver. Someone who believes in enjoying himself, someone with a passionate enthusiasm, a fanatic. An early recorded example is 'I actually did begin to be a raver for these weekly meetings' (MacInnes: *Absolute Beginners*, 1959). It is not necessary, however, to be a 'raver' for anything in particular. One can simply be a 'raver' – 'The Soho Fair was a festival of the ravers' (Nuttall: *Bomb Culture*, 1968). Now somewhat dated.

Rave-up. A noisy party. An expression of the 1960s and 1970s – 'He admits he doesn't look his best after an all-night rave-up' (*Pelham Pop Annual*, 1970). It is now dated.

Real. Very. Much used in the USA since the late 19th century, 'real' was adopted by 'advanced' British teenagers in the late 1950s – 'Eccles is fab and Bluebottle real switched on' (*Jackie*, 2 Oct 1965) – and gradually phased out during the 1970s, although it still continues as a joke-word. In '. . . distinguished by some real cruel lyrics' (*Sounds*, 21 July 1979), 'real' is being used only semi-seriously.

Really. Very much. 'Really' became an extremely popular feature of teenage speech in Britain in the 1960s, and remained so until very recently, although it is now showing signs of obsolescence. It was hardly ever used in this way by anyone who, in 1960, had left their teens behind them, and marks a sharp and important dividing line between the generations. Usually, it was nothing more than a meaningless intensitive – 'When I played it to Col, he really liked it' (*Jackie*, 24 Jan 1981); 'The bike is good and I really feel I can put it all together this year' (*Motor Cycle Weekly*, 31 Jan 1981); 'I really liked his image, too' (*Sounds*, 11 Dec 1982).

Record player. A gramophone with an electric pick-up and amplifier. The term has passed through two stages. The first, which began in the mid-1930s, referred to a record-playing unit which played records through a radio. The second, from the mid-1950s, was a unit intended only for playing records electronically, with its own built-in amplifier and loudspeaker. Pop music would have been impossible without record players, which made it possible to play records loudly – 'Everyone in Britain possessing a record-player . . .' (*New Musical Express*, 5 Dec 1958).

Red. Barbiturate. 'Red', 'red-bird' and 'red-devil' are American terms, first used there in the early 1960s and soon part of the vocabulary of drug-takers throughout the English-speaking world – 'Mixing reds and alcohol can lead to a one-way trip' (*Oz* 21, June 1969).

Reefer. A cigarette containing marijuana. Used in the USA in the early 1930s, the word had spread to the UK by the late 1950s. After the early 1960s, it was rarely used by people who actually smoked such cigarettes, but it continued to form part of the vocabulary of knowledgeable and would-be knowledgeable journalists – '. . . prosecuted for selling reefers to unsuspecting teenagers' (*Zigzag*, Aug 1972).

Relate to. To feel sympathetic towards, involved with. A fashionable word among sociologists, welfare workers, hippies and sub-intellectuals since the 1950s, in a world where the individual content to be on his own, thinking his own thoughts and living his own life, is regarded with some suspicion, a world in which 'relationships' have become a cult – 'More and more young people are unable to relate to Fleet Street' (*Oz* 34, April, 1971); 'Certain people's music that I just can't relate to' (rock musician, in Gold: *The Road to Rock*, 1976).

Right On. Exactly, precisely, to the point, very hip and trendy. This black American expression continues, more than ten years after its importation into the UK, to be used self-consciously by most white people. Sometimes this is shown by inverted commas, as in 'His performance as interviewed as 'right-on'' (*Gay News*, 23 Feb 1981), sometimes not – 'A hip lady who sends right-on letters' (*Spare Rib*, Sept 1979).

Righteous. Perfect, excellent. An American expression of the early 1940s, it became the highest compliment a Hell's Angel could pay – 'They believed they were as tough and as righteous as the American brothers' (Mandelkau: *Buttons*, 1971). It should be noted that 'righteous', in this context, carries no moral or religious connotation whatever. The righteousness that is implied is entirely pagan and amoral. Nowadays, it can be used ironically, as in 'It is far too righteous a song' (*Sounds*, 11 Dec 1982).

Rip off. 'Rip off', an American creation of the late 1960s, is a true child of the Permissive Society, in which all decisions tend to be pragmatic and notions of right and wrong are extremely flexible. The basic meanings are 'to steal' and 'something stolen', but to translate the phrase is to bypass the fact that, as with 'shoplifting', the blunt term is not being used in the first place. 'Stealing' is something which belonged to the old society, in which theft was regarded as morally wrong. 'Rip-off', by contrast, states the fact, but makes no attempt to castigate. As a picturesque euphemism, it is typical of its age.

(*i*) To steal. Once a youth-word, it has now settled down into much more general use among people of a much wider age range – 'Are you good at anything? Yes, ripping off bikes' (Mandelkau: *Buttons*, 1971).

(*ii*) To copy, without permission or acknowledgement – 'It was all ripped off from Tchaikovsky' (*Zigzag*, July 1973).

(*iii*) Something which is overpriced, bad value for money – '. . .

without the rip-off we've had in the past' (*Oz* 41, April/May 1972).

(*iv*) Thieving, plagiarizing – '. . . the rip-off artists who kill many good talents' (*Attila*, 22 Oct 1971).

Ripped. High on drink or drugs. An American expression of the 1960s, it was being used by British addicts by the early 1970s and is still current – '. . . with the ruling classes ripped out of their heads on the good stuff' (*Home Grown*, No. 3, 1978).

Roach. The butt of a cigarette, especially one containing marijuana. The word first appeared in this sense in the USA towards the end of the 1930s and was being used in the UK by the mid-1960s. It is unlikely to be used by people who do not take drugs themselves – '. . . making a mainline out of a roach clip' (*Home Grown*, No 2, 1977).

Roadie. The road manager of a pop/rock group, the person who does the driving and is responsible for the equipment. The term began to be used in the USA about 1968 and in the UK two or three years later – 'Ben Palmer on piano (later Cream's roadie)' (*Zigzag*, Aug 1972). The word appears to have become a permanent and essential part of the pop-musician's vocabulary – 'The big black roadie rushes forwards to stop Dave Wakeling being pulled over-enthusiastically into the cauldron of high-stepping Glasgow fan-lava' (*Sounds*, 11 Dec 1982).

Rocker. Someone who plays, sings or enjoys rock music. 'Rock' and its derivatives and compounds is almost worthy of a dictionary of its own. The history of the word is as follows. In the mid-1940s, 'rock' was used in the USA to mean a jazz form characterized by a strong beat. Later, about 1950, 'rock and roll' appeared, pop music with a heavy beat and simple tune, with frequent echoes of the Blues. By the mid-1950s, 'rock' was being used as a synonym of 'rock and roll', especially in compounds, such as 'rock guitarist', where the full form, 'rock and roll guitarist', would have been cumbersome.

'Rocker' came to have two quite distinct meanings: (*i*) A performer of rock and roll music, an enthusiast for it – 'I'm a rocker, but I like Crosby types of light song' (rock and roll singer, quoted in *New Musical Express*, 14 Feb 1958).

(*ii*) A motorcycle enthusiast of the Hell's Angel type – 'If I told them I had a '58 Cadillac, they would have thought I was a rocker' (rock musician in Gold: *The Road to Rock*, 1976).

Rock machine. The rock music business. Used mainly by journalists and by those earning a living from pop music, the word carries more than a hint of the seedier, wheeling and dealing aspects of the pop world – '. . . the most accurate and sustained satire on the rock machine and some of its more ludicrous principals' (*Melody Maker*, 27 Jan 1979).

Rootsy. Genuine, traditional, reminding one of its origins. This American word is little used or understood in the UK outside groups, such as pop music and films, which have strong links with the American way of life and much sympathy with it – '. . . a respectably rootsy piece of reggae' (*New Musical Express*, 7 March 1981).

Rudy. The super-cool, unsophisticated hooligan who always comes out on top. This Jamaican word describes a style of appearance, attitude to life and taste in music fashionable among both black and white youths during the 1960s and 1970s – 'Sunday's Specials gig at the Lyceum was populated not by skins or modes or rudies, but wave after wave of soul types' (*Sounds*, 1 Dec 1979).

Rules OK? An expression first found among gangs of young football fans in the UK during the 1960s. These youths were and still are much given to writing statements like, 'Arsenal Rules OK?' on city walls as a gesture of solidarity and a provocation to the supporters of other teams. The phrase is no longer the monopoly of football supporters and has become merely a challenging way of stating something which one believes to be true and which one is willing to defend – 'Pragmatism Rules OK?' (*Sounds*, 21 July 1979).

Rush. The feeling of euphoria, the adrenalin flow, as a stimulant drug begins to have an effect – 'Then he got blown to pieces, probably taking it for an extra-strong rush' (*Home Grown*, No. 2, 1977).

Before the American drug world took it over in the 1960s, 'rush' was a rushing sensation of any kind. The word can still be used in this general sense.

S

Salt. A female sexual partner. 'Salt' has had sexual connotations for a long time. From the 17th to the 19th century it was commonly used to mean 'amorous, lecherous', as was 'salt-water', for 'an act of sexual intercourse'. In the 1960s, after many years, quiescence, it emerged as a youth-culture word, with a sense not previously used – 'I had a game of soccer this afternoon and afterwards popped a bit into my salt' (letter to *Oz*, June 1969). 'Salt', one should observe, is used here in the old sense of 'salt cellar'. The association of ideas is obvious.

Scene. An activity or where it is carried on, a situation, an experience, an event, a way of life, a style. The word was originally, in the 1950s, associated with the American world of jazz, beatniks and hippies. It had arrived in the UK by the early 1960s and it was soon in general use among the younger and trendier sections of the population, although half-informed journalists of a different culture and generation continued to place it within the jazz/hippy field it had occupied ten or fifteen years earlier. The following meanings can be distinguished in the UK.

(*i*) An area of activity, interest, style of living. 'The Scene' is where the interesting activities are to be found. People 'on the scene' are visibly and consciously fashionable in appearance and habits – 'Mods who are always on the scene' (*Jackie*, 18 Jan 1964); 'Whatever scene you're on, you're likely to discover things aren't happening quite as they should' (*International Times*, 14 Oct 1966); 'If we want to copy someone else's scene . . . '(*Oz* 33, Feb 1971); 'It was the typical student scene' (*Zigzag*, Aug 1972).

(*ii*) An area of activity, place to live, which one enjoys and feels at home in – 'The Costa Brava isn't necessarily your scene' (*Pink*, 12 May 1979); 'I much prefer Japan anyway. The scene there is incredible' (*Jackie*, 24 Jan 1981).

(*iii*) Style – 'It wasn't her usual scene, picking up strange men in the launderette' (*Woman's Own*, 13 Jan 1979).

(*iv*) A sexual relationship, usually of a homosexual nature – 'Musicians that the author had a scene with' (*Zigzag*, Sept 1973).

(v) What is currently fashionable – 'The scene till now has been accumulatively negative' (Nuttall: *Bomb Culture*, 1968).

In all its meanings, 'scene' is a word to handle with great care. It is subject to frequent and rapid changes of fashion and, although those who belong to 'scene' using groups will have a sure touch in the matter, outsiders, such as parents, journalists and novelists, can all-too-easily find themselves speaking and writing yesterday's English in ignorance, which can be embarrassing.

Scene, bad. A problem, trouble, disagreement. See also SCENE. 'All the right wing bulldogs came beating along and there were some pretty bad scenes there' (*International Times*, 31 Oct 1966).

Schizo. An abbreviation of 'schizophrenic'. The British definition is much narrower and more precise than the American, a fact which has influenced the meaning of the abbreviation in the two countries. In the UK, 'schizo' has been used by 'serious' novelists and other writers since the mid-1940s. The Americans have been more inclined to use 'schiz', a form which has hardly been heard in Britain at all. 'He was certified as a schizo' (*New Musical Express*, 1 Jan 1979) follows the British tradition, but American influence has been at work among the young here, producing a much wider and looser popular definition, suggesting madness and disassociation of a more general kind – 'Schizo eyes staring out at nothing' (Cohn: *Awopbop*, 1969).

Schmaltz. Literally, 'fat, dripping', and hence sentimentality. 'Schmaltz' was originally German and Yiddish, the figurative meaning gaining wider circulation via Jewish comedians and the musical press. In the 1960s it became part of the language of the pop music world, as an apt description of sickly playing and singing – '. . . his nightclub schmaltz' (*Oz* 41, April/May 1972), and 'For every track of Four Tops schmaltz, a track of Four Tops power' (*The Soul Book*, 1975). 'Schmaltz' is not merely a journalists' and critics' word in the UK. It is used in conversation, especially by the more educated and disapproving members of the public.

Schmaltzy. Grossly sentimental. *See* SCHMALTZ. '. . . the largely schmaltzy remainder' (*Sounds*, 24 Jan 1981).

Schmuck. An unpleasant person, an underhand individual, a con-man. A Yiddish expression, it has been in general use in the UK since the 1950s, especially in the entertainment world – 'Isaac Hayes is a monstrous schmuck' (*Oz* 41, April/May 1972).

Schmutter. Clothing. Originally Yiddish, the word passed into general use in London and the South East of England during the 1940s and afterwards became fashionable among young people in the UK – '. . . some very fancy schmutter: massive tuxedo, lace shirt, varnished pumps with bows . . .' (MacInnes: *Absolute Beginners*, 1959).

Score. Of American origin in all the following senses:
   (*i*) To acquire, steal, buy, borrow – 'Dennis made his chick and kept her busy, while Kate and I scored his Travellers Cheques and passport' (parody of hippy language in *Oz* 8, Jan 1968). In use in the USA about 1914, this sense was not found in the UK until the early 1960s, when it arrived as part of the verbal furniture of the hippies.
   (*ii*) To buy or acquire drugs – 'At least five people approached me attempting to score' (*Schoolkids Oz*, April 1970); 'If you land on a named square, you can score ounces up to the amount shown' (instructions for game in *Attila*, 16 Dec 1971). In use in the USA about 1935, in the UK in the early 1960s.
   (*iii*) A person who sells drugs – 'Your next score doesn't like your face. No score' (*Attila*, 16 Dec 1971). The noun appeared late, by comparison with the verb, in the USA about 1950. It was in the UK by the late 1960s.
   Both (*ii*) and (*iii*) have been used almost entirely by people who take and supply drugs.
   (*iv*) To have sexual intercourse. The word has the flavour of obtaining something or somebody much wanted, of achievement – '. . . those sort of women, one he scores, one he don't (interview with rock group in *Zigzag*, Sept 1973) and, intransitively, 'She dances with this guy who's absolutely convinced he's about to score' (*Sounds*, 21 July 1979).

Screw. (*i*) To have sexual intercourse. An old term, of purely British origin, which dates back to the late 18th century, possibly earlier. An important change of usage has occurred in recent years, however. As part of the new freedom of expression conferred by the Permissive Society, it is now widely used by the young, especially the working-class young, of both sexes – 'Do they shut their eyes and think of England when they screw?' (*Brighton Voice*, July 1973); 'Loving (non-screwing) relationship' (advert in *Sounds*, 3 March 1979).

(*ii*) To eye, look someone up and down – 'I saw four mods come out. They started screwing me' (Mandelkau: *Buttons*, 1971). Of British origin and commonly found since the 1950s, especially among the more violent and uneducated young.

(*iii*) To exploit someone – 'Who's screwing who?' 'headline in *Brighton Voice*, March 1973); '. . /. end up with nothing, because they've been screwed all the way down the line' (*Zigzag*, Feb 1973). In use in the USA in the 1930s, but in the UK not until the 1950s, when it tended to be used by students, the political Left, and the lower end of the business community. It is now almost Standard English.

(*iv*) A warder, prison officer. First recorded in the early 19th century, the word was used until the late 1950s only by those with personal knowledge of the criminal world. In recent years, however, it has formed part of the hate vocabulary of those sections of British society which are instinctively opposed to anything and anyone concerned with the maintenance of law and order and social control – 'Employment for vast numbers of pigs, lawyers, judges, screws, prison governors' (*Oz* 33, Feb 1971).

Scrummy. An abbreviation of 'scrumptious'. Wonderful, delicious. This is an expression with an interesting history. 'Scrumptious' was in use in the mid-19th century, as a recent import from the USA, and 'scrummy' was being used by middle-brow writers, including John Galsworthy, about 1920. It had passed out of adult use by 1940, but was revived as a novelty among the 8–14 age-group, and by the journalists meeting their needs during the 1950s – 'Scrummy pin-ups' (*Oh Boy!*, 19 Jan 1980).

Self-styled. This became a favourite *Private Eye* word during the 1960s, describing someone who made extravagant and often ridiculous claims as to his importance and status – 'In comes self-styled South African, Peter Hain' (*Private Eye*, 8 June 1970). The expression, which was never used in speech, was in perfect accord with the demolition tactics in favour among 'progressives' at the time. Celebrated people were suspect because of their celebrity and in constant need of being investigated and trimmed down to human size.

Sell out. (*i*) Something which compromises principles for money or expedience. The phrase is British in origin, but subsequently percolated to the USA and elsewhere in the English-speaking world, where the need for it was quickly realized. Its history reveals a welcome cynicism towards current commercial practices. When it first appeared, about 1930, it meant, with no sinister overtones, 'a sporting fixture for which all seats have been sold'. This was later taken to imply that the impressive success of such an occasion was due to forceful and possibly unscrupulous promotion, rather than to any intrinsic merit, and from this point it was only a short step to its new meaning, which became extremely popular among the power-suspicious young of the 1960s – '. . . a feeling that anything in the charts must be automatically a sell-out' (Cohn: *Awopbop*, 1969).

(*ii*) To compromise one's principles for the sake of money – screaming that we'd sold out' (*Zigzag*, July 1973); 'This is not a policy of selling out, of giving whitey what he wants' (*The Soul Book*, 1975). The history of the verb is similar to that of the noun.

Send. To make excited, to move. This expression most frequently refers to the effects of music or musicians. It was common in American jazz circles in the 1930s, used by pop music fans everywhere in the 1950s, and survived as a teenagers' word in the 1960s – 'I went to see Jimmy Young recently and he sent me' (*New Musical Express*, 13 July 1956); 'I'm not normally a Kitt fan, but Eartha sends me with this sizzling song' (*New Musical Express*, 14 Feb 1958); 'A film we went to ages ago that rather sent us' (MacInnes: *Absolute Beginners*, 1959).

Sent. Infatuated. Originally used by jazz musicians – *see* SEND – it was taken up by teenage girls in the 1950s to describe swooning emotion of a delectable kind – 'I'm sent and I don't ever want to come back' (*Jackie*, 18 Jan 1964).

Session. A recording session, where professional pop musicians are hired for the occasion, often playing with people with whom they have never played previously. The word has been confined to musicians, ultra-keen fans and the press which serves them both – 'Legend has it that you got into sessions' (*Zigzag*, Dec 1972).

Sessioneer. A session musician – '. . . the career of Studio One's leading young sessioneer' (*Black Music*, Dec 1979).

Set. A group of musical numbers, a performance. This is an inside-word, used from the 1960s onwards by musicians, musical journalists, and fans – 'the big groups would never do more than a thirty minute set' (*Zigzag*, Aug 1972); 'The Car's set was infinitely more satisfying to my ears' (*Melody Maker*, 7 Oct 1978); 'We're still looking for someone who actually saw her set' (*Sounds*, 1 Dec 1979). It is not in general use, even among the young.

Sexism. Discrimination on the basis of sex. This heard-everywhere term was used first and particularly by militant feminists in the 1950s, concerning the alleged oppression of women by men. It is now used more generally, and often vaguely, in the discussion of sex stereotypes – '. . . keeping children out of nurseries for fear of the sexism they'd be subjected to' (letter to *Spare Rib*, Sept 1979) implies that both boys and girls are subjected from their earliest years to pressures which make them conform to traditional views of roles played by males and females in society.

Sexist. Possessing, displaying or encouraging attitudes which reinforce sexual stereotypes, refusing to admit that women are in every way the equals of men – '. . . the whole problem of sexist bands being booked for college gigs' (*Melody Maker*, 20 Jan 1979).

Sex object. A man or, more usually, a woman, who is regarded and treated primarily as a source of sexual gratification. First used by feminists in the 1950s, these are still the people who provide the expression with its main market – 'Pop lyrics present women as sex objects for men' (*Spare Rib*, April 1975).

Shag. To have sexual intercourse, have sexual intercourse with. This 18th century term has remained in common use until the present day, but one important change has taken place during the past 30 years. Until about 1950 only men had full rights to the word. A man could 'shag' a woman; a woman, no matter what her age or social class, could neither 'shag' a man, nor 'shag', although she might, as a token of her passive stereotype, 'be shagged'. The post-war campaign for women's rights and the rather more tolerant attitude towards sexual behaviour hae brought about some change in the situation. 'Woodbine Lizzy. Shags like a rattlesnake, doesn't she?' (Waterhouse: *Billy Liar*, 1959) would not have been possible 20 years earlier. But the extent of the change should not be exaggerated.

Shagged. Exhausted. This was a public school expression in the 1920s and was in general middle-class use from the 1930s onwards. By the 1950s, however, it was possible to observe a marked movement down the social scale – '. . . after we'd shagged ourselves out running or jumping' (a Borstal boy, in Sillitoe: *The Loneliness of the Long Distance Runner*, 1959).

Shit. While preserving its basic meaning, 'excrement', this word has undergone many changes of figurative usage since World War II. As an expletive, it was never as strong or as socially disreputable in the USA as in the UK, and its fading strength and taboo value in the UK in recent years may owe a good deal to American influence. Most remarkable, however, is the way in which 'shit', especially as an interjection and the phrases embodying it have become part of the normal vocabulary of a great many women and girls, a phenomenon which constitutes a sharp division between the pre- and post-war generations.

The greatly increased use of the word during the past 30 years reflects the steady impoverishment of vocabulary among those whose culture lies along the pop-aggression axis. The more basic one's language, the more convincingly one is a member of the tribe. The following special senses merit individual explanation.

(*i*) A despicable person – 'Isn't Quentin Hogg an unremitting shit?' (*International Times*, 27 Oct 1967).

(*ii*) Cannabis, hashish – 'Many are serving life-imprisonment, caught with 50 kilos of shit' (*Oz* 15, July/Aug 1969); 'This place is an Italian prison . . . naturally I'm here for shit, 52 grams to be exact' (*Oz* 34, April 1971).

(*iii*) Nonsense – 'He doesn't take any shit from the Motown money man' (*The Soul Book*, 1975).

(*iv*) Organization – 'When are you gonna get your shit together and get your distribution sorted out' (meaning get yourself organized) (*Superbike*, Sept 1978).

There are numerous compounds of this all-purpose, all-meanings word, which can be used equally well as a noun, verb or adjective, or as a fairly forceful interjection. None of them, however, form part of the day-to-day vocabulary of ordinary English people, no matter what their age, sex or social class. Used in innocence by a foreigner, they would sound doubly strange.

The more frequently found Anglo-American creations of the past 20 years have been the following:

Shitheels. An idiot – 'The Turks are portrayed as sadistic shitheels' (*Rolling Stone*, 11 Nov 1978).

Shit-hot. (*i*) Very good – 'He's a shit-hot mechanic, too' (*Attila*, 16 Oct 1971). (*ii*) Very well – 'They made us play shit-hot every night' (*Zigzag*, April 1973).

Shitless. Always used, as an intensitive, in conjunction with 'scared', the alliteration no doubt adding to the total effect – 'The bosses are all scared shitless' (*Attila*, 13 Nov 1971).

Shitlist. A blacklist – 'If you're important enough to be on the GCHQ's shitlist, you've already made a lot of mistakes' (*Undercurrents*, July/Aug 1974).

Shit, beat the. To beat someone extremely viciously – 'We spent the whole evening beating the shit out of him' (*Zigzag*, July 1973).

Shit, give a. To give a damn, not care in the least – 'John still in the madhouse and nobody giving a shit' (Nuttall: *Bomb Culture*, 1968); 'I don't give a shit about any of that' (*Sounds*, 3 March 1979).

Shit on. To abuse, treat like dirt, exploit – 'Blues was and is the music of the black man who has been shat on since he was born' (*Attila*, 23 Oct 1971).

Shit over. To treat someone badly, crookedly – 'He shat all over the Beatles' (*The Road to Rock*, 1974).

Shit, scare the. To terrify – '. . . raucous, screeching music. It usually scares the shit out of cats' (*International Times*, 27 Oct 1967); '. . . scare the shit out of a lot of chickens' (*The Guardian*, 12 March 1979), and hence

Shit-scared. Terrified – 'I've never been so shit-scared in all my life' (*New Musical Express*, 7 March 1981).

Shoot up. To inject a drug, usually heroin – 'They sneaked out to the toilet to shoot up more crystal' (*Oz*, Winter 1973).

Shower. An undesirable, despicable person, a group or collection of such persons. This purely British expression has been known since the early 1950s. For a while, its use was confined to the more educated youngish males of the middle-class, but since the mid-1960s it has been entirely classless and equally popular with both males and females, although the range of users tends to be on the young side – 'I hear you're going out with a shower' (*Jackie*, 2 Oct 1965); 'Student Power – what a shower' (line from song, 'Student Power', by the Angelic Upstarts, 1979).

Side. A recording, a record. In this sense, the word has very rarely been used by anyone other than pop musicians and by the journalists associated with them – '. . . sides began to be recorded using 'soul' as part of the title' (*The Soul Book*, 1975).

Side-kick. A companion, helper, person playing a secondary role. The word has been common in the USA and in Australia since the early 1920s but, until the mid-1940s, it was generally felt to be an alien expression, with film and gangster associations. By the 1960s, however, it was being used in the UK with reference to women and girls, as well as to men, especially by young people – 'It was Liz, my side-kick, who dared me' (*Jackie*, 29 Feb 1964); 'His sugar-and-spice side-kick, Pamela Pearl' (*Melody Maker*, 24 Jan 1981). It is now almost part of Standard English.

Sigh-guy. A man attractive to teenage girls. The word was coined by American journalism in the late 1950s and was found in the UK not long afterwards – 'That sigh-guy may get round to asking for a date' (*Jackie*, 15 May 1965), and 'Newest sigh-guy on the scene is 18-year-old David Essex' (*Jackie*, 26 Feb 1966). It has now practically vanished.

Sit-in. See -IN. A form of protest involving the occupation of a building of some importance and a refusal to move out until demands have been met. The word originated during the student troubles in the USA in the 1960s and subsequently became much used among students and factory workers in the UK – 'The sit-ins, riots and marches at Berkeley failed' (Nuttall: *Bomb Culture*. 1968); 'We asked a student where the sit-in was' (*Attila*, 6 Nov 1971). 'Sit-in' is now Standard English. There is no other word for the event.

Skin. The 1960s produced three new meanings for this adaptable word.
 (*i*) A skinhead, who might be defined as a teenage male, who has his hair cut very short, is greatly addicted to violence, possesses a very

small vocabulary and, indeed, is not much given to speech at all. After his first appearance in the early 1960s, the skinheads slipped somewhat into the background in the early 1970s, to experience a strong revival at the end of the decade – 'The Subs have a skin following, who come to see us' (*Melody Maker*, 19 May 1979); '. . . hot line buzzing from half the skins in London' (*Sounds*, 1 Dec 1979).

(*ii*) Paper used for rolling cannabis cigarettes – 'The police managed to find a very small amount of pot and some skins' (*Oz* 15, July/Aug 1969), and 'Contented murmurings, rustle of skins, stoned sighs' (*Attila*, 23 Oct 1971).

(*iii*) Drums. A word used only by initiates. '. . . by appointing Terry Chimes to pump the skins' (*Sounds*, 28 April 1979). The word is used only by those within the perimeter of the musical world.

Skin mag. A pornographic magazine. This is entirely a journalists' term – '. . . in possession of the skin mags' (*Private Eye*, 15 Jan 1971).

Skull. One's head. The word, now obsolete in this context, was used during the 1960s and early 1970s, in phrases describing drug highs, especially from amphetamines – '. . . warring kids, up to their skulls in amphetamines' (Nuttall: *Bomb Culture*, 1968).

Slacks. Nowadays, trousers for casual wear. The word was used in the early 19th century as a colloquialism to describe trousers in general and, later, trousers worn by soldiers. It had become Standard English before World War I. With the develop of unisex habits of dress in the 1950s and 1960s, 'slacks' became the garment worn by girls – '. . . durable boots, slacks and jacket' (*Jackie*, 18 Jan 1964); 'This super trouser suit with a cotton top and rayon slacks . . .' (*Jackie*, 15 May 1969). Long since abandoned by teenagers, the word is now used only, if at all, by middle-aged women and very conventional men's outfitters.

Slag. To insult, abuse, castigate. This sense of the word originated in the UK, apparently in the 1960s, and it has continued to be widely used ever since, more particularly by younger people and non-Establishment journalists – 'The interrogators often attempt to induce guilt in them by slagging them as shits and whores' (*Spare Rib*, Jan 1979), and 'Sweet have always been slagged very heavily by the press' (*Sounds*, 3 March 1979). But, before this, the word had had a strongly pejorative atmosphere surrounding it for many years, with 'slag' as 'a coarse, loose woman', and 'slagger', 'a brothel-keeper'. One can notice this sense continuing in the UK today, among males at the lower end of the social scale – 'All the niggers at the discos and white slags hanging about with them' (a skinhead, reported in *New Society*, 26 June 1980).

Slag off. To criticise adversely, to damn. The phrase has been a favourite of pop musicians since the early 1970s – 'You used to slag off a lot of your records' (*Zigzag*, July 1973); 'That's the reason why people slag off other bands, 'cos they're scared of them' (*Melody Maker*, 20 Jan 1979). It is used by British youth of all classes and by journalists of all ages – I don't like slagging off people's work' (*Soundmaker*, 4 Dec 1982).

Smack. Heroin. A word current among addicts in both the UK and the USA – 'The clinic in Sussex that helped him kick smack' (*Sounds*, 24 Jan 1981).

Smoke. To smoke marijuana. Very widely used, especially by the drug-consuming fraternity, for more than 30 years, this is an entirely neutral word, with no overtones of praise or blame – 'We smoke up at this geyser's house where we get it from' (*New Society*, 7 Feb 1980)

Smoochy. Suggesting and encouraging kissing and cuddling, referring especially to music – '. . . all sentimental and smoochy' (*Melody Maker*, 24 Jan 1981). The word has an interesting history. In the 1890s 'smoodge' appeared in Australia, probably as a variant of 'smooth', with the meanings 'ingratiate oneself, kiss and caress'. It is still used in Australia in this way.

The Americans borrowed the word from the Australians, spelling it 'smooch', and keeping the Australian meaning. In the UK, however, it acquired two extra senses during the 1960s, 'to dance slowly and lovingly', and 'a piece of music played for this style of dancing'. But, as the spelling shows, 'smooth' and its derivatives, 'smoochy' and 'smooching', certainly arrived here from the USA, not Australia.

Snicker. Giggle. This alternative to 'snigger' was, until recently, purely American, but it is now used by British people, especially musicians and their hangers-on, who pride themselves on their American connections – 'no-one but Cornwell could get away with such languid husky vocals without a snicker' (*Sounds*, 24 Jan 1981).

Song, on. At the top of one's form. The expression is purely British and is much favoured by sports journalists – 'Mike Bailey's team are really on song at the moment' (*Shoot*, 31 Jan 1981).

Speed. Amphetamines. A term used by drug addicts and by those who have some reason to refer to such people in a knowing way – 'Speed has become much more common' (*New Society*, 7 Feb 1980).

Spicey. A pornographic magazine. 'Spicy' (usually spelt in this way) was in colloquial use in the UK, with the meaning 'titillating, sexually exciting', from the 1870s. More recently, it has acquired the additional sense of 'suggesting something scandalous or sensational'. As a noun, 'spicey' is very much a working class/lower-middle class word, much less likely to be used by the young than by their parents – 'I do a good round in spiceys' (Terson: *Zigger Zagger*, 1967).

Spiel. Sales talk, writing or speaking aimed at persuasion, lengthy explanation. More often than not, the word suggests both dishonesty and long-windedness. It was being used in this sense in the UK by the 1950s, as an import from either the USA or Australia, and coalescing then with the existing British senses. The use of the term by members of the younger generation reflects their realistic belief that all sales-talk and advertising is, by definition, suspect – 'For once the fan club spiel is justified' (*Oz* 43, July/Aug 1972).

Spiked. Drugged unknowingly, laced (of a drink). Originally part of the Anglo-American drug-taker's specialized vocabulary, it has since achieved much wider currency – 'Almost immediately, I was spiked with wine and acid' (Mandelkau: *Buttons*, 1971).

Spin. To play a record. The expression, first found in both the UK and the USA in the 1950s, is now almost obsolete. In its day, it was used mostly by disc jockeys and pop fans – 'Most of the discs that Alan liked to spin . . .' (*New Musical Express*, 21 Sept 1956); 'Her mum said, 'Hold on, she's spinning some discs''(*Jackie*, 15 May 1965). 'Her mum' was certainly doing no more than repeating a phrase she had heard her teenage daughter using. 'Spinning some discs' was certainly never part of the day-to-day vocabulary of 'her mum's' generation.

Splif. A cigarette containing cannabis. American in origin, the term was in general use among drug-takers on both sides of the Atlantic.

Nowadays it is mostly confined to West Indians – 'He'd just been dragging on a splif' (MacInnes: *Absolute Beginners*, 1959).

Split. To leave, usually, but not always, precipitately. The word has been much used in the USA since the mid-19th century, with the meaning 'move fast'. In the 1950s it acquired the more specific sense of 'get out or away quickly', and emigrated in this form. During the 1960s and 1970s the expression was a great favourite of the Alernative Society, the members of which were constantly obliged to leave somewhere with all possible speed – 'One fuzz takes down some of our names and gives us a warning about trespass. We split' (*Schoolkids Oz*, April 1970); 'They all split for Istanbul' (*Brighton Voice*, Sept 1973).

Square. Conformist, conventional; an old-fashioned, reactionary person. One early 19th century meaning of the word current in the UK was 'honest, straightforward'. The modern sense, first heard in the 1950, is a development of this. A teenager at that time was likely to apply the word to anyone of his or her parents' generation. The expression lingered on through the 1970s, but is found much less frequently nowadays – 'You really are an old square. Can't you see she's in love?' (mother to father, about daughter, in a *Boyfriend Annual* story, 1963, with the mother being careful to use her daughter's idiom); 'You can be the envy of your friends – as they say in square adverts.' (*Melody Maker*, 27 June 1964); 'Ultimately the Model Citizens try too hard to be cool, and end up as laughable squares' (*Melody Maker*, 12 May 1979).

Stake-out. Being watched by the police. This is an American expression. When it found its way to the UK in the 1960s, it carried with it the flavour of cops and robbers television serials. It has never been widely used or understood in the UK outside the circle of professional police-haters of the more trendy kind – '. . . tapping for political surveillance purposes may be done without all the paraphernalia of stake-outs' (*Undercurrents*, July/Aug 1974)

Stand-out. A distinctive person, something outstandingly good. This expression, current in the USA since the 1920s, is used only in the pop world and its environs in the UK – 'Henderson's contributions include a stand-out, 'Full and Satisfied'' (*Melody Maker*, 19 May 1979).

Star-trip. To behave like a star, get excited at the idea of being, seeing or hearing a star. The term crossed to the UK from the USA in the early 1970s over the familiar pop-music bridge – 'They were star-tripping like crazy. They thought he was going to do a Midas' (pop musician in *Sounds*, 28 April 1979). 'Star-trip' is not yet in general use.

Stash. (*i*) To hide, put in a safe place – '. . . you collect £100 and stash your dope' (*Attila*, 16 Dec 1971).

(*ii*) A cache, something hidden away for safety – 'The New Moon on Thursday is good news for your sterling stash' (horoscope in *Sounds*, 28 April 1979).

'Stash', in this sense, is an American colloqualism, little used in the UK, except by those who belong to the pop music/drug complex.

Steady. A regular girl/boyfriend – 'I'm seventeen and my steady is 20' (letter to *Jackie*, 25 Jan 1964). The noun is no longer used by teenagers, but the verbal phrase is still in common use – 'I'm free at weekends, now I'm not going steady with Alison' (*Jackie*, 12 May 1979).

Steamed. High on drugs. The term, which originated in the USA is used only by addicts and sympathizers – 'They were steamed out of their boxes'(*Sounds*, 3 March 1979).

Steamed up. Sexually excited. This phrase is of British origin. In the 1930s, 'steamed up' meant 'tipsy', and was much more common in Scotland. From being alcoholically excited to being sexually excited was a natural progession and one which accorded with the changing spirit of the age. This meaning dates from the late 1950s – 'It shouldn't get him too steamed up' (*Jackie*, 26 Sept 1964).

Steam in. To move in, become involved. A British expression, much used by teenage fighting tribes – 'If there's a ruck, we steam in' (rocker football fan, quoted in *New Society*, 13 Sept 1979).

Stick up. To reprimand, punish. A reshaped and figurative version of the old-established, 'to give someone the stick', meaning 'to beat'. Widely used since the early 1970s, the phrase is used mainly by those most likely to find themselves at the receiving end of official disapproval – 'They're marvellous, she says – they've never given her any stick about having time off for running' (*Honey*, June 1979).

Stiff, a real. Something exceedingly boring. In the USA, a 'stiff' has been a corpse since the 1850s and the word has been used occasionally in the UK with the same meaning since about 1914, the expression 'to bore one stiff' being first found at about the same time. In its figurative sense, however, as in 'The song is a real stiff' (*Sounds*, 3 March 1979), the noun is American and modern. It is not widely found in the UK outside the usual highly Americanized circles, such as the musical part of the entertainment world.

Stoned. High on drugs, drunk. 'Drunk', came first, about 1920, 'high on drugs' only in the 1960s. Nowadays the word is used in the sense of 'drunk' only by people who are unaware of its association with drugs – '5000 stoned, tripping, mad, friendly hippies' (*Zigzag*, Aug 1972); '. . . listening to every record stoned' (Gold: *The Road to Rock*, 1976).

Stoned out. High on drugs or alcohol. This is a slightly stronger term than 'stoned' – '. . . stoned out on meth, threatening to toss bombs at the Russians' (*Oz*, Winter 1973).

Stone-funk. A very earthy kind of rock music, often played and sung by blacks. 'Stone' means 'very', as in 'stone-dead', 'funk' is a special brand of rock music – 'They maintain the drive wih a deliciously sly, stone-funk encore' (*New Musical Express*, 12 May 1979). The expression is technical and professional.

Storm, go down a. To receive a rapturous reception. An expression current during the 1960s and 1970s in the pop/entertainment world – 'We just blew the place apart . . . went down a storm' (*Zigzag*, Nov 1972). Unlike its synonym, 'go down a bomb', it has not been generally adopted by teenagers, or indeed by any other age-group in the UK.

Straight. One of the key UNDERGROUND, Alternative Society words. In the following senses both in the USA and in the UK, it summarized during the 1950s and 1960s many of the characteristics of the Enemy, the Establishment, everything that was unfriendly and intolerant.
   (*i*) Not under the influence of drugs or addicted to them – 'The buzz of all buzzes which is the thing that is Gold – you've got to be straight to get it' (*International Times*, 19 May 1967).
   (*ii*) Heterosexual. For some unexplained reason, this emerged later than its opposite, 'bent', meaning 'homosexual' – '. . . if he satisfies a straight woman' (*International Times*, 5 Jan 1968); 'The man

I've met has a largely straight circle of friends' (*Gay News*, 23 Feb 1978).

(*iii*) Conventional, Establishment. Used by Alternative people to describe everyone but themselves – '. . . those hippie shops and hippie enterprises which have to survive in the grab-world of straight society' (*Oz* 9, Feb 1968); 'I kept bumping into straight friends' (*Schoolkids Oz*, April 1970).

(*iv*) A conventional person – 'That's all right', says the younger of the two, 'We'll con some straight'' (Neville: *Playpower*, 1970).

Street. Popular, acceptable to and understood by 'real' urban youth. Originally black American, it is now a catch-all adjective, used by trendy people to establish their credentials – 'Levine has real street credibility' (*Sounds*, 1 Dec 1979); 'They were street people. I could relate to them' (*Blues and Soul*, 1 Jan 1980).

Street rocking. Demonstrations aimed at bringing about some form of social change. An American expression of the mid-1970s, it was installed among the disaffected young of the UK by the end of the decade – 'The only way change'll come is through some sort of street rocking' (*Sounds*, 27 Jan 1980).

Stretch. A particular enthusiasm. An expression used by teenagers during the 1960s – 'Science fiction's my stretch' (*Jackie*, 8 Feb 1964) – but never heard now.

Stroke. Technique, approach, method. The derivation is either from the American use, with the meaning 'persuasion, flattery', or from the Anglo-American rowing term, meaning 'style'. In the UK, however, the word is little used in this sense, despite the efforts of pop journalists – 'It's different strokes for different folks' (*Sounds*, 11 Dec 1982).

Strung out. Tense, obsessive, often as the result of taking drugs – 'I don't believe in drugs. It takes so much time and you get strung out' (*International Times*, 28 April 1967); '. . . strung out on some form of micromadness' (*Oz 43*, July/Aug 1972). The phrase has been used since the 1960s mainly by people whose own lives contained a strong possibility of becoming strung out from time to time.

Stud. For 200 years, the Americans, but not the British, have used 'stud' as an abbreviation of 'stud-horse', meaning a stallion. From there, the transition to 'man of exceptional sexual activity' was easy and natural, but 'stud' was also, during the 1950s and early 1960s, used to mean 'boyfriend conscious and a little overproud of his manliness' – 'The chick sits on cushions in the front part with a brolly and her stud heaves the thing along with a hop pole' (a teenager in MacInnes: *Absolute Beginners*, 1959).

Stylist. A musical performer. This is an American hyperbole, part of the publicist's toolbox of meaningless expressions. Within this field, it has been in use, both in the USA and in the UK for 30 years, an exceptionally long time for a piece of jargon – '. . . glamorous young vocal stylist' (*New Musical Express*, 17 Aug 1956); 'Marvin Gaye, one of the most lauded stylists in black music' (*Rolling Stone*, 30 Nov 1978).

Suede. An apt description of the very short haircuts of the Mods of the mid-1960s – '. . . the new mods, suede heads and crombie boys' (*The Soul Book*, 1975). The word disappeared at the same time as the haircut.

Super. Good, exciting, outstanding. This is and always has been a very British expression. Originally, during the years immediately following World War II, it was a very upper- and upper-middle class word. Pronounced and stressed in a characteristically debutante or Guards officer manner, it became a rather overdone joke among other sections of the community. The written record is likely to provide a very unreliable record for posterity on occasion, for example – 'Here's a super game to play. All you have to make are the paper flowers you see below' (*Judy Annual for Girls*, 1968). The journalist responsible for this presumably chose 'super' because he or she assumed that all young girls used the word at that time. This was a complete misapprehension. Not one per cent, if that, of the readers of *Judy Annual* would have had 'super' in their active vocabulary then, except possibly to poke fun at upper-class snootiness. Five years later, however, the situation would have been different, since by 1963 'super' had moved a considerable way down the social scale.

As a prefix, 'super', implying superior size or quality, was in limited use before World War II, but it has really come into its own during the past 30 years. It is, however, no longer the word it was. Its tedious overemployment, especially by journalists and professional publicists,

has worn it out and removed much of its original force and appeal –
'. . . super-established names' (*Zigzag*, April 1973); 'Lawyers have
obviously been to her a superbreed' (*The Guardian*, 19 May 1979);
'. . . motor cycling's super-hero' (*Daily Mirror*, 22 March 1979).

One or two of the apparently endless series of 'super-' compounds
deserve individual treatment.

Supergroup. A name given by the pop music business to a
phenomenon of the mid-1960s, when the most talented member of a
famous pop group would join up, perhaps only temporarily, with his
counterparts from other groups to form a Supergroup – 'The leap from
the Small Faces to the supergroup, Humble Pie, was far greater than a
mere change of groups' (*Friends*, No. 1, Jan 1969).

Superspade. The archetypal black, full of sexual vigour, animal
energy and cool. Also to play the part of such a person – 'Buddy is
superspading three quarters of every number' (*Oz* 18, Feb 1969).

Superstar. Someone very famous or very accomplished, or both,
usually in the field of entertainment or sport – 'Roger has no need of
superstar trappings now he has God on his side' (*New Musical
Express*, 12 May 1979).

Surreal. Dreamlike, disjointed. Surrealism was a favourite, if not
always well understood, style among the hippies and pop poets of the
mid-1960s. 'Surrealist' and its rather barbarous abbreviation,
'surreal', were used by them to describe anything associated with the
visual/verbal aspects of drug experiences – '. . . autobiographical
statement frequently couched in surreal lyrics' (*The Soul Book*, 1975).

Surrealist. *See* SURREAL. 'Instruments and voices move around the
room in an amazing surrealist manner' (*International Times*, 27 Oct
1967) and, from the same source, 'The lyrics are Dylanesque, that is,
they range across the surrealist spectrum' (*International Times*, 2 June
1967).

Suss. An entirely British abbreviation of 'suspect', but with a much
wider range of meanings than the full word. The sources which follow
provide clues to the users.

(*i*) To realize, figure out – 'Young bands have sussed that the
imagery of new wave is a much more attractive proposition' (*Melody*

Maker, 12 May 1979); 'Does the romance test beat you every time or have you got it sussed?' (*My Guy*, 11 Sept 1979).

(*ii*) The adjective, suspect – 'The people I used to regard as suss have since fell (sic) to bits and become drips' (*New Musical Express*, 12 May 1979).

(*iii*) Intelligence, wisdom, perception – 'The guy has proved he has enough ability and suss . . .' (*Sounds*, 1 Dec 1979).

Suss out. *See* SUSS (*i*). 'It took me a lot longer to suss it out than he did' (pop singer in *Friends* No. 1, Jan 1969) and, to illustrate the stamina of the phrase, 'Concentrate on getting your cash flow sussed out this week' (*Sounds*, 23 April 1979).

Sweat, no. Without effort, difficulty or problems, easy. Mainly American but, as an export, it has been much used since the mid-1970s by disc jockeys, run-of-the-mill salesmen and others in the UK whose maket value is reckoned to be increased by the use of Americanisms – 'But there's no sweat, Honda's spokesman assures us' (*Superbike*, 1 Sept 1978).

Sweetheart. Used to emphasize the sarcasm of one's reply, without the slightest feeling of endearment and often in a threatening way. The usage is American, and familiar to British people through films and television programmes. It has never had more than a very limited market here, but it has value for those who see an advantage in cultivating a tough, hardboiled, gangster-like image – 'He walked out of our concert on Saturday. Did I tell you that? Yes, sweetheart' (interview with rock group in *Zigzag*, July 1973).

Sweetie. A form of greeting, not necessarily endearing, which is common among homosexuals and among actors, dancers and other people in the entertainment industry – 'The Hoplite gripped my arm. 'Oh no,' he cried, 'didn't I tell you, sweetie? It's all over between him and me" (MacInnes: *Absolute Beginners*, 1959).

Swing. To go smoothly, be stimulating. An Americanism, commonly found in the UK in the 1960s and early 1970s among the young and 'progressive', but very rarely today – 'We haven't found a common direction, but it swings all right' (*International Times*, 29 May 1967).

Swinger. Someone lively, modern, young, up-to-date, out to have a good time. See SWING. 'The young are getting richer and the old are getting older. You're either on the side of the swingers or you're dead' (letter to *Oz* 3, Aug 1967). The expression is obsolete, except among those who do not realize that it is obsolete.

Swinging. Fashionable, lively, entertaining, exciting, ready and anxious to enjoy oneself. Among the young, the word is now very dated, but it is still found among people who look back longingly to yesterday and their youth. The heyday of 'swinging' was the 1960s and early 1970s – 'I'm seventeen and up until the day I met Tony I had a swinging time' (*Jackie*, 17 Sept 1966).

Switched on. Aware of current trends, fashionable, enthusiastic. A catch-phrase of the 1960s and early 1970s – 'Eccles is fab and Blue-bottle real switched on' (*Jackie*, 2 Oct 1965).

Syndrome. Ideas, behaviour, type, group, complex. During the 1960s the word was much used by the more intellectual and trendier underground press and its readers, often very loosely and with little clear meaning – 'Kesey wound up the Acid Tour syndrome with what was billed as a huge 'Trips Festival' (*Oz* 4, Sept 1967); 'It was unusual to hear somebody other than the Peel of Drummond syndrome getting into a little head music' (*Oz* 26, Feb 1970).

Synthetic. Artificially blended and constructed; lacking in originality and vigour. 'Synthetic' is a favourite pejorative among rock musicians, who consider themselves superior to those who earn a living from pop music – '. . . the blandest, most synthetic music of the moment' (*New Musical Express*, 20 Jan 1979).

Synthesist. A phoney, someone wih nothing genuine or original about him, a mere amalgam of bits and pieces. Common in the pop music world, but not elsewhere, and derived almost certainly from the items of electronic equipment used by pop musicians, which creates sounds artificially. Applied to people it is derogatory at best, abusive at worst – 'They're a bunch of raving synthesists' (*Sounds*, 24 Jan 1981).

T

Tab. A tablet, pill. The abbreviation has been used by takers of LSD from the 1960s onwards to describe a dose of LSD, but not of other drugs which come in tablet form – 'If you really feel together, a wee half tab of acid can do wonderful magic' (*Attila*, 23 Oct 1971).

Talent. Sexually attractive members of the opposite sex. Used by members of both sexes, 'talent' was a youth word of the 1960s – 'Sandra was right about there being loads of talent at the dance' (*Jackie*, 2 March 1968).

Tart. A flashy, pretentious person of either sex – 'All those laser-toting tarts' (*Sounds*, 1 Dec 1979). This modern meaning is easily confused with the two older-established senses of the word, 'girl' and 'prostitute'.'Tart' would appear to be losing a little more of its vigour and precision with each decade that passes.

Tasty. A primarily British term, but known and used in the USA in both the following senses:
   (*i*) Excellent, in a flavourful, interesting way – 'They had a countryish guitarist who was very tasty indeed' (rock musician in *Zigzag*, Feb 1973).
   (*ii*) Physically attractive. The word has been used in this sense since about 1890, but only recently about men – 'Ted, the tasty young Swedish singer' (*My Guy*, 12 May 1979) would not have been possible 30 years ago.

Techno-rock. A type of pop music with a very mechanical sound to it, the result of complicated electronics and mixing – 'The obscured forms of Kraut techno–rock' (*Sounds*, 1 Dec 1979)

Ted. A Teddy Boy, a youth phenomenon of the late 1950s, characterized by a vaguely Edwardian style of dress. Young people themselves would always use this abbreviation. Only outsiders and those unsympathetic to this breed of teenager wrote 'Teddy Boy' in full. So, from a writer who was a well-wisher, 'Standing about on corners, and outside their houses there were Teds' (MacInnes: *Absolute Beginners*, 1959)

Teddy boy. For the difference between the full form and the abbreviation, see TED. 'Ban the Teddy Boys' (Fabian of the Yard, quoted in *New Musical Express*, 21 Sept 1956).

Teen scream. A teenage idol who receives screams of excitement and adulation from his fans – 'I got out of my early environment by being a teen-scream' (pop singer in *Friends*, No. 1 Jan 1969). The expression has now passed into history.

Teeny. An abbreviation of 'teeny-bop'. A very young teenager – 'At the London concert, it was the tiny teenagers, the teenies, not the intellectuals, who left in disgust' (*Friends*, No. 1 Jan 1969) and, away from pop music, 'The prospective teeny buyers' (*Superbike*, Sept 1978).

Teeny bop. *See* BOP. Very young and very fashion-conscious in all things – 'It was easy to trap a large crowd, mostly teeny bop freaks and park hippies' (*Oz*, Winter 1973). The teeny bop wave has come and gone now with only a few stragglers left behind.

Teenybopper. *See* BOPPER. A very young teenager of either sex, with a precocious and passionate interest in pop music – 'At the risk of seeming a teeny bopper, he frequents concerts by Quintessence' (*Schoolkids Oz*, April 1970). In an advanced state of obsolescence.

Thing. A way of life, interest, phase, obsession, phenomenon – a vague term, very popular during the 1960s and 1970s, which could mean all of these and many more, according to the context – 'He did a religious thing and left the group' (rock musician, in *Zigzag*, Feb 1973); 'We were into a heavy pills thing' (rock singer in Gold: *The Road to Rock*, 1976); 'We didn't want to be sucked into the new-wave thing' (*Melody Maker*, 12 May 1979). As with many verbal fashion-accessories of this kind, 'thing', together with the definite or indefinite article preceding it, can usually be omitted from the sentence without the sense being disturbed in any way.

Thing, to do your own. To go one's own way, be completely individual. The expression started life as an axiom of American hippiedom and then became part of the creed of the international youth movement throughout the world – 'To me the answer is, stay out of the way, do your own thing and keep growing' (letter to *Attila*, 6 Nov 1971).

This. The, a certain, someone called. 'This' has been used extensively by the young and their spokesmen for more than 20 years to refer to and make more interesting someone or something which/who is known to the speaker but not to the listener – 'But things changed pretty quickly after she met this Ally' (*Jackie*, 2 March 1968); 'He has this big smile' (*Sounds*, 3 March 1979). Something in the nature of a confidence trick is involved; 'this' brings the reader or listener from outside a situation into its centre and transforms him/her immediately into a friend.

Thrash. A rather amateur musical performance or recording. A useful term, but one little used outside the pop music business – 'The charmless thrashes they intend to release and the ones they don't (*Sounds*, 24 March 1979).

Thrush. A female pop singer. The word is used only by journalists and frequently, if not normally, in combination with 'cute'. A 'cute French thrush' (*New Musical Express*, 27 July 1956); 'I met that cute thrush' (*Jackie*, 8 Feb 1964).

Tight. Controlled, precise, keeping to an exact beat and structure. The term is used frequently in the musical world, as a compliment to performers and bands who sound well-rehearsed and at ease – '. . . a tight crew of seven musicians' (*Rolling Stone*, 25 Jan 1978), and 'Wanted urgently good tight drummer' (*Melody Maker*, 19 May 1979).

Together. A hippy, Alternative Society word from the USA which has insinuated itself gradually into the general vocabulary of the young. It is used in two senses.
   (*i*) Organized, self-confident, purposeful – 'If someone can get a reasonably together sound out of one of these . . .' (*Attila*, 23 Oct 1971); 'I could never get my act together enough to do cabaret' (pop singer in *Sounds*, 21 July 1979).
   (*ii*) Calm, sophisticated, knowing – 'A cool, rather snooty together look turns a lot of boys on' (*Jackie*, 1 Sept 1979).

Togs. Clothes. The social rise and all of this entirely British word makes an interesting story. It was first recorded about 1809. For the whole of the 19th century it remained a working-class word, but early in the 20th it began to go up in the world, until by the 1930s it had acquired a strong public school flavour. In the 1950s it greatly extended its range of users, as teenagers of all classes became attracted to it – '. . . town-type togs' (*Jackie*, 8 Feb 1964). During this new phase of popularity, which did not outlast the 1960s, it was used rather more by girls than by boys but, for both sexes, it was then pushed firmly out of the way by GEAR. It is now used rather tongue-in-cheek by trendy journalists – 'If you've got some new togs to show off' (*Time Out*, 10–16 Dec 1982).

Toke. A drug-taker's word, born in the USA in the 1960s and soon exported. It can be used both as a verb and a noun.
(*i*) To inhale from a cannabis cigarette – 'American students, toking on a more or less legal joint' (*Home Grown*, No. 2, 1977).
(*ii*) An inhalation from a cannabis cigarette – 'Another toke on the passing joint' (*Attila*, 13 Nov 1971).

Ton. A hundred, usually referring to either money or speed – 'Bluebird, new and gleaming, was doing a ton' (*Jackie*, 15 May 1965); '£250 went down after that through to about a ton' (*Zigzag*, July 1973). By about 1975 it had passed the peak of its popularity and one hears it very little nowadays.

Ton-up. *See* TON. Travelling at a very high speed, usually on a motorcycle – 'I don't think I'm a ton-up merchant' (*Jackie*, 11 Jan 1964).

Tool. A weapon. Originally a rockers' word, it is now in general use amongst the more violent members of British society. 'We grabbed our tools and by then the Mods were at the end of the street' (Mandelkau: *Buttons*, 1971).

Tool up. To arm oneself. After its introduction in the 1960s, the word was soon being used by the criminal underworld, as well as by rockers – 'We tooled up immediately in a nearby building yard' (Mandelkau: *Buttons*, 1971).
More recently it has been used figuratively, in the sense of 'equip, prepare oneself' – 'Spielberg is theoretically tooling up for his climax

when the director becomes a conceptual engineer' (*Sight and Sound*, Summer 1978).

Too much. The phrase, which came to the UK from the USA in the early 1960s and can now be considered dead, was used in two senses: (*i*) Unbearable! 'Ugh! Too much, so that cat is cutting out' (*International Times*, 5 Oct 1967).

(*ii*) Wonderful. Really. 'Well, actually I'm a model. Too much!' (cartoon in *Oz* 8, Jan 1968); 'There are so many good groups in the States. Procul Harum are just too much' (musician in *Oz* 18, Feb 1969).

Originally a hippy expression, 'too much' was, understandably, much parodied and it may well have been laughed out of existence.

Toot. Cocaine. Cocaine is the caviare of drugs, much favoured nowadays by the well-to-do and not physically addictive, or so it is claimed. 'Toot' is the up-to-date euphemism for this expensive recreation – 'You can find a 'toot' in London's West End, a 'line' at a party in suburbia, a 'snort' in Manchester, a 'blow' in Edinburgh' (*Daily Express*, 23 Nov 1982).

Top, go over the. To become crazy, uncontrollable – 'Our fans go completely over the top' (rock musician in *Sounds*, 3 March 1979). The phrase originated during World War I, when troops left the protection of their trenches and 'went over the top' to engage the enemy. Between World Wars I and II, it was much used in the figurative senses of 'lose one's temper', 'drink excessively', and the transition to the modern meaning was then an easy and natural process.

Tranny. A transistor radio. The word, always used endearingly and jokingly, is believed to have been invented by the disc jockey, Kenny Everett – '. . . my first tinny tranny, confiscated for surreptitiously listening via earphones' (*Sounds*, 28 April 1979).

Trash. (*i*) To make insulting remarks about something, to treat as useless – 'Vivien Goldman trashed Marvin Gaye's new album' (*Melody Maker*, 20 Jan 1979).

(*ii*) To wreck, ruin, vandalize – 'Whether he trashes his hotel before leaving it or not . . .' (*Sounds*, 1 Jan 1979).

The word, in both senses, is of American origin and has so far been little used outside *Melody Maker* circles. It means exactly the same as 'rubbish', which is British and which may well, as an equally recent introduction, block the progress of 'trash'.

Trendy. When it first appeared in the early 1960s, 'trendy' meant simply 'fashionable', and had no derogatory overtones – 'She thinks toothpaste should be trendy, too' (*Jackie*, 2 Sept 1967). Soon, however, it came to mean 'self-consciously, often ridiculously fashionable' – 'Terson's criticism of the trendy vicar' (Michael Croft's introduction to *Zigger Zagger*, 1970), and those who behaved in such a way were equally laughed at – 'We are left with the well-off trendies' (*Cracker*, No. 1 1972). Few colloquialisms have lost face so quickly and so thoroughly. There is nothing to praise or admire in 'The wettest of the trendy white funk crew' (*Time Out*, 10–16 Dec 1982).

Trip. All the 'trip' meanings which follow started life in the USA, all crossed to the UK wih the hippy-drug cult or with its watered-down sequels.

(*i*) An experience brought about by a drug, usually LSD or mescalin – 'When you take a trip, you need to be very careful of the people around you' (*International Times*, 28 April 1967). Originating with the users of the drugs this quickly became the only respectable term.

(*ll*) An obsession. 'The sheriff didn't care. He was on his power trip' (Mandelkau: *Buttons*, 1971).

(*iii*) To take LSD – 'Smoked at 9, first tripped at 11' (*Schoolkids Oz*, April 1970).

(*iv*) Enthusiasm, 'cup of tea' – 'If eco-explo isn't your trip, I suggest you turn the page' (*Oz* 34, April 1971).

(*v*) Attitude, way of life – 'Most of us try to lay our trip on others most of the time' (*Attila*, 25 Nov 1971).

Although far from obsolete, the 'trip' series no longer possesses the freshness and the power to seize the attention that it had in the early 1970s. It seems likely that drugs and drug metaphors are being found increasingly boring and commonplace.

Tripped out. *See* TRIP. The expression, during its heyday in the 1960s and 1970s, had two meanings:

(*i*) Under the influence of LSD and, from this, having the senses disturbed from any cause – 'You'd be tripped out on sound alone' (Cohn: *Awopbop*, 1969).

(*ii*) Possessing the approved hippy awareness and senses of values –
'. . . a transparent dress designed by two tripped out chicks'
(*International Times*, 30 Jan 1967).
Now dead.

Trucking. Moving in a free and easy fashion, enjoying oneself. In the
UK, this Americanism has not strayed very far from the entertainment
field, even in the catch-phrase 'Keep trucking' – 'Keep on trucking
with the Durriti' (*Attila*, 16 Oct 1971); 'If you're truckin' along to
Capital Radio Jazz Festival . . .' (*Sounds*, 21 July 1979).

Turn it up. Paradoxically, to stop doing something, not, as one might
have guessed, to do something all the more. Originally, in the 1950s,
this was a London expression, but as with many others, the pop music
business, which eats and spits out new words at a frightening rate,
picked it up and gave it mass circulation – 'You get some chick
screaming and you tell her to turn it up and she does' (pop singer in
Friends, No. 1, Jan 1969). It is no longer in fashionable use.

Turn on. In the late 1950s and early 1960s, the American hippies
busily establishing a new world of their own, discovered the delights
of, among other things, cannabis. From this period came the first sense
of 'turn on' –
(*i*) To smoke cannabis, which was part of the vocabulary of drug-
takers in the UK by the middle of the decade – 'They turn on blatantly'
(*Oz* 18, Feb 1969).
At the same time, the transitive possibilities of the verb were being
developed, producing –
(*ii*) To make excited, sexually or otherwise – "Eli' is nothing less
than brilliant if it turns you on' (*Oz* 33, Feb 1971); 'Here's one blowing
gently in your ear trying to turn you on' (*My Guy*, 19 May 1979).
'Turn on' can also be used as a noun –
(*iii*) Something or someone which stimulates – 'Is the turn on dope
and not beer?' (*Attila*, 23 Oct 1971).

Turned on. *See* TURN ON, the American hippy origins of which it
shares.
(*i*) Excited, stimulated. 'Everybody is turned on by IT'
(*International Times*, 28 Nov 1966).
(*ii*) Aware of the real circumstances – '*The Times*' reporters were
just turned on enough to realise . . .' (*Oz* 33, Feb 1971).

The corresponding and older-established British phrase is 'switched on'. The fact that the Americanism has competed so successfully with it, at least among the young, is both curious and interesting.

Two-time. To have two girl/boy friends at the same time and to deceive them both. This American term, associated with such transatlantic habits as 'dating' and 'steadies', had a short life in the UK in the 1960s – 'Recently I two-timed my boy' (*Jackie*, 24 July 1965).

-type. A meaningless suffix, popularized by Mr Jinx, of the long-running American strip cartoon, Pixie and Dixie. It spread into the UK via the tabloids, which took this syndicated cartoon, and achieved a limited success among teenagers during the 1960s and 1970s – '. . . a fun-type mood' (*Jackie*, 18 Feb 1964); '. . . a red-herring type rumour' (*Zigzag*, Feb 1973).

U

Ultimate. The very best. This general-purpose superlative, bred in the USA, has been much used since the early 1970s by media people, whose living depends on superlatives, and by teenagers, who enjoy tweaking the tail of media people without being observed – 'He's the ultimate guy who'd give you the shirt off his back' (rock star in *Zigzag*, April 1973); '. . . the ultimate one-piece suit' (advert in *Superbike*, Sept. 1978).

Ultra. Very, extra. A form of exaggeration fashionable among teenagers, 'ultra' is usually found as the first element in a compound adjective, but sometimes on its own, for example, 'He's really ultra' – 'The ultra-big pads have been divided . . .' (*Home Grown*, No. 2, 1977).

Uncool. Not the done thing, foolhardy, displaying too little confidence and too much emotion, overdone. The word is used by those for whom to be COOL is the most desirable of all states – '. . . he closed and clutched at an imaginary guitar like a Status Quo fan. Clouds swirled across the stage and it all seemed most uncool' (*Melody Maker*, 12 May 1979).

Underground. The international 'progressive' movement and subculture, embracing, inter alia, left-wing, anti-authoritarian, anti-capitalist, anti-Establishment, revolutionary views, unlimited tolerance in sexual matters and considerable sympathy towards drug-taking. The word seems to have been first used in New York in the mid-1960s, when 'Underground' was characterized by duplicated magazines and home movies – 'That unpopular label, 'underground' believes that once you've blown your own mind the Bastille will blow itself up' (Neville: *Playpower*, 1970).

Unhip. *See* HIP. Unfashionable, naive, suggesting the wrong lifestyle. The first sense is illustrated by '. . . a fine view of their stiff white collars and Turkish bathed necks and unhip Jermyn Street hairdos' (teenager in MacInnes: *Absolute Beginners*, 1959). 'He's so unhip that he gave an exploding cigarette to an arbiter of taste on the NME' (*Melody Maker*, 31 March 1979) contains the 'naive, out of touch' meaning.

Untogether. Disorganized, unaware. This, like its opposite, 'together', began life as a hippy word but is now an everyday term among those who cluster around rock and pop musicians – 'I gather you were thrown out of Hawkwind for being too untogether' (interview with rock musician on BBC Radio One, 13 July 1980); 'We started off with Steve New, but he was a *little* untogether' (*Sounds*, 24 Jan 1981).

Up-beat. Cheerful, optimistic. During the 1960s and part of the 1970s, this expression had a certain vogue among youth-journalists and, by imitation, among young people themselves – 'This up-beat mood will last all week' (*Jackie*, 25 Jan 1964). The fashion has now completely passed.

Up-front. Open, honest. Originally an American hippy term, this is now used much more widely, among the hippies' modern descendants, who represent a rather broader band of society – '. . . clear up-front vocals' (*The Soul Book*, 1975); 'He's quite upfront about pirating various punk band designs' (*Home Grown*, No. 3, 1978).

Uptight. Tense, anxious, bad-tempered, repressed. Originally used by hippies to describe the mental state they would least like to be in. The word is perfectly respectable, 20 years later, although a little daring when spoken in an educated voice – 'I was pretty evil during the session, so uptight and shouting at everyone' (rock star in *Zigzag*, April 1973); 'The umpire's being quite firm. Mark Cox is getting quite uptight about it' (BBC commentary at Wimbledon, 25 June 1979).

Use. To take drugs regularly – 'Some are still using and unhappy' (*International Times*, 13 Feb 1967). Always an inside word to describe the habit, it is still occasionally found.

V

Valid. Worthwhile, meaningful. A trendy journalists' borrowing from the social sciences, a rich quarry for such people nowadays – 'I think it was one of our most valid albums' (*Blues and Soul*, 1 Jan 1980).

Veggy. Vegetarian. This is a middle-class student type of abbreviation – 'We ate beautiful veggy food' (*Undercurrents*, Oct/Nov 1978). Social historians of the future may well note that vegetarianism is extremely rare among members of the British working class, where one's sense of well-being is directly related to the quantity and quality of one's meat consumption. In the UK, whatever the situation may be elsewhere, vegetarianism is a very middle- and upper-class affair.

Vibes. Feelings, sensations, atmosphere, relations, omens. This word, an abbreviation of 'vibrations', came into use simultaneously in the early 1960s among American hippies and pop musicians. Both in the USA and abroad, it has always been used only semi-seriously by other people. Vibes, it should be noted, are either good or bad, with nothing in between – 'Perfect vibes between audience and group' (*Zigzag*, Aug 1972); 'Everything oppressive will automatically collapse through the accumulated good vibes' (*Spare Rib*, Feb 1979); 'Good vibes for going places on Friday evening' (Horoscope in *Sounds*, 24 March 1979). The word can also be used in the singular, with the same meaning and associations – '. . . so that we can play in the corner of the pub or in a hundred thousand seater and still get the same vibe' (*Melody Maker*, 24 Jan 1981).

Vibe up. To stimulate. The verb is not common outside musical circles. 'Vibing up the senile man' (record title, 1979).

Vibrations. The early form of VIBES, still in use in the UK in the early 1970s – 'The vibrations which they give off are almost always very loving and good' (*Oz* 43, July/Aug 1972).

-ville. A place, state of affairs, condition. This is a left-over from

188

American BEAT language. In the UK, it was only ever used by those, such as disc jockeys and certain journalists, who make a practice of using American expressions – 'From that night on it was lonesomeville for me' (story in *Jackie*, 2 March 1968); 'Thankfully no-one was hurt. A cranium connexion would have meant instant snuffsville' (*Sounds*, 1 Dec 1979).

Vinyl. A record, vinyl being the substance from which the record is made. The word has been used in and around the pop music business since the mid-1970s – 'He committed himself to vinyl' (*The Soul Book*, 1975); 'The vinyl inside both these jackets fits the presentation' (*Melody Maker*, 20 Jan 1979).

W

Wacker. The Liverpudlian equivalent of 'mate', and an example of the many Liverpool expressions which came briefly into teenage fashion with the Beatles – 'Don't worry, wacker' (*Jackie*, 15 Feb 1964).

Wally. A stupid person, someone with an inflated sense of his own worth. Exclusively British, this popular teenage word is much used by football fans – '. . . those over-publicised wallies from Shepherd's Bush' (letter to *Foul*, June 1974); 'I hate Mitchell and Twigger and all that crew. Talk about wallies!' (*New Musical Express*, 12 May 1979).

Wank. To indulge oneself, go on and on about a particular topic. Now very common among the young and fashionable and with older trendies. The figurative meaning is not found before the mid-1960s, and then only in the UK. Before that time, the only meaning was 'masturbate' – '. . . intellectually wanking over the sexual imagery, political leanings and revelatory nose-pickings of Medicine Head' (*Oz* 34, April 1971); '. . . the boring old wank of Left versus Right' (*Attila*, 23 Oct 1971).

Wanker. An incompetent, dull person, someone incapable of originality or creativity. Particularly popular with football crowds – 'They're just a bunch of wankers who see us as a way of making money' (pop group, quoted in *New Musical Express*, 6 Jan 1979).

Wank mag. A pornographic magazine, with strong echos of 'Yank mag' – '. . . cleaned-up versions of adverts from the wank mags' (*Sounds*, 28 April 1979).

Wanky. Self-indulgent – 'The last quarter of the record's given over to wanky "jazz-rock"' (*Sounds*, 21 July 1979).

Warpo. Weird, freaky. This abbreviation of 'warped' (compare

CHEAPO) is found only among the trendier young – '. . . any kind of warpo image of his own' (*Sounds*, 3 March 1979).

Warp out. To deviate from, abandon, water down. For the range of users, *see* WARPO – 'Karl had warped out on the DIY punk ethic' (*Sounds*, 24 Jan 1981).

Waste. To beat up. The word comes from the USA where, in gangster talk, 'waste' means 'kill', and in the UK it is used only by those elements in society for whom beatings up are an exciting and inevitable fact of life – 'The Mods waste an entire café of rockers before setting on the police' (*New Musical Express*, 12 May 1979).

Wax. To record. This is a hardy perennial among journalists in the pop music business, popular even now, when records have long since ceased to be made of wax – 'The disc waxed by Frankie Vaughan in the United States is disappointing' (*New Musical Express*, 14 Feb 1958), and 'The Knack will enter the studio sometime in March to wax their debut album' (*Melody Maker*, 27 Jan 1979).
   It also means a record – '. . . the best girl on wax today' (*New Musical Express*, 6 Jan 1956).

Waxing. A recording. The same considerations apply as for WAX. So, 'His latest waxing on Columbia' (*New Musical Express*, 16 Nov 1956), when the days of wax were not long over, and '. . . the most notable of which was his premier waxing with M' (*Sounds*, 28 April 1979).

Weed. Marijuana. For decades, the 'weed' was tobacco. When the drug habit changed from tobacco to marijuana, it was almost inevitable that 'weed' would accompany it. By the mid-1960s, however, it was dead, except as a joke. In 'It's smoking weed' (MacInnes: *City of Spades*, 1957), the word is to be taken straight. In 'President Brezhnev foresook the weed two years back' (*Home Grown*, No. 2, 1977), it means tobacco, but the writer is playing with words, so that 'marijuana' is also implied. In 'Eleven States have already decriminalised possession of the weed' (*Rolling Stone*, 30 Nov 1978), one can feel the inverted commas in the author's mind as he wrote.

Weird. Peculiar, strange, inexplicable. This sense of the word existed in the UK in the mid-1920s, but at that time and until after World War

II it was used mainly by the British upper classes. During the late 1950s, it was taken up by the American hippies and applied by them to anything they found out-of-the-ordinary or interesting. Afterwards, in the mid-1960s, it became almost as popular with the post-hippy generation – 'It's a very weird scene, because the Stones and the Beatles got screamed at far more than us' (pop singer, quoted in *Friends*, No. 1, Jan 1969); 'It was too weird to make another album at that time' (rock musician, in *Zigzag*, April 1973).

Weirdo. Odd, freaky. 'Weirdo' is post-hippy, and current among the kind of people who were using 'weird' in the 1970s – 'The avant-garde/ classical weirdo scene' (*Zigzag*, Aug 1972), and 'Devo, the weirdo band . . .' (*Rolling Stone*, 30 Nov 1978).

Weirdy. Someone of particularly strange appearance or behaviour, especially of a hippy or bohemian kind – '. . freaky sax-blowing weirdies' (*Zigzag*, Aug 1972).

Whack. A hearty, a jovial extrovert – 'The saloon bar was full of whacks, burbling over jolly pints of E.' (Nuttall: *Bomb Culture*, 1968).

Whacked. Exhausted. A 19th century word, which is used today mainly by older people. When it formed part of the teenage vocabulary, in the 1960s, there was usually a feeling of quotation about it – 'It made me feel whacked, just watching' (*Jackie*, 18 Jan 1964). The use of any of the 'whack' series of words demands the greatest care nowadays, if embarrassing sniggers are to be avoided, because echoes of the teenage expression, 'whack off', meaning 'masturbate', are never far away.

Whack off. Masturbate. An expression common among teenagers of both sexes since the 1960s – 'Her mother catches Janis in the bath singing the Kozmic Blues and whacking off' (*Oz*, Winter 1973).

Whacky. Jolly. During the 1960s and 1970s this was a word much loved by the younger art, literary and television critics – 'Whacky dislocated collages of original writing and corny old novels' (Nuttall: *Bomb Culture*, 1968).

Where it's at. What is important or true, what one believes in, is interested in, is capable of. Of American hippy origin, this phrase has since been very widely used by the UNDERGROUND everywhere – 'In this way you can become free, that's where it's at' (*Oz* 6, 1967); 'If you're the shy type and can't make it to where gay people are at . . .' (advert in *Spare Rib*, April 1975).

Where one's at. What one believes it, is interested in, is involved in – 'He knows, more than the vast majority of musicians suddenly caught up in the the frenetic whirlpool of 'pop' success, exactly where he's at' (*Friends* No. 1, Dec 1969), and 'If you're the shy type and can't make it to where gay people are at . . .' (*Spare Rib*, April 1965).

Wild. Crazy, extraordinary, fantastic. This American import was much used by the more advanced British young and their journalistic courtiers in the 1960s – 'Here it is – the wildest competition of them all' (*Melody Maker*, 27 June 1964).

Wimp. A failure, someone with no strength of character. In the USA from about 1920 a 'wimp' was a girl, and from there the word came to mean 'a weak man'. It was used in the UK in this sense by about 1965 and is still current among journalists and the more word-conscious young. 'Does this man look like a terminal wimp to you?' (*Sounds*, 21 July 1979) could cause problems for the older generation.

Wimp out. Capitulation, giving in without a struggle. 'And if you think that means an overtly bland wimp-out, you're wrong' (*Sounds*, 24 March 1979).

Wimpy. Naive, wet. A term of abuse now common among the young and unknown to most of their elders – 'I hate all these fresh-faced young bands, all these wimpy bands' (*Sounds*, 11 Dec 1982).

Wipe out. To exhaust. Introduced into the UK from the USA in the 1960s, it is still far from being the most widely used term for this state among young people in the UK, although it has powerful backing from the America-facing entertainment industry – 'She wipes you out, leaves you amazed and glad you were there' (*New Musical Express*, 12 May 1979); 'Maybe I was just wiped out' (*Sounds*, 24 March 1979).

-wise. In the way of, so far as this or that is concerned. A tiresome suffix beloved first of American journalists and then by journalists outside that great word-factory – 'Why has perfume such a devastating effect male-wise?' (*Jackie*, 11 Jan 1964); 'Image-wise, Thelma Houston remains middle of the road' (*The Soul Book*, 1975). Outside journalism, '-wise' had a considerable vogue during the 1970s among industrial, commercial and other not fully literate people, in such compounds as 'personality-wise', and among students, who said it tongue-in-cheek.

With it. In fashion, aware. Originally a jazz word, it had a short but vigorous life among British young in the 1960s, with the 'in fashion' meaning, although older people and journalists continued to use it for much longer. It is still used by teenagers, however, in the sense of 'understanding what is going on, knowledgeable' – 'This is no time for thinking, smile, get with it' (girl to boy in story in *Boyfriend Annual*, 1963), and 'Here's a quickie quiz to see who's with it popsterwise' (*Jackie*, 11 Jan 1964).

Wog. A derogatory, but usually not unfriendly British term for a non-white foreigner. Originally a sailors' term for an Indian shipping clerk – the British put the coloured races firmly in their place in Victorian times – 'wog' is considered nowadays by the middle-class young, the Left and the trendy to be certain proof of a reactionary and racist attitude, although it is still widely used by the working class of all ages – 'Muscles like yours still have the power to turn the wogs into custard' (Terson: *Zigger Zagger*, 1967).

Workshop. Any form of group activity involving study or discussion. The term is much used by members of the Alternative Society and the Left generally, mainly no doubt because it sounds busy and productive and gives mere talk the cachet of solid manual work – 'The fluid situation of largely unprepared workshops did not alienate many people' (*Spare Rib*, April, 1975).

Wow. This very American-sounding and feeling word was in use in the USA in the mid-1920s, meaning 'a great success'. It became a popular youth and journalists' word in the UK in the 1960s, when it was used both as a verb and a noun.

(*i*) To arouse great admiration – 'Want to really wow them this summer?' (*Jackie*, 30 May 1964). This usage is now virtually obsolete.

(*ii*) Someone or something very exciting, attractive. This is much favoured by journalists writing for the teenage market, but often contains an element of sarcasm when used by the British young and one does well to be sensitive to this possibility – 'At 41, he knows why he's such a wow with women' (*Oh Boy!*, 19 Jan 1980).

Y

Yak. To chatter, ramble on. First observed in Australia about 1880, 'yak' became popular in the U.K. in the 1950s – 'This feller kept me yakking about jazz all day' (*Jackie*, 25 January 1964) – and it appears now to be a permanent part of the language. There is usually an implication that the talk is lengthy or boring, but this is not necessarily the case, as the following example shows – 'I was yakking to the Paramounts' (*Jackie*, 6 June 1964).

Yonks. Years, ages. First used during the 1960s by young people of the student type, the word then had wider popularity among the same age group for a while, but is now rarely heard, except from people closely resembling the original users – 'One of the best heavy metal albums I've heard in yonks' (letter in *Sounds*, 28 April 1979).

Yucky. Messy, revolting. A teenager word of the 1960s and apparently entirely British – 'Use flesh-tinted creams to cover up – much less yucky than spot creams' (*Jackie*, 20 December 1969). The interjection 'Yuck!', meaning 'disgusting', is a back-formation from this.

Yummy. (*i*) A vague and rather childish adjective indicating pleasure of some kind, often in connection with food or sexual attractiveness. Originally this very British expression was used only by younger teenage girls and by the magazines catering for them, but its market has recently expanded – 'What a yummy place to work' (*Jackie*, 15 February 1964); 'The yummy Leif Garrett' (*Pink*, 12 May 1979); '. . . the gorgeous girls and three yummy hunks of manhood on the stage before you' (*Sounds*, 24 January 1981).

(*ii*) A sexually attractive young girl. This usage has been confined to young men in their twenties – 'What a little yummy!' (*Oz* 43, July/Aug 1972).

Z

Zap. An Americanism in both its senses.

(*i*) To attack. This has been used since the late 1960s by people of all ages who are enthusiasts of the Superman cult – 'I am zapped by a succession of weirds' (*Attila*, 13 Nov 1971).

(*ii*) To send, throw – 'Simply zap them back with a covering letter' (*Sounds*, 24 Jan 1981).

'Zap' can also be used as a noun, with the meaning 'excitement, enthusiasm, high quality' – '. . . and picks out the wheat from the chaff, the leaven from the lump, or whatever the phrase is that media people currently use' (*Soundmaker*, 4 Dec 1982).

Zonked. High on drugs. Used only by those who consider they belong to the drug milieu – 'Everyone in the audience got zonked out of their minds on LSD' (*Oz* 4, Sept. 1967); '. . . a lonely Hell's Angel without a bike, zonked on methedrine' (*Fanatic*, No. 5, 1977).

A Note on Sources

For nearly 400 years, the raw material of dictionaries has been the printed and written word. With rare exceptions, living speech finds its way into dictionaries, even slang dictionaries, only if somebody has written it down, a form of hit and miss documentation which few people nowadays would claim to be satisfactory. In an ideal world, there would be a considerable staff of trained people, employed by the state, whose full-time job would be to maintain a running record of the words and expressions they heard around them and to note the kinds of people who used these words. This, and only this, would allow the history of the language to be written in a continuous manner, with changes and innovations reported as they happened. The project would be extremely interesting and correspondingly expensive, but anything else can be only a second best.

There is, however, something to be said in defence of printed sources, which are those on which *The Dictionary of the Teenage Revolution and its Aftermath* has been forced to rely. They are certainly better than nothing at all and, used with imagination and with a will to understand the subtleties of an idiom which is not one's own, they can provide a useful, if not faultless, picture of the earlier stages of a revolution in language and linguistic attitudes which began in the 1940s and which is still in progress. There is some value in talking to people who were teenagers in the 1950s and 1960s and who are now, inevitably, middle-aged, but one has to treat their reminiscences with considerable discretion. Asking anyone to recall how he talked 30 years ago is unlikely to produce results which are any more reliable than what is to be found in the magazines of the period. And until a time machine is invented, which will give one the power to return to the past and to take part in conversations with the people of our choice who were alive then, the written record, together with a certain amount on film, tape or disc, is all that is available to us. We must make the best of it.

In any case, the national stock of recorded sound is of very little use to anyone who wishes to study the language of the teenagers of 20, 30 and 40 years ago. The recordings kept for posterity are largely those of the great and famous, together with people who happened to be part of news stories. The speech of ordinary people has been preserved mainly by accident and in very small gobbets. The difficulties of locating these fragmentary offerings are immense, not least because they are usually indexed under quite different headings.

So printed material for the most part it has to be. My most often quoted periodical is *Jackie*, a weekly published from 1964 onwards. Intended primarily for girls aged 12–16, it has always had a large readership and it must have had considerable influence, both in reflecting and in forming the tastes and habits of this age-group. *Honey*, a monthly magazine for rather older girls, sells getting on for 250,000 copies and is no doubt read by almost double that number of people. Many girls graduate, via their mothers, from *Honey* to *Woman's Own*, a weekly which dates from as far back as 1932 and which now has a circulation of more than 1,500,000. Less important, but still influential within the same field are *Judy*, a weekly for the lower age end of the *Jackie* market, which has been appearing since 1960, and the associated *Judy Annual for Girls*, 1968 onwards. *My Guy* is a more recent (1978) monthly, read mainly by girls in their middle and late teens. It sells more than 250,000 copies. *Oh Boy!* (1964) and *Fab* (1966) were both aimed at 14–16-year-old girls. They combined in 1976, to form *Oh Boy with Fab*, which is bought by about 150,000 teenagers, a figure reached in the 1960s by *Boyfriend* (1958), which also had an annual, *Boyfriend Annual*.

There has been nothing for boys in any way comparable to *Jackie* or *Honey*. *Pink* and *Mates*, 1970 and 1976 respectively, were read by both boys and girls, although probably more by boys. It is a difficult market and the two amalgamated in 1975, to produce a magazine with the curious title of *Mates with Pink*. It has a circulation of about 100,000. *Mates Annual* was published in August each year from 1965 until 1978. It is now extinct.

Among the special interest magazines read by boys in their teens and early twenties, I have made use of the football weekly, *Shoot*, which began its career in 1969 and has now reached a circulation of over 300,000, and its more recent and smaller-selling rival, *Foul* (1979). *Motor Cycle Weekly* goes back as far as 1903 and now sells rather fewer than 100,000 copies. *Bikes* began publication in 1980 and no circulation figures are issued for it, although they are probably similar to those of *Superbike* (1976), which averages 90,000 copies.

Jazz and pop music magazines form a class of their own. *Melody Maker* has been going since 1926 and now sells 140,000 copies each week, rather less than *Sounds* (1970), with its 160,000, and very much below the 230,000 of *New Musical Express* (1962). The very successful American fortnightly, *Rolling Stone* (1970) is coy about revealing its British sales, but they are probably about 25,000. The more specialized *Black Music and Jazz Review*, originally *Black Music* (1973) has a circulation of about 50,000 a month, and *Blues, Soul and Disco Music Review*, originally *Blues and Soul* (1966) manages only 3,500 a fortnight. The monthly magazine, *The Gramophone* (1923) and *Sight and Sound*, published quarterly by the British Film Institute since 1932, have both shown great stamina, but their appeal has always been to a more educated public and their circulation correspondingly small.

Of the various annuals connected with pop music, I have used only the *Pelham Pop Annual*, which ran from 1966 to 1975.

It should be noted that the bigger selling periodicals of this kind are not concerned only with music. They regularly include articles on other subjects which are reckoned to be of interest to their readers, not infrequently venturing into a discussion of social and political problems. They have as fair a claim as any to reflect the general culture of teenagers and young adults.

Another broad group of publications has emerged to meet the tastes and requirements of people who, for one reason or another, feel themselves to be out of tune with the established order of society. *Undercurrents*, published monthly since 1972, deals with 'scientific ideas and technological proposals that make possible a richer life style for individuals in a decentralised ecology'. *Attila* (1971) is a go-your-own-way monthly which has shown unusual stamina for a magazine of this type. It survives in a world where a short life is normal and where *Cracker* (1968), *China Cat Sunflower* (1970) and *Fanatic* (1965) have long since gone to the wall, as has *Brighton Voice*, a publication which appeared somewhat sporadically during the late 1960s and early 1970s. What began as *Friends* (1969–71) and then became *Frendz* (1971) has done surprisingly well. Published monthly and advocating 'the Alternative Life Style', its circulation reached 20,000 in 1980. It is, by the way, rare for this type of magazine to issue any circulation figures to carry out its legal responsibility to deposit copies in the statutory national libraries. The files held at Brighton Polytechnic are altogether exceptional.

Home Grown (1961) catered principally for drug-takers. It did reasonably well for five years and then faded out as the police became more interested. *International Times* (1967) and *Zigzag* (1969) were on the side of drug-taking and other anti-establishment habits and ideas from the beginning, but both survived their dangerous infant years. *Zigzag* now sells 32,000 copies a month, which makes it not only a commercially viable proposition, but on the verge of prosperity. *International Times* was first published in 1967, as a fortnightly. In 1970 it was rechristened *IT* and its circulation has on occasion gone as high as 50,000. From the beginning, it had an anti-authoritarian approach to everything. It faithfully reflected the attitude of its mainly young readers, it was written in language they could understand, and it gave them a sense of belonging to the tribe.

Of the numerous irreverent and satirical magazines which have come and gone and in one or two cases stayed, I have made particular use of *Oz* and *Private Eye*. *Oz* was the brainchild of a group of expatriate Australians, led by Richard Neville, who edited it from its birth in 1967 until its death ten years later, after he had become bored with it. For a time, it was one of the most successful monthlies of its day, reaching a circulation of 80,000 in 1972. It symbolized, reflected and advocated nearly every form of opposition to tradition and the Establishment. Associated with it was a less successful venture, *Schoolkids Oz*, which made somewhat irregular appearances between 1968 and 1973.

Private Eye, a fortnightly, has been in existence since 1961, and now sells a remarkable 160,000 copies an issue. It specializes in ridiculing members of the Establishment, especially where their domestic life and business dealings are concerned, and in exposing financial and political scandals. The great and powerful are frightened of it, the literate young love it. Many of its turns of phrase have become part of the language.

Time Out (1968), a weekly with a readership which overlaps to some extent with that of *Private Eye*, combines a detailed listing of events and activities with comments on the current scene. It has had its ups and downs, including a period when it ceased publication altogether, but it now has a very respectable circulation of 80,000 which makes it a social force to be reckoned with.

Gay News (1972) and *Spare Rib* (1972) are both essential reading for anyone who wishes to keep up-to-date with the terminology employed by homosexuals and lesbians and to be aware of the finer shades of meaning which are so important among these sensitive and easily affronted people. *Gay News*, a fortnightly, does not publish its circulation figures, but *Spare Rib*, which appears monthly, has no reason to be dissatisfied with its 30,000.

Of the publications intended primarily for adults, but with a sizeable readership among older and more intelligent teenagers, I have used *The Alternative* (1972), published by the Union Movement, a British fascist organization, leaflets put out by the National Front, also fascist, and the monthly *National Front News* (1976). *New Society* (1962) deals each week with sociology and social happenings in a popular way and with a fairly obvious bias towards the mid-Left and to the general ideals of the Welfare State. Its circulation fluctuates between 30,000 and 35,000. *Playboy International* (1954) is nudist, male chauvinist, and what its title suggests, with articles of general interest by American-type intellectuals to keep up the tone. *The Listener* (1929) is the vehicle created by the BBC primarily to reprint the texts of broadcast programmes, as a whole or in part. Its quality and interest has varied a good deal, according to the Editor, but over the years it has been a useful mirror of the changing habits of the British, with much useful information about the teenage world. Its circulation is now hovering around 35,000, but in the past it has been considerably higher. *The Spectator* (1829) is a serious-minded weekly, nowadays fairly well to the right of centre. Like all periodicals of its type, it has found the going hard in recent years and just about manages to get by with its 30,000 circulation.

The *Dictionary* contains the odd reference from *The Lancet* (1823), a professional monthly produced for the surgical end of the medical profession. It sells 27,000 copies and sometimes includes articles covering a broader field.

Four daily newspapers have supplied quotations for the *Dictionary*. The *Daily Mirror* (1903) usually has its head and heart turned towards the Left, without being to the slightest degree Marxist. With a circulation of 3,500,000 it is certainly entitled to call itself popular. The *Daily Express* (1900) is well to the Right, believes in Putting Britain First, and sells about 2,000,000 copies. *The Daily Telegraph* (1855) is strongly Conservative and achieves a circulation of not quite 1,500,000. *The Guardian* (1959) has a much smaller readership of just under 400,000. A high proportion of its readers are young. It is popular among students, media people and the Liberal Left.

Of the three radio programmes mentioned, Radio One is the pop music channel, Radio Two is mixed pop and talk, and Radio Four is middle-of-the-road in all things. The audience for Radio Four is markedly older than those for Radio One and Radio Two.

The books from which examples of teenage speech have been taken for the *Dictionary* are all by people who have shown a strong sympathy for teenagers and their preferred way of life, with a good ear for the idiom of the streets, cafés and discos. In both these respects, Colin MacInnes was outstanding and I have made much use of his *City of Spades* (1957) and *Absolute Beginners* (1959). Nik Cohn's *Awopbop* (1969) and Jamie Mandelkau's *Buttons* (1971) are both treasure-houses of the kind of language I have been looking for, and I have also dug deeply into Keith Waterhouse's *Billy Liar* (1959), Alan Sillitoe's *The Loneliness of the Long Distance Runner* (1959), Peter Terson's *Zigger Zagger* (1967), Richard Neville's *Playpower* (1969), Jeff Nuttall's *Bomb Culture* (1968), Mick Gold's *The Road to Rock* (1976) and Sean Hignett's *A Picture to Hang on the Wall* (1966). The odd example has also come from John Le Carré's *Tinker Tailor Soldier Spy* (1974), Peter Wilmott's *Adolescent Boys in East London* (1966), Ronald G. Corwin's *Education in Crisis* (1974), Ann Garner's *Monkey Grip* (1977), Graham Greene's *Brighton Rock* (1938), *The Soul Book* by Ian Hoare and others (1975), Bill Mather's *The Wort Papers* (1972), and Tim Myer's *Fast Sam* (1975).